GERMANY AND YUGOSLAVIA, 1933–1941

The German Conquest of Yugoslavia

FRANK C. LITTLEFIELD

EAST EUROPEAN MONOGRAPHS, BOULDER
DISTRIBUTED BY COLUMBIA UNIVERSITY PRESS, NEW YORK

1988

EAST EUROPEAN MONOGRAPHS, NO. CCXLIV

CONTENTS

PREFACE

This book was written to answer several questions. 1) Exactly what were Hitler's plans for Germany's relations with the other European states? Did he plan to conquer all Europe, part of it or set up a system of political and economic control and domination? Most people think he had a well thought out plan for a German empire stretching to all parts of Europe. Actually his ideas on the future Reich were little different from the German war aims in the first world war. The rest of Europe would be allies or under the political or economic domination of Germany. Yugoslavia would be one of those countries designated to supply Germany with food and raw materials. Hitler well appreciated the part shortages of these things played in the defeat of the Central Powers in World War I. That must not happen in his new war.

2) The evolution of the nationality problem. Yugoslavia was made up of many different peoples who had gone through their own historical and cultural evolution. The most serious problem faced by Yugoslavia throughout its history has been how to keep all these people together in one state. The most divisive group has been the Croats. Their desire for independence has been so great that in the 1920's and 30's they were even willing to invite foreign conquest as a way of getting rid of the Serbian dominated state of Yugoslavia. Hungary, Italy and Germany were all made use of throughout the period to aid in the destruction of Yugoslavia and the creation of an independent Croatian state. Croatian revolutionaries assassinated King Alexander I with the help of Italy and Hungary and the Croats assisted Germany in its conquest in 1941. As a reward, they were allowed their own autonomous state afterward. Only one other conquered people were given such a reward. The Slovaks were allowed an autonomous state after the conquest of Czechoslavakia. I wanted to see why this happened in the case of the Croats from both sides.

3) The question then arises; how did the Croatians fare in Yugoslavia? What was government policy and how thoroughly was it

carried out? What sort of government system did various people and groups hope to create in the area? Could the Croatian grievances have been assuaged in any sort of federal state where they were not dominant? Was there some other sort of government that might have worked?

4) What was the German attitude to Yugoslavia specifically? Could an independent Yugoslavia continue to exist in a German dominated Europe? We asked the question generally about Europe as a whole but the question still exists about his plans for Yugoslavia itself. In other words, just what did Hitler plan to do with it? Would it be conquered or allowed to retain some kind of independence in Hitler's new Europe?

5) What was the attitude of Italy? Italy had dreams of an Italian empire in the Danube basin and the Balkans. How did this relate to growing German interest in southeast Europe? Was an Italian Balkan empire consistent with German plans?

In attempting to answer all these questions, I found three works which have contributed a good deal to this paper. They are the books by Hoptner, Maček and Ristić.[1] They all illustrate, however, the major problems in writing the history of the Balkans. There, simply, is little unbiased material to use. Nearly all books on the area's modern history were written by participants who were trying to appear in the best light and defend the movements of which they were part. The governments of which I am writing obviously failed since the country was conquered by the Germans. For reasons best known to themselves the post war governments have published almost nothing of the documents. Thus, we have to rely on the large number of memoirs and defence briefs put out by the participants during and after World War II.

J. B. Hoptner is the only person who has attempted to write a complete history of this period in Yugoslav history in any language. It grew out of a visit to Yugoslavia in 1946-47. When his book was published in 1962 much material was not yet available. In the succeeding years a mountain of new material has come out which modifies or changes many things Hoptner says. For instance, the German documents for much of the period, particularly for the coup and German invasion, were not yet published. Apparently the author made no effort to find such unpublished material. He also made much use of materials from the Nurnberg Trials which appear to be contradicted by documents from the German Foreign Ministry Archives that have since appeared. The British archives have been largely opened now for that period so that more trustworthy materials are available.

In purely internal Yugoslav matters Hoptner was sometimes forced to rely on one witness. Most of his story about the events leading up to the signing of the Tripartite Pact came solely from talks with Vladko Maček, the Croat Peasant Party leader. Maček is sometimes contradicted by other participants. Also, the German ambassador seems to have been quite well informed about matters. His reports at times give the story of an event that throws a different light on them than that of Maček and apparently a more trustworthy one. On the coup, Hoptner relied entirely on Brigadier-General Bora Mirkovic. The general apparently convinced Hoptner that he was the one who planned the coup against the regency government of Prince Paul, organized it and carried it out from behind the scenes. Again, from more recent material, this seems quite wide of the mark.

Although everyone who writes about Yugoslavia in this period must rely heavily on Hoptner, it is evident that in part his work needs revision. This was the starting point of my own work. My hope was to make better use of the great volume of German, British and French materials which he either did not have or barely touched. The most important additions are new material from Yugoslavia.

Among those working in Yugoslavia today Ferdo Čulinović[2] and Dusan Biber[3] have written the best books. Čulinović's book is a general history of Yugoslavia from 1918 to 1941 but concentrating on the period from 1938 to 1941. It is the most sober and least tinged with Communist ideology of any history written in Yugoslavia since 1945. It is looked upon as quite reliable. Again he accepts Hoptner's work as his starting point whether or not he condemns it for its capitalist orientation.

Biber's book is on the effect of Nazism on the german minority of Yugoslavia, particularly those in Slovenia. He recounts the effect Hitler's appearance and success had there and recounts the growth of a local Nazi movement going on to tell of its use by Hitler in 1941 and the fate of those Germans as the war went against them. It is an excellent study of one german minority throughout the Hitler period.

Johann Wuescht's[4] book and collection of documents tells the story from the other side. He was a slovenian german driven out after the war. This book purports to be a documentary history of German-Yugoslav relations from 1933 to 1945. It is largely a defense of the Germans in Yugoslavia and their conduct during the occupation. It, therefore, becomes condemnatory of the Yugoslavs. Despite its very evident bias, it is a valuable collection bringing together many documents difficult to obtain otherwise.

Vladko Maček's memoirs largely repeat the story told in Hoptner. Despite the time that has elapsed, he has not changed his story. His book, therefore, becomes an amplification of Hoptner on certain aspects of his story. He recounts these important events in such vague terms, however, that one is still left puzzled as to what happened and why.

One of the most important books by a participant in these events is that by Ristić. He was aide de campe to General Simović during the coup against Prince Paul. Furthermore, he had full access to the unpublished memoirs of General Simović. The story he tells contradicts that of Maček and Hoptner in a number of ways. While Maček tends to be vague and superficial, Ristić tells his story in detail and with confidence. It bears the stamp of greater reliability. Another valuable study is that by Roberts[5] on the assassination of King Alexander. Unfortunately it contains no footnotes or bibliography. I have, therefore, been forced to use it sparingly.

One of the most important controversies in studying Yugoslavia in the interwar period is the character of King Alexander. Very few writers, if any, are neutral on the subject. Their opinions range between portraying the king as a power hungry despot on the lines of a king Carol of Rumania who took his country on the road to dictatorship. Some call him a fascist and equate him with Mussolini and Hitler. He, therefore, worked for friendship with them because they were kindred fascist states. The opposite view is that the king was a democrat and parliamentarian who was forced to adopt a position which he himself deplored because events forced him to do so.

The most notorious example of the first school is Svetozar Pribičević[6]. He had become a leading politician in Croatia and the Austro-Hungarian Empire before World War I. Like most others of the kind at the time, he was for a federalized Yugoslavia when it came to forming the new state. He, therefore, opposed the Serbians who wanted a centralized government. Later, after agreeing to proposals from the Serbians which created a more centralized federation than the Croatians wanted, he claimed he had been tricked. No one seems to know why he agreed to these proposals. He became a bitter opponent of the king and all he did. He was one of the foremost advocates of the proposition that the King was a fascist. One with similar ideas who was very popular in the United States was the Communist writer, Louis Adamić.[7] Between them they were largely responsible for the almost universally held view in the West that Alexander was a species of Fascist or at least closely sympathetic to them.

On the other side was Stephen Graham[8]. His biography of the king is a hymn of praise to a king who could do no wrong. He was constantly working for nothing but the good of the country. His opponents wanted nothing but their own selfish good, or most commonly, were working for others. He usually means Italy when he says this.

Between these extremes a good example of a more judicious view is Hamilton Fish Armstrong[9]. He had developed a close relationship with the king over a period extending from the end of World War I to the king's death. He found him a congenial person who believed in parliamentary government and constitutional monarchy. He believed the king was forced by events to do as he did. Nevertheless, Armstrong says the king was wrong to institute the dictatorship. He should have used persuasion and consultation since the only result of his actions was to alienate those who should have been helping to correct the problems. Despite all this, Armstrong believed Alexander was the only hope of the country if it was to pull itself together and become a community. Only Tito since had the ability to do so but even he has not permanently cured the nationality problems of the country. If Alexander had had another ten years, the added hatreds produced during World War II might never have happened and so made the cure easier to obtain.

A number of major problems arose in making this study. Among them was the question of Fascism in Yugoslavia. Did a true Fascism exist in Yugoslavia and, if it did, what social and political groups supported it? This breaks down to the study of three groups. 1) The dictatorship of King Alexander. Was it like that of King Carol of Rumania or Admiral Horthy of Hungary? 2) Milan Stojadinović's Green Shirts. This was the nearest thing to a true fascism but was clearly modeled exactly on those of Germany and Italy. 3) The Ustaša. This was the only one in the group of native origin.

When one analyses the Ustaša, it appears less likely that it was a true fascist movement. Ideologically it was based on little more than desire to see the return of the Habsburgs. It was confined almost entirely to Croatia, an area that had been ruled by the Habsburgs. Socially its followers came mainly from groups that had lost out by the incorporation of Croatia into Yugoslavia. These were certain parts of the middle class in Croatia and Slovenia as well as the remains of the old landowning class expropriated by the land reform instituted soon after the creation of Yugoslavia. It also included some peasants who saw the prices of their crops drop when easy access to the markets of Vienna was lost.

Its main motivation was anger at the disappearance of an old, secure way of life; a nostalgia for what could never return. They looked on Yugoslavia with hatred because they blamed it for all their problems. The Ustaša had no constructive ideas or positive program. Because of that it had no chance to spread to other discontented groups. Throughout the 1930's its membership remained stable. Outside the problems caused the government by its use of terror, it was a negligible force.

Externally it was another matter. It soon became apparent that it was receiving considerable support from foreign governments, namely Italy and Hungary. The constant violence they unleashed in Yugoslavia caused relations of Yugoslavia with those countries to worsen. Contrariwise, those countries encouraged the Ustasa to increase their violence whenever they wanted to put pressure on the Yugoslav government.

One of the major questions about the Ustaša I set out to examine in this paper was what relationship they had with Germany. Many of the accounts by Yugoslavs who had anything to do with these events, as well as western newsmen, blame the Ustasa for the entire breakdown of the country and the shortsighted view of the whole thing taken by certain rather slimy politicians. The entire thing, they say, was a german plot and done directly at Hitler's orders. It seems now impossible to resolve the matter but I have gone into what I consider the balance of probability.

The problem for Yugoslavia, then, was not an attraction to Fascism but a more basic problem. That was simply the difficulty of bringing together people of similar cultural and racial roots but who had come to differ profoundly over a long historical time. In fact, many of them had become irreconcilably hostile to each other. Many even came to prefer the alien rule of Italy or Germany rather than that of the dominant Serbs in Yugoslavia. This willingness to endure a foreign rule illustrates how profound the hostilities were and are. Somehow this problem has to be solved if Yugoslavia is to continue.

Another problem is, of course, the question of the attitude of the Allies in stopping aggression. As is shown in the paper, Yugoslavia found herself with no meaningful support from France or England throughout the period. She was left on her own resources for defence. She hoped to use a policy of divide and conquer against Italy and Germany, entangling them so much in their conflicting ambitions that they would leave Yugoslavia alone. This worked for a while because Mussolini was too dependent on Hitler and was willing to trust him a certain distance. When his ambition and jealousy became too great and he tried his Greek adventure, Hitler had to change his views and actively intervene in the Balkans. Italy after that became a subordinate and had no chance to adopt her own policy in the Balkans.

Then the Allies again took an interest. But, they showed no knowledge of the area or anything but a desire to use the area to achieve their own ends. The fate of Yugoslavia and Greece in 1941 illustrates this. Probably someway could have been found not to make the area a battlefield. War came in 1941 only because the Allies hoped to catch the Axis in the Balkan morass, not because they genuinely hoped to achieve the independence of those states. The unrealistic way the Allies encouraged the Yugoslavs to resist the Axis Pact must bear some of the blame for what happened. Hitler might have merely aided Mussolini instead of mounting an invasion of Yugoslavia and Greece if the British had stayed out of Greece.

The real problem then becomes these conflicting ambitions of Italy and Germany. If Germany had been able to control Italy Yugoslavia might have been left alone as were Sweden and Switzerland. She would have been forced to continue to send all her raw materials and agricultural products to Germany but could have remained independent. The adventure in Greece that Italy could not handle and then British involvement to aid Greece made German pressure on Yugoslavia inevitable. The only way German aid could go directly to the front in Greece was through Yugoslavia. A way around might have been found without British involvement. This was like a red rag before a bull to Hitler by this time. Given all this, Yugoslavia was faced with certain German control.

Thus, the fact that Italy wanted an empire in the Balkans and Mussolini felt left out of Hitler's Europe together with the rather cynical involvement of Britain in the area were the problem. The nationality problem in Yugoslavia becomes a tool all of them used to achieve their ends. None of them cared what happened to the various peoples concerned. Their dreams and hopes, thus, seem more and more like living in a dream world far removed from the politics and realities of the time.

Like so many others around the world, these Yugoslav politicians had little comprehension of what Fascism was all about or what sort of men they were trying to work with. As I say many times in my book, they thought they were working with the same sort of trust-worthy German leaders they had always known. As with the others, they had to learn from bitter experience.

CHAPTER 1
THE YUGOSLAV PROBLEMS TO THE ASSASSINATION
OF KING ALEXANDER

The country we now call Yugoslavia is one of the states created as a result of World War I. Its creation made almost as many problems as it was meant to solve. The principal problem for the new state was the national question. Yugoslavia was formed from several areas which had had the most diverse political, religious and national development. All but one of these areas had had some kind of independent political life in the Middle Ages. After the conquest of the Balkans by the Ottoman Turks in the 14th and 15th centuries, Serbia and several areas inhabited by people of Serbian stock remained under their domination until the 19th and even 20th century. Slovenia, the westernmost of the Balkan slavic areas, never was independent. After Turkish rule, they were conquered by the Habsburgs in the 15th and 16th centuries. Croatia, after a short period as the ruler of a rather extensive state, joined Hungary in the 12th century. It had, therefore, become part of the Habsburg Empire in the 16th century along with Hungary. The Kingdom of Montenegro was the only state in the Balkans to retain at least a semi-independent condition throughout the period.[1]

The religious situation was even more involved. Croatia and Slovenia were almost wholly Roman Catholic while Serbia and Montenegro were Orthodox. In addition, there was a large Mohammedan minority scattered all over the country but found in its largest numbers in Macdeonia and the south.

These religious differences caused a great deal of hostility between the parts of the new state founded after World War I. Politically Serbia was still very oriental. The top political leadership still came from the old leadership groups. That is, the almost illiterate landlord or chieftain class who had mainly now become professional politicians or army officers. The membership of the parties, however, increasingly came from those who controlled business and from the growing middle class which developed phenomenally after 1918. It was a parliamentary state but these upper classes controlled the Skupstina (the name of the Serbian parliament later taken as the name for the Yugoslav parliament) through their domination of the peasantry.[2] Croatia had long taken part in the parliamentary traditions of Austria-Hungary. There was a very strong group of parties based on popular support widely distributed among all parts of the society. The parties, however, were controlled by the upper classes.[3]

In most cases these upper class politicians were quite unable to work in a true parliamentary system, particularly in Croatia. Their brand of politics under Austro-Hungarian rule was opposition and obstruction against the Germans and Hungarians. The nationalties hoped to obtain self rule and realization of their dreams for their own governments in their own states by these means. When these people went into the Yugoslav parliament they knew no other way to carry on political action except the promotion of parliamentary chaos. "Thus only parliamentary sabotage was developed and none of the finer statecraft of piloting legislation to successful enactment."[4] Therefore, they were glad of the excuse to show that the new state was not allowing the Croats their full place and so went over again to a policy of opposition. As could be expected, the political solution favored by these politicians was a new dualism of Croatia and Serbia.[5]

The Serbian parties were little better. They supported a Great Serbia policy whereby the new state was to be regarded as a Serbian empire. The premier of Serbia, Nikola Pasić, was a leading exponent of that idea. He had been a leader in the movement for a greater Serbia for some years before World War I.[6] Much of the sympathy for this expansion among these politicians came from a desire to line their own pockets. Political life in Serbia was corrupt in the extreme and so the new acquisitions were regarded as a wonderful windfall. Much of the anti-government feeling in the new areas can be directly traced to an experience of the corruption of the new government. This is not to say, however, that it was wholly or even largely corrupt but there was a significant percentage of corrupt individuals. These people had ample opportunity for corruption because of the structure of the country. Most of the local power was in the hands of bureaucrats appointed from Belgrade. Their actions were aften very arbitrary. In addition most were Serbs and allowed anti-Croat prejudice to influence their actions.[7]

As one can see from what has already been said, the nationality question was responsible to a large degree for the lack of support for the new country. South Slav nationalism was among the various brands of nationalism which appeared in the 19th century. Those who held to this looked to the unification of all the Slavs in the Balkan area into one state. However, after the formation of the independent states of Serbia and Bulgaria all hopes of such a solution disappeared because of their rivalry over Macedonia. Any sense of solidarity they may have had soon waned and ended in the Balkan Wars of 1912. From that time on, the South Slav ideal was the union of all the Slavs of the Balkans except Bulgaria. The Serb-Croat Question largely arose over the structure of the new state. This began in the period 1914-1918 when it first became of practical importance. At one pole was the Radical Party of Serbia under Nikola Pasić. He, as we saw earlier was a passionate believer in a strongly centralized state under the control of the Serbian government. At the other pole were the Croats who wanted an autonomous Croatia. They based this hope on the claims of "the historic state," since they felt Croatia had never lost its identity as a separate state. It is true that it had been part of Hungary since 1102. The Croats said their joining Hungary had been entirely voluntary on their part and certain rights had been reserved to Croatia. Therefore, it had never ceased to be a separate state.[8] Some of them wanted to make Croatia a monarchy so that their union with Serbia would be a purely personal one, based on having the same king, as was the union of Austria and Hungary in the Ausgleich of 1867. Others wanted a Croat republic within the yugoslav monarchy. There were only a very few who wanted an entirely independent country.[9]

The vast majority of people were, however, in favor of this new state not only because they favored the union but became of the esteem in which the king was generally held. Alexander was a generally popular king throughout his life and trusted by the people in what he did. This was due not only to his personality and attitude to his office but mainly because he had been head of state during World War I. His father, King Peter I, was officially king until 1921. He had, however, become king in 1903 as a result of a coup d'etat when he was already 60 years old. In 1914 he had become too ill to fulfill the functions of his office and so made his son, Alexander, the regent. In the popular mind he was identified with the highly popular struggle against Austria and Bulgaria in World War I and received the credit for victory even though he was only regent.[10]

Some writers were hostile to him almost from the foundation of Yugoslavia. Among them was the Croatian politician, Svetozar Pribičević. At the key moment in the formation of Yugoslavia he brought his influence over to support of Alexander's plans for a centralized state rather than the federal one most Croatian politicans had wanted. This was crucial in winning most Croatians to accepting it. Apparently later Pribičević came to the conclusion that he had been tricked and came to hate Alexander bitterly. Unfortunately, for a long time his biography of Alexander was the only one known outside the country. Thus, its picture of a monster consumed by personal ambition and dictatorial desires was accepted as true. To Pribičević he was the same as Hitler and Mussolini.[11]

Before going into the development of the king's personal rule, it will be well first to discuss the political groups that were to be found in the new state. The party which had championed the Yugoslav Idea before World War I, the Democratic Party, had begun in Croatia but spread to Serbia as well. In other words, it was a Yugoslav party rather than one belonging to any specific national group. This ideal had not been realized when the new state was formed. With its failure the party collapsed in Croatia. The party survived in Serbia. There was also a small splinter group called the Independent Democratic Party.[12]

In Croatia the Democratic Party lost all its adherents to the Croatian Peasant Party founded in 1905 by Antun and Stjepan Radić. By 1933, when it had become the champion of the idea of federation and the defender against Belgrade, some 90% of the Croats voted for this party. It had been founded on the idea that, since the peasants were the largest part of the population, they, rather than the upper classes, should control the government. Their program was based on green socialism.[13]

In addition, there was the Croat Party of the Right founded by Antun Starčević. This party rose in reaction to Austro-Hungarian domination and Serb nationalism. As such, it was one of the most popular parties before World War I. It based its appeal largely on the religious differences between the Serbs and Croats. Later it became very conservative. Its official name was Pure Party of the Right.

After the death of Antun Starčević the party split, one part becoming known as the Francovci because their leader was Dr Joseph Frank, a Zagreb lawyer. They became the symbols of the most reactionary ideas, among which was their advocacy of the return of the Habsburgs.[14] The Frankovci broke up after World War I but was reconstituted when the national question broke out again in 1929. It was re-formed under the leadership of Dr Ante Pavelić, another Zegreb lawyer, on 7 January 1929 in Zagreb. It was far from a mass party but came to have great importance, as we shall see. Its membership was made up of a few small merchants, artisans and middle class youths in a few large towns as well as a few village priests and rich kulaks. From this you can see that it resembled Fascism in that its members came from similar social groups. Like Fascism, its favorite type of political action was terrorism. Officially it was the Croat Revolutionary Organization although popularly called the Ustaša.[15]

In Serbia the two major parties were the already mentioned Democratic Party and the Radical Party. It should be mentioned here that neither one followed the principles one would expect from its name. The Democrats favored a strong, centralized state, as long as they controlled it. The Radicals had also become quite conservative by this time. The Radicals now represented vested interests as well as a policy of uniting all Serbs to the Piedmont of Serbia. The party had been founded in 1881 as a genuinely radical and revolutionary party to represent the interests of the peasants and for radical reform of the state. The person most people associated with it from the beginning was the man who wrote its platform originally and only gave up its leadership on his death, Nikola Pasić.[16]

The other major political group in the new state at the moment of its founding was the Communist Party. In 1920, in the first national elections for the Skupstina, they received 58 seats. This has been called the only completely free election in Yugoslav history. It made the Communists the third largest party in the Skupstina. This largely reflected the fact that many small national groups were not allowed to put up slates of their own and so voted Communist as a means of expressing their opposition. Also most of the other parties had left social reform for nationalism, the main exception being the Croat Peasant Party which had both. This tremendous vote so frightened the other groups that the Communists were immediately persecuted and later in the year they were outlawed. Many intellectuals joined Communism thereafter as a means of expressing their disenchantment with the status quo rather than any love for the principles of Karl Marx. Until the revolt against the Germans during World War II, the Communists had little practical importance.[17]

The parties described above were those that aroused most interest although there were many other parties, largely based on national or religious principles. The number was so large because the electoral procedure was by proportional representation, copied from the French system.

The national question, thus, pretty much dominated all political life during the 1920's. Nikola Pasić's control of politics assured that his idea of a unitary state controlled by Serbia would remain dominant. After his death in 1926 the situation got more and more out of hand. There was no one with his grasp of politics or who had the strength to dominate events as he had. The corruption mentioned earlier became worse and worse. The situation finally came to a head on June 20, 1928. On that day the head of the Croat Peasant Party, Stjepan Radić, and four other deputies were shot in the Skupstina by another politician who thought he had been insulted by Radić.[19]

The successor to Radić as leader of the Peasant Party was Dr Vladko Maček. He was a much less able man than his predecessor, as his whole attitude from then on was to show. In meetings with the king on January 4 and 5, 1929 Maček made the following demands to achieve a reconciliation. There were to be elections for a new constituent assembly to revise the constitution; Croatia was to receive her full independence during this period of reorganization; the connection to Serbia was to be a purely personal union in which the king of Serbia would also be the king of Croatia. This would be the only tie between the two countries. This was not to be the case for Croatia only. The entire country was to be split up into its 7 parts (the king modified this to 5 by splitting Bosnia between Serbia and Croatia and giving Macedonia to Serbia without informing Maček). There was to be no national army. Each federal unit would have its own.[20] To the king these demands were equivalent to destroying the country. The very next day Alexander established his personal dictatorship. The establishment of the royal dictatorship has been loudly denounced by nearly all the Yugoslav writers who have published in the West.[21] Under the new system, the king was to be the complete leader of the country. On January 8 all parties organized on a religious or "tribal" basis were suppressed. On January 24 the same fate was meted out to the Serbian parties. Also a censorship was set up. The country was divided to provinces entirely controlled from Belgrade.[22]

Looked at without bias, the king's actions can be seen perhaps in a better light. The political life of the country up to that time was not such as to make anyone see much hope for democracy. The actions of the skupstina were not very much calculated to promote the good of the country but rather the good of the politicians.

The deliberations of the skupstina seem like those of the Austro-Hungarian parliament in its last years. Little could be done because of the constant opposition of the Croats. After the assassination of Radić this became much worse since the Croats went over to total opposition.[23] They blamed the government for allowing his murder to happen and even tried to say that the assassin was a tool of the king.[24]

This is all nonsense, however, as Alexander was raised in traditions of political and personal liberty. He always greatly admired England. Under the conditions rapidly coming to the fore in Yugoslavia he could see no hope for a liberal parliamentary system unless the government was cleansed and the people educated up to the level where they could understand and appreciate what democracy really was. This was what he hoped to do under his dictatorship. He stated that his action was only temporary and that a new constitution would be drafted.[25] Alexander summed up his desires for the country in the following statement, "What I require is forty years of peace in which to build up a tradition of honest administration."[26]

The people seem to have accepted the dictatorship much more readily than the professional politicians. The people as a whole had not become politically conscious enough as yet to want freedom at the expense of efficient, trouble free administration. They saw a decrease in graft. Many highly popular measures that had been blocked for years by the obstructionist tactics of the parliamentarians were at last implemented. Also, they found they liked efficient government by experts. Even the average Croat liked the king more than could be believed by reading the dispossessed parliamentarians. This is particularly shown by the greeting the king received on his visit to Zagreb in 1933.[27] The reason for the people's favorable response seems to have been that it put everyone on the same footing. All were ruled equally by the dictatorship.

Had the king lived beyond 1934, the evidence seems to show that there would have been a trend toward liberalization of the regime. The constitution of 1931 was a step in this direction as it made at least a facade of democracy. In 1932 came a reform of the laws on political parties, elections and association. There are some reports that he intended to end the dictatorship altogether on his return from his fatal trip to France.[28] At the least, his regime did stifle disunity. If he or another strong hand had remained at the helm, there is hope that the various groups might have learned to work together. The communist regime has somewhat realized his dream but only by using harsh repression. But the prevalence of anti-government terrorism around the world shows that separatism still exists.

The greatest problem of Yugoslav history in the 20th century is that major questions never could be worked out because foreign states hoped to use them to control or even conquer the country. Through the 19th and 20th centuries the Balkans had been the cockpit of European quarrels. The states of the area have had little chance to decide on their own destinies unhampered by outside interference. Yugoslavia has been the focal point for this because of its very important geographic position. Austria, Hungary, Imperial Russia, Italy, Germany and Soviet Russia all sought to use the national question for their own ends. The effectiveness of this technique as used by Nazi Germany in World War II is notorious. Nevertheless, it has never been studied in a dispassionate way as a whole. Much is accepted as truth which is dubious, to say the least. As I have attempted to show already, most of what has been published in western languages about the problem was done for political reasons. My hope is to sift through this material and present a less biased account.

In this paper I am concentrating on the Croatian problem. Some of the other national groups presented as much, if not more, of a problem but the size of this group, its relatively advanced political consciousness and consequent leadership on opposition to the state make it the most important for such a study. This is not meant to denigrate the Slovenes, Macedonians, Albanians or the German minority, to mention only a few. But, their importance was largely local and could not so much effect the existence of the state.

The hard core of opposition came from certain Fascist, or really semi-Fascist, organizations whose membership was largely Croatian and meant to transform the state on Fascist lines. They were used by the Germans and Italians after the conquest to rule Yugoslavia and were even allowed to retain a semi-autonomous state of their own based on the medieval kingdom of Croatia. This and the state of Slovakia, carved out of Czechoslovakia, are the only instances of this sort done by Hitler during the war. Thus such a national movement, seen by Hitler as so trustworthy that they could be allowed so much autonomy, takes on a peculiar interest.

The group in Croatia most vociferously friendly to Fascism was the Ustaša. The origins and beliefs of this movement have already been described. As far as membership is concerned, they were quite insignificant. They took the lead in strong denunciation of the regime, however, and this had an effect on many people who could not accept their other ideas. The noise they made and the notoriety they attained gave them a greater importance in the eyes of the world than they deserved. Hitler realized this and never made use of them exclusive of other groups or leaders. In fact, for some time he refused to use them at all despite the urging of Mussolini, because he regarded them as a distinct liability.[29] His early efforts were directed toward influencing the government through trade, offering protection against Italy and Hungary and giving them the example of his new political system. The Ustaša was kept as an auxiliary on the side. It was only with the development of the Greek situation and British involvement there as well as the breakdown of attempts to recruit Yugoslavia into the Axis that the Ustaša took on importance in Hitler's eyes. As shown by what happened in Czechoslovakia or Norway, he never did trust or like native Fascist movements. His usual attitude was to use them as tools to back the resistance of more important groups and then forget them.

Hitler realized, however, that this movement had little influence in the country and was even looked on with hatred and fear by the great majority, even in Croatia. Therefore, his major effort in Croatia was to work with the Croatian Peasant Party. Radić, its founder, had had no sympathy for the growing Nazi movement in Germany. His successor, Maček, was not as quick to see the evils and dangers of cooperation with Hitler. His one aim was freedom for Croatia to manage its own affairs within the monarchy. He thought, or made himself think, that Germany was only interested in helping him attain this. Then too he seems to have retained the old idea of Italy as the traditional enemy even after the Anschluss had placed the German frontier right on that of Yugoslavia.[30] Hitler was very clever at using the various changes of the internal situation in Yugoslavia for his own advantage.

Up to the Anschluss, Italy was the major enemy of Yugoslavia in truth. Since the 19th century Italy had a great interest in expansion into the Balkans. One of her major goals in entering World War I on the side of the Entente was to gain substantial parts of the area. Her wishes had been agreed to by the allies in the Treaty of London in 1915.[31] It was only with the greatest difficulty that Yugoslavia had on to most of this territory after the war. Mussolini inherited a great deal of hatred for Yugoslavia when he took control of Italy. His interest in D'Annunzio and the Fiume Question illustrates this. Therefore,

Mussolini maintained the same bad relations with Yugoslavia as had governments before him. It was his hope to somehow gain the territories that Italy had claimed and, perhaps, all of Croatia, Montenegro and Albania thus cutting Yugoslavia off from the sea. The rump left would then be totally dependent on Italy for its trade and even continued existence.[32]

Mussolini could find few groups in the country willing to support him. The tradition of mutual hatred between the Italians and the Balkan peoples goes all the way back to the 15th century at least and the Venetian Empire which then controlled Dalmatia. The only friends he could find were those who openly sympathized with the fascist viewpoint, that is the Ustaša. Stephen Graham, the biographer of Alexander, claims they did not even have a real philosophy of government or social reform. They were out for nothing but their own private gain.[33] Ernst Nolte in his book on Fascism also does not regard them as real Fascists. One of the major reasons for this was their lack of support at home and their subordination ideologically and in ideas on organization and method to outside examples.[34] After the group was reformed by Pavelić after World War I, they were forced to flee the country and had to pursue their goals from exile.[35]

This dependence can be seen in the fact that they tried to gain the support of every group interested in revision of the status quo in Yugoslavia. Pavelić was interested in modeling his group on IMRO and worked to gain their support.[36] At first the Ustaša was supported by Hungary.[37] The old Frankists had been Habsburg legitimists. Therefore, Hungary hoped to use the Ustaša for her own advantage to regain the territories lost after World War I. Later on Mussolini also cooperated signing a secret military convention in 1929 with Hungary for mutual aid in taking over Croatia. Secret arrangements were made with Austria for the transit of troops and munitions across the country. In 1931 these arrangements were expanded in a convention for policial cooperation as well.[38]

All of this received its great impetus from the crisis of 1929 caused by the assassination of Radić and the start of the royal dictatorship. The Ustaša was organized in that year.[39] Mussolini also saw the dictatorship as his golden opportunity to realize his ambitions.[40] The assassination of Radić and then the setting up of the dictatorship alienated nearly all Croats from the regime to a certain degree. The Ustaša was only a tiny group that advocated violence and the use of terror as their primary weapon. They did not care who outside the country gave them help in their scheme to entirely wreck the monarchy. They had to recognize after all that they had almost no support at home.[41]

The fact that the Ustaša leaders went first to Hungary for aid shows the kind of regime they visualized. Their early hope was for a revival of the Habsburg monarchy but in a federalized form so that Croatia could govern herself. The fact that this could not be realized came home to them early and then they simply settled down to the destruction of Yugoslavia. Help would be accepted from any source. They did not seem to consider that they might fall under a worse tyranny when their schemes had been accomplished. The average Croat seems to have had little sympathy for the Habsburg revival. What support Mussolini gave seems to have been because it provided the most understandable source of opposition to the Yugoslav monarchy.[42]

The use by Mussolini of the Ustaša at this time was blocked by the strong response of King Alexander himself. By 1932 the relations of Italy and Yugoslavia had deteriorated to a very low point. The king decided something must be done about this and so he tried to set up secret discussions with France and Italy in order to create a bloc based on the peace treaties of 1919. His hope was to unite these states once again on the old basis of preventing Germany from upsetting the order of Europe. Italy would be unable to attack Yugoslavia and might forget her because of being so involved in the larger problem. Italy refused to take part because in June there had been an outbreak from the Ustaša and Mussolini expected the country to fall apart. By November he had moved to provoke the proclamation of a Croat republic in the vicinity of Fiume. His scheme was to have the Ustaša invade Yugoslavia and proclaim an independent Croatia to which he would immediately grant recognition. The Yugoslav intelligence service learned of these plans and the massing of Italian troops on the border. Mussolini was forced to back down when he received a message from the king saying that he would regard any outbreak by the terrorists as an attack by Italy and would act accordingly. At the same time he would bring the matter before the League of Nations, accusing Italy of aggression.[43]

Thus, Alexander took a strong line in protecting his country against this long standing problem. Because of the attitude of the people he was able to act in this way. As I have tried to show, the people were essentially behind the king. He definitely reflected the opinion of the people when it came to foreign policy and relations to Italy. The support was particularly evident when he tried to strengthen the Little Entente and founded the Balkan Entente.

The Little Entente was originally set up by Czechoslovakia, Rumania and Yugoslavia to maintain the status quo in the Danube basin. This meant it was directed against those states in Central Europe and the Balkans which desired a revision of the Versailles Treaties. Most of the countries felt they had most to fear from Hungary. France took an important hand in achieving this system and then took care to maintain it. Her interest was, of course, twofold. It was part of her effort to ring Germany inside a wall which would prevent her from breaking out again. It was also part of her effort to isolate Communism within Russia.[44]

Between 1924 and 1927 the relations of the Little Entente and
Hungary considerably improved to the point where an agreement was
made with Yugoslavia. This good beginning was destroyed when
Hungary decided to base her alliance on a great power instead. She
chose Italy and so destroyed relations with Yugoslvia. It marks the
fact that Hungary had decided to return to a strong revisionist position for which she needed the aid of a great power.[45]

Hungary saw certain weaknesses in the Little Entente and set out
to exploit them for her own interests. These essentially were two in
number. 1) Internal instability in the member countries. 2) Divergent
interests of each in the international sphere. Czechoslovakia was
threatened by Germany, Rumania by Russia and Yugoslavia by Italy.
It was hoped that these other dangers could be maneuvered into the
foreground and so make the danger from Hungary seem less immediate. Thus, the solidarity against her revisionism could be broken and
Hungary could move ahead. This was the reason for the rapprochement with Italy. The difficulties in the relations of Italy and Yugoslavia
were regarded in Hungary as the weakest link in the Little Entente.[46]

Another reason for the rapprochement with Italy was that Yugoslavia did not fear a German takeover of Austria. To both Czechoslovakia and Rumania this was a positive evil but in Yugoslavia it
was regarded as a good thing. She did not think of Germany as having
ambitions in the Balkans. Even if Germany did have these ambitions,
it would still be good because she was bound to clash with Italy whose
ambitions also looked toward Austria and the Balkans. Thus, she as
a great power could be used to block the desires of Italy against
Yugoslavia.[47]

This is, of course, where a good part of the problem arises later
on. Yugoslavia was unwilling to join any combination planning to
frustrate Germany because the only result of such action, as far as
she could see, would be to leave her at the utter mercy of Italy. Her
problem came to be that she could not see how to live without Germany
as a neighbor. But then came Hitler and she then began to wonder
equally how she could live with her. Then came the frustrating attempt
to play off one against the other in the hope that they would come
to forget her and let her live on. Once the unity of the Entente was
broken and any hope of action was gone, the rest of the story almost
appears inevitable and a certain element of hopelessness enters the
picture.

This is, at least, the way it presents itself to us now from the vantage
point of hindsight. To the leaders of the time, it appeared that there
was little danger to be expected from Germany for some time. Ever
since Bismarck there had seemed little German interest in southeast
Europe except as a communications link to the east and as a market
for German goods. As a consequence, the Yugoslavs did not regard
the domination of Austria by Hitler as the opening wedge in a drive

for political control of the Danube basin. Thus, when the Little Entente was destroyed it did not appear tragic that they were now forced to look to Berlin for protection against Italy and Hungary.

All of this presented major problems for Yugoslavia's chief ally, France. Her international position was based on containing Germany by a ring of alliances of which the Little Entente was a major part. Without Yugoslavia the Little Entente would be useless. However, Italian hostility toward Germany particularly over Austria was also very important in French eyes. Therefore, the problem for France became how to keep Yugoslavia happy despite her constant cries for proection and help against Italy while retaining the support of Mussolini.[48] This began to become increasingly important, as we shall see, when the assassination of the king of Yugoslavia occurred soon after the attempted coup against Austria, and the attempts to bring Italy into a general disarmament scheme designed to pen Germany up and control her. Thus, the Yugoslavs saw themselves increasingly neglected. The value of the connection came under fire more and more as France showed herself incapable of stopping Hitler. Furthermore, France and England showed themselves unable or unwilling to solve Yugoslavia's greatest economic problem of the 30's which was how to sell her products on the depressed international market. Thus, the action which would could help her seemed as time went on to be to desert the unnatural connection with France and accept the natural one with Germany.

Nonetheless, the Little Entente remained effective for some time yet. There was in addition to the Little Entente another regional Balkan group formed at this time which played an important role in these events. This was the Balkan Entente formed on 9 February 1934 composed of Yugoslavia, Greece, Rumania and Turkey.

This league was formed as a result of several problems. One was fear of the increasing strength of Germany and a consequent desire to provide for their own defense by an organization similar to the Little Entente. The other was their fear of a Great Yugoslav State due to the increasing friendliness of Bulgaria and Yugoslavia. This lead to a recurrence of the old fear that union of all Slavs in the Balkans into one state (which, of course, was the old dream of South Slav nationalism before World War I) would result in the domination of the area by such a large state. Rumania and Greece thought it necessary to get together to prevent such an event.[49]

Corruption and bad government were so widespread in Bulgaria that a number of reform groups appeared, all of which were at least quasi fascist and which were all so similar in program that they can be called one. The first was the Reserve Officers' League. The other was a group of intellectuals called the Chain (Zveno). Both were formed by army officers in 1930.[50]

Because their programs were, on the whole, needed, they came to have the support of the mass of people. They were rather authoritarian and fascist. It must be remembered in this regard that although the term democracy was used to describe the Bulgarian system, it merely served as a facade for the most rank corruption. Democracy was, despite words, all but dead. Their program called for dissolution of the Sobranye (the name for the parliament), dissolution of the political parties and trade unions and the establishment of authoritarian rule from above by the Zveno and its army friends. This was to be done through a new Sobranye elected in a corporative manner. The Fascists always denied it was a true fascist state and it is true that it did not take on most of the trappings. In addition, it oriented its foreign policy towards anti fascism and was in favor of the Great Yugoslav idea.[51]

By the beginning of 1933 they had most of the country back of them and proceeded to try to implement their policy. This was aimed particularly towards friendship with Yugoslavia. France and Britain encouraged this scheme from a desire to lessen tension and to increase the numbers in the anti fascist camp. King Alexander was certainly not averse to receiving Bulgarian overtures and continued to encourage them.[52]

From the Yugoslav point of view, it had long been imperative to come to an understanding with Bulgaria because of the difficulties with Italy and Hungary. The main point of difference between them was Macedonia. Both had long claimed the area and, as the Ottoman Empire had collapsed, each put forward its claims. Neither would relinquish its claims so that the result had been war in 1885 and again in 1912. The result was partition of the area which satisfied no one.

One result of this partition was the formation of a terrorist organization in Bulgaria. It was called the Internal Macedonian Revolutionary Organization or IMRO for short. It was anti Yugoslav and used frankly terrorist methods to bring about the ''return'' of all Macedonia to Bulgaria. It was not run by the Bulgarian government but controlled the government through fear of assassination by IMRO's agents and other brutal methods. Efforts had been made by the Bulgarian government to control IMRO but its wide following in the officer corps and its popularity among large and important segments of the population rendered these efforts futile.[53]

Both countries were becoming convinced by the 1930's that a settlement of their differences was necessary because the tension in both countries was becoming intense over IMRO acts of terrorism on their mutual frontier.[54] Furthermore, Italy saw how useful this state of turmoil could be in her efforts to realize her aims in Yugoslavia. She carefully supported Bulgarian claims to territory lost to Yugoslavia by the Treaty of Neuilly, engaged in a great deal of propaganda and subsidized IMRO.[55] The IMRO question was so explosive internally in Bulgaria that the first efforts at an understanding had to be limited to smaller problems. There were, thus, quasi governmental conferences and visits by the monarchs. These resulted in such non-political results as a project for a chamber of commerce and industry, a medical union and an agricultural union. The problem of a political pact eluded them, however, since Bulgaria refused to sign such a document thinking this would force them to recognize the territorial status quo. This Bulgaria refused to do while any land which had been part of Bulgaria in 1914 was in the hands of others.[56] There were, however, several factors which made a rapprochement more likely. One was the pact signed in June 1933 between Great Britain, France, Italy and Germany. In it these powers agreed to consult on all matters of common interest, to cooperate within the framework of the League of Nations in maintaining the peace, and together to consider ways to make the covenant of the League effective. In effect it created a directorate of Europe forcing the small states under the tutelage of the large. As such it aroused strong distrust in Yugoslavia and Bulgaria.[57]

King Alexander regarded this pact as an attempt by Italy and Germany to revise the peace treaties and particularly to change Yugoslavia's frontiers. He immediately entered pacts to prevent any danger of having to counter this act alone. On July 4, 1933 Yugoslavia signed a convention with the other Little Entente states as well as Turkey and the Soviet Union. In it the signatories defined various aggressive acts and stipulated that a country has the right to defend itself. Part of it seemed to point directly to Bulgaria in that it defined as an aggressor a state which supports on its territories armed bands whose only purpose is the invasion of another state, and which does not take measures to stop their activities upon representations from the endangered state. This could only point to IMRO.[58]

This made clear to Bulgaria that the raids by IMRO must be suppressed. Events in that country soon made this possible. In May 1934 a coup took place which resulted in the Military League and Zveno seizing power. One of their first acts was the interning or arrest of IMRO members in the country. Within a year Yugoslavia and Bulgaria signed a pact for joint operations to suppress IMRO activities along their common frontier.[59]

Greece and Turkey were, however, immediately alarmed at this seeing it as the prelude to the Great Yugoslav state they feared so much. Therefore, complicated maneuvering began. In May 1933 Greece and Turkey announced a treaty guaranteeing their common frontier. Bulgaria was invited to join, but in such a way as to make it seem that the whole thing was designed to embarrass her, because it would force her again to recognize her territorial losses. The final treaty was restricted to mutual guarantees against aggression by a Balkan state or its neighbors. In the conditions of the time this could only mean Bulgaria. Bulgaria did refuse to join as she was to refuse to join all these pacts. She felt she could not recognize in such a way the mutilated condition in which she had emerged from World War I.

The pact was signed nevertheless on September 14, 1933. M. Titulescu of Rumania then stepped in contacting all the countries except Albania to try to get them to sign similar treaties of non-aggression which would be crowned by a multi-lateral treaty of mutual guarantees. A Rumanian-Turkish and Yugoslav-Turkish set of treaties was soon signed and completed the network of treaties by which the four major states of the Balkans were joined, largely at the expense of Bulgaria. When it came to the larger treaty, Greece and Turkey were willing to sign if it was restricted to the Balkans. Greece was close to Italy and feared her very much while Turkey was much concerned about her neighbor, Russia. Alexander refused to yield preferring an attachment to Bulgaria rather than to a weakened general alliance. His interest, as formerly pointed out, had been to end his squabble with Bulgaria in order to present a larger front to Italy. This was just what Greece could not allow because of her fear of Italy. Nevertheless, with the seizure of control in Bulgaria by the officers' groups, there was a suppression of IMRO, which had been the immediate goal of the rapprochement. Nonetheless, a beginning was made in bringing Bulgaria over to a larger view of a Balkan pact when the personal animosity of Kings Alexander and Boris was changed to friendship after a visit by King Boris to Belgrade.[60]

King Alexander subsequently visited the capitals of the other states involved. The kind of pact he wanted against both internal and external aggression could not be obtained, however. Bulgaria finally refused to join while there was any hope of revising the Treaty of Neuilly and Greece refused to broaden the treaty to include mutual guarantees against aggression coming from outside the Balkans as well as within. Thus, the treaty took the form demanded by Greece and Turkey in the first place: that is, to isolate Bulgaria, especially from Yugoslavia. This extremely shortsighted view of her interests by Greece prevented formation of a new grouping which might have been decisive in the coming struggles.[61] This was merely another sign of what a shortsighted attitude the states of Europe took. It is one of those ironies of history that Greece succumbed to an attack initiated by Italy. If Southeast Europe had been long prepared for joint action, there might have been no attack.

The major watershed in the pre-war history of Yugoslavia is the assassination of King Alexander on October 9, 1934. While, as we shall see, the king was not averse to improving relations with Germany, he would probably have resisted German aggression into Southeastern Europe. He was a strong man who understood the realities of power and would not have hesitated to act if necessary. Since King Alexander's son was underage, the period after his death (1934-1941) was a regency under the dead king's brother, Prince Paul. He had neither the ability nor the strength to rule, especially in a country as divided as Yugoslavia. The situation could only go downhill

under those circumstances. It seems likely that if Alexander had
retained the throne an accommodation might have been worked
out on the nationality issue and firmer actions might have been
taken in the international sphere. Since the only really constructive
French statesman between the wars shared Alexander's fate on
that day, chances for containing aggression were considerably lessened.

The group responsible for the assassination of the king and M.
Barthou, the French foreign minister, was the Ustaša. As was said
earlier, this was at least a semi-fascist organization, taking its example
directly from Italian Fascism, according to one of the more important exile writers on this period. The post war regime of Marshal Tito
and his successors has called it nothing else than fascist.[62] There is
considerable controversy on the point. Nolte regards it as only semi-
Fascist, if that.[63] Little if any study of it as a fascist movement has
been done. Its one really strong point was a fanatical nationalism and
an attachment to monarchy. Essentially they hoped to create a Croatian state under a monarchy, possibly headed by a member of the
Habsburg dynasty. It is true that its membership came from those
social groups which supplied the classical fascist parties in Italy,
France and Germany; the middle class, civil servants, the wealthier
peasants and the conservative classes in general. However, these
classes were quite small in Yugoslavia although larger in Croatia than
most of the country. Croatia was probably the most economically and
socially developed part of the country from its days under the Habs-
bugs. Thus, its source of possible adherents was small. Its philosophy
remained reactionary in that it did not even give lip service to social
reform but advocated a return to the good old days of the Habsburgs.
If not them, they at least wanted a conservative monarchy. With all
this, it could only appeal to those who had lost something by the
dissolution of the Habsburg state. They made no real effort to state
their program in terms that could appeal to a mass audience, as did
Fascism and Naziism. Its following was always infinitesimal but cor-
respondingly fanatical. Its weapons were those of the terrorist. These
were so much a part of its makeup that, even when it achieved its
own state in 1941, it could not forget them and so could be called
responsible for destroying itself by 1944.[64]

The Ustaša was refounded, as previously stated, on January 7, 1929,
the day after the proclamation of King Alexander's dictatorship. Officially it was named the Croat Revolutionary Organization with Ante
Pavelić as its first leader.

From the first, the organization was under foreign pay. Its Frankist
antecedents assured that it would be attracted to Hungary. The
Frankists were for the old Habsburg Empire but based upon a new
trialist system that would create a self governing south slav bloc. This
made their name practically synonomous with revisionism. Since

Hungary was the most revisionist of the old Habsburg dominions the two were bound to come together.[65] Italy came into the picture in 1919 because of its efforts to expand at the expense of the new Yugoslavia. It was natural for these two revisionist states to team up for the realization of their aims. Both were glad to make use of this divisive force in Yugoslavia which was, on the other hand, using them for its own purposes.[66] They, at least, recognized there was small chance for them to bring off a popular revolt on their own. It has been stated that they were very much a minority party with no chance to become the majority given their rigid program and the social composition of the country. Therefore, they quite cynically sold out their nationalism to the highest bidder. At first Hungary and then Italy were only too glad to use them for their own ends.[67]

The question of whether Germany made any use of them in turn is, of course, an important one. It would seem that Hitler did not have to use them as the European situation was bringing Yugoslavia closer to Germany and breaking their contact with France. The result of the assassination was to accelerate this motion. It only worked to the harm of Italy, Hungary and France. The first two had to give up any hopes of a rapprochement with the Balkan states which they had been endeavoring to arrange. France pursued the killers in such a dilatory and timid fashion that Yugoslav confidence in her ability or willingness to protect them suffered a sharp drop. Germany was quick to step in and take advantage of the situation.[68]

It would have seemed that Yugoslavia should have been alarmed by the recurring German efforts to absorb Austria. Yet, just the opposite was its real effect. Relations had never been very friendly between Belgrade and Vienna. Intrigue against Yugoslavia had often originated there. The takeover of Austria by Germany seemed to end this. For another thing, Alexander admired Hitler. He found him a man of his own type, direct and seemingly with no subterfuge, knowing his own mind, or so Alexander thought. Most importantly, Hitler forced all Pavelić's agents to stop their activities and leave Germany. Nonetheless, we now know that this was not true. There were numerous trips by Pavelić and other important members of the group to Berlin. Also Alfred Rosenberg kept contact with the whole balkan revolutionary movement through a group under his control called the Croatiapress. Just what all this meant is still a mystery since the papers to do with the group were either destroyed or are in the East.[69]

However, there is one clue that does seem to show that Germany may have had a hand in the assassination. For one thing, Pavelić was in Berlin just prior to the assassination and left hurriedly just a day or two before for Italy. Furthermore, Goering is quoted by François-Poncet as saying to him just after the assassination that Rosenberg had slipped up.[70]

This, of course, could be interpreted several ways. First of all, it is notorious that Hitler preferred to keep everything on the foreign policy level in his own hands. Thus, it frequently happened that someone in the Foreign Ministry did something entirely contrary to a policy long pursued by Hitler simply because Hitler never told underlings what he himself did. The frustration in the Foreign Ministry was great as a consequence. The same thing frequently happened to Rosenberg, especially since he handled slavic affairs, the area that especially interested Hitler. It may have seemed wise to Rosenberg to back the Ustaša as a divisive force from motives similar to those of Mussolini while Hitler pursued an entirely opposite policy.

It is also well known that Hitler was an opportunist in finding ways and means for carrying out long formulated plans.[71] Thus, despite his opposition to the Ustaša because of their pro-Habsburg stand, he may have allowed Rosenberg to keep up these contacts secretly. This could have been either as a means of keeping contact in case they might prove useful, or in order to control them and prevent them from doing anything against German interests. If the last were his desire, he does not seem to have told Rosenberg about it or matters got out of control.

Another motive may have been the hostility that existed between Rosenberg and Goering. The spreading of such stories to such a man as the French ambassador may have been designed to embarrass Rosenberg and lead to his dismissal. They had long been rivals for control of the East so that Goering could have seen this as a means of getting control from him of eastern affairs.[72]

Whatever is the true explanation, I think that Hitler had no desire to see Alexander off the throne. As I have mentioned before, Alexander considered Hitler a kindred soul. While he recognized that Hitler posed a threat to peace, he thought that Hitler could be contained. He was willing to work with Hitler and allow him a certain latitude. Furthermore, Yugoslavia's position would put her right between Italy and an enlarged Germany if Anschluss were carried out. The history of German-Yugoslav relations seemed to show that Germany had no ambitions as far as Yugoslavia was concerned. They could, therefore, play off Italy against Germany.[73] Why then should Hitler want to remove Alexander? His departure would mean the restoration of the Habsburgs to the throne of Croatia. This could only be an extreme liability to Hitler in the rest of Central Europe.

This was perhaps the greatest liability to the formation of any fascist or semi fascist movement in Yugoslavia at this period. Hitler could get what he wanted by manipulating the legal government. A fascist regime simply was not necessary. This shows the fact pointed out by others that Hitler did not like foreign fascist movements and treated them with disdain, if he recognized them at all.[74]

It would seem to me, therefore, that there was no deliberate part played by Hitler in the assassination. The aftermath was quite different. He was singularly able in seizing an opportunity when it presented itself. At any rate, all he had to do was be prompt with condolences and sit back collecting the laurels.

A further example of this idea may be seen in Hitler's attitude to revanchism in Hungary. There had been some disagreement in Hungary about the course to follow in orienting their policy to the emerging power blocs. In 1932 many wished to base their policy on France. It was hoped that she could be persuaded to desert the Little Entente and base her central european policies on Hungary and Austria. Gömbös put an end to this hope by definitely going over to Mussolini. To France and the Little Entente this merely proved that Hungary could not be trusted. This reaction impelled Gömbös to move even closer to Italy, the one great power that was Hungary's friend. Such a necessity also impelled government orientation even more to the right giving Gömbös and the Fascists more power. It, of course, was also done to deprive his enemies of power, who were largely francophile, by depriving them of the backing of France.[75]

Along with this, Gömbös had come up with the idea of an axis composed of Hungary, Italy and Germany that would be essentially concerned with Danubian problems. This reflects the opinion Gömbös had of the power of Germany at this time. He regarded Germany as distinctly second rate in such a combination. At any rate, Hungary and Italy could always team up and out balance Germany. The only bad point about this scheme, as far as he was concerned, was that Mussolini consistently opposed letting Germany into the Danube area, regarding it as his own area of expansion. He, further, demanded Hungarian help in keeping the Germans out.[76]

Gömbös approached Hitler about his axis idea as soon as Hitler was in power. Hitler showed an interest in it. However, here we can see the sort of place Hitler had in mind for Yugoslavia in his new Europe. He insisted on a place for Yugoslavia in this axis. He particularly respected its army which he thought would be useful in keeping Italy in order. If Italy took the wrong course, as far as his control was concerned, he would then abandon her in favor of Yugoslavia. In return for German friendship, Hitler insisted that Hungary leave Yugoslavia alone. Gömbös protested this in vain.[77]

There is no talk here of Yugoslavia changing to a fascist government before she could be brought into such a system. It is plain that Hitler had achieved a modus vivendi with the royal government. This appears to have been a misreading of the actions of the Yugoslav government and their whole purpose. Nevertheless, he does not seem to have contemplated conquest or seen its need. His idea was the same as for Hungary or Rumania. That is, to draw her into the German orbit thereby controlling her but allowing her the letter and illusion of her freedom.

One of the very interesting points is the rivalry over the area with Italy shown at this very early point. It would appear to be stronger on Hitler's part than usually appears. That is, that he did not even regard Italy as such an important prospective ally as Yugoslavia. Despite his reverence for Mussolini as the founder of Fascism and his teacher, he always held him in contempt as a practical man and held the Italian people in complete contempt. Here we can see this in budding form. Obviously he has much greater respect for the Yugoslav army than the Italian.

It is interesting to contrast this view with that of Hoptner. He says that Alexander hoped to use Hitler to keep Mussolini out of his country. It would be a return to the classic Yugoslav policy of playing off Austria against Italy. Here Germany takes the place of Austria. The danger of this plan was recognized but they thought they could make it work.[78] Indeed, if the relative strengths of Italy and Germany had remained the same and they had gotten together, and Alexander had lived, it might have worked. The tragedy is that after his assassination the regency did not have the strength or intelligence to do so.

The task of the revived Ustaša began right away in 1929 under Hungarian and Italian tutelage, promoting ill feeling between Croats and Serbs, turning this into an armed rising by the Croats and so causing the destruction of Yugoslavia. 1929 was, of course, viewed as a particularly good time for this with first the assassination of Radić, the leader of the Croatian Peasant Party, and the subsequent founding of King Alexander's dictatorship. National feeling ran high because of these events.[79]

To show the foreign character of the new movement, we might look at the nationality of some of the founders (or refounders). General Serkotić, late of the Imperial Austrian Army, never gave up Austrian citizenship. Gustave Perchets was an intelligence officer in the Hungarian Army. Pavelić and the other member, Branimir Jelić, were Yugoslav in nationality. Nevertheless, two out of the four founders never gave up foreign citizenship and were known to have gone into the movement in the first place to realize ambitions that had nothing to do with Yugoslavia but had the goal of realizing Hungarian revisionism.[80]

Since this was very plain, they could get almost no support from the other major political figures. Radić, before he died, said all Croats regarded them with shame and that their support from Hungary and Italy precluded any kind of mass support. Every group refused to join them, including Maček, the new leader of the Peasant Party, after the assassination of Radić. Thus, their demands had to change in the hope of provoking and stampeding the Yugoslavs into civil war. Pavelić hoped to be able to organize just over the border in Hungary and Italy, carrying on raids like the IMRO in Bulgaria. As it was, he had very little support. In 1930 he had only 30 members. There may have been hundreds of sympathizers across the border in Croatia but they did nothing to help, if they even existed. The greatest effect of the Ustaša was on Croats abroad who had very little contact with home. The Ustaša did publish several periodicals which had a wide popularity among these people. Since this was all the news they could get about affairs in Yugoslavia, it is not surprising that they did not understand how little truth there was in what they were told.[81]

The assassination also is connected to the european situation at the time in another way. That is through the history of France. The last large scale attempt to settle the German problem had been undertaken by Aristide Briand. His attempt at a Franco-German rapprochement failed with the rise of Hitler as did also his attempt at the disarmament of Europe. In 1932 he was driven from office and soon died with the vision of all he had tried to accomplish in ruins around him.[82]

He was succeeded by Pierre Laval and a stream of other nonentities incapable of reacting effectively to the danger presented by the Third Reich. The French allowed their fears to be allayed by Hitler's protestations that he was for lasting peace. The right wing especially heaved a sigh of relief when he did not immediately attack France. They found themselves with little reason to fear him but rather shared his ideas on anti-Communism, anti-Semitism and opposition to democratic government.[83]

The situation seemed ready for change when Louis Barthou became Foreign Minister in the Domergue government early in 1934. Even though he was of the right, he envisaged a new policy involving the ringing about of Germany by the smaller states, backed and directed by France and Italy. In a tour of eastern Europe he reinvigorated the Little Entente and took the first steps towards reinstituting the Russian Alliance. Mussolini was becoming particularly alarmed at the moves Hitler was making toward Anschluss with Austria. Thus, the moment for such an action seemed to be perfect.[84]

The problem was, however, the relations of Italy and Yugoslavia. It was equally important to Barthou's plan to bring Yugoslavia into his new system. To Italy such a new friendship with Yugoslavia could only seem as though she were guaranteeing the status quo between Yugoslavia and her other particular friend, Hungary. This could end all Italy's plans in the Danube Basin by alienating Hungary. To Yugoslavia it, of course, appeared as though she were asked to sit down to the table with the wolf and appear to smile as she was eaten. It appeared all too likely that this might be the prelude to France giving Yugoslavia to Italy in return for her adherence to the alliance. The Yugoslavs thought Barthou would do almost anything to get Italy's support against Hitler. Thus, both states which were the cornerstone of Barthou's plan refused to join while the other was in.[85] This mixture of hatred for Italy and distrust of France was leading them to look for another great power to protect them with which they had no differences. This could only be Germany, as we have seen. The king did not wish to hinder France's efforts but he saw it as his duty to get ironclad guarantees from Italy on the independence of the Balkan states. Barthou finally invited Alexander to France to try to settle these problems and he landed at Marseilles on 9 October 1934. Both he and Barthou were assassinated by a member of the Ustaša while riding from the dock in an open car.[86]

Despite the overwhelming evidence, there still seems to be a question about how much Mussolini was involved in the assassination. Sir Ivone Kirkpatrick, in his biography of Mussolini, says that Mussolini's closest associates who have survived are convinced he had nothing to do with it. If this is true, it shows that the Ustaša hid their plans from everyone. On the other hand, Armstrong is still convinced that they were but a tool of Mussolini. This, of course, would be typical. There are many examples of such occurrences.[87]

As I have said before, the Ustaša was reformed in 1929. Its leaders had to flee almost immediately to Vienna. Two of them went to Bulgaria where they reached an agreement with IMRO for joint terrorist activity to liberate Croatia and Macedonia. These were Percec and Pavelić. Later Pavelić went to Italy while Percec established a training school for terrorists at Janka Puszta in Hungary.[88]

It is interesting that the Croatian Peasant Party also took part in some of this sort of work at this time. It shows the wrench the establishment of Alexander's dictatorship had caused. They met in 1929 with Baron Apor, a representative of the Hungarian Foreign Ministry. It was agreed that the two countries would cooperate in liberating Croatia. Italy was dragged into this and a secret Italian-Hungarian military convention was drawn up to which Croatia was made a consulting party. Secret arrangements were made with Austria for the transit of troops and ammunition. In 1931 this was expanded into a secret agreement for political cooperation.[89]

This resulted in action by the Ustaša with the help of, or at the instigation of, Hungary and Italy. The attempts went on throughout the period after 1929, Italy taking the lead in using the Ustaša. One occurred in June 1932. There was a revolt of the Ustaša that Mussolini expected would cause the country to fall apart. In November Mussolini moved to expand this by getting the rebels to proclaim a Croat republic in the vicinity of Fiume. The plan was to have a large force of Croats from the training camps in northern Italy invade Yugoslavia. Mussolini would immediately grant the new state recognition. The Yugoslav intelligence service learned of this. Mussolini had to give up his plans when he received a secret message from Alexander saying that he would regard any attack by the terrorists as an attack by Italy and would act accordingly. Not only that, but he would accuse Italy as an aggressor before the League of Nations.[90]

Again in August 1934 after the assassination of Dollfuss, Chancellor of Austria, it was learned that Mussolini intended to move troops into the Drava Valley to block Hitler and link up with Hungary. Again Alexander warned him this action would mean war. This last is again very interesting as showing the attitude of the king to Germany coming into the area. She was not regarded as an enemy the way Italy was.[91] Thus, the question of who planned the murders is a very open one. As we have seen in the foregoing, Italy had been the one to use the Ustaša up to that time. Mussolini had, however, experienced nothing but failure in using them. Furthermore, he seems to have had an interest in fostering Barthou's anti-Nazi coalition.[92] Therefore, it seems unlikely that he would encourage the assassination plans. He may have decided that a subservient Yugoslavia in such a coalition would be better for his interests. This seems highly unlikely, however. It is true that the Germans were the only ones to benefit from the affair. The fact that they were the first with their "sincere" condolences and that they pushed for international investigation and action while France tried to hush it all up worked for them in appearing as the only real friends the country had in its hour of need. Hitler beyond all doubt showed his great ability in profiting from events, whether the whole affair was a mistake by Rosenberg or the Ustaša acted entirely on their own.

We have seen the start of the political problems Yugoslavia had to face but it is in the economic sphere that these political problems expressed themselves. The foundation of the major foreign problems was her economic position which allowed her hardly any latitude in the actions she could take. The real effect of the end of the common market of the Habsburg Empire, the depression of 1929 and the lack of industrial development could be seen in Yugoslavia as she tried to keep her independence in the 1930's.

In 1920 at least 78.8% of her population was engaged in agriculture. In 1931 this had only decreased to 76.5%.[93] It has been calculated that she had a surplus agricultural population (that is, surplus farm population to total farm population) in 1921 of 41% which rose to 43% by 1930.[94] These figures were arrived at by comparing yield per hectare in France and Yugoslavia.

FIGURE I
YIELD PER HECTARE

Country	date	percent[a]	number[b]	A Y W[c]	A Y P[d]
Yugoslavia	1931	76.5	140	10.5	58.8
France	1931	28.0	48	15.5	110.5

a) percent of total population dependent on agriculture.
b) number of people per 100 ha. of cultivated land
c) average yield of wheat (quintals per hectare).
d) average yield of potatoes (quintals per hectare).

Thus, with one third the workers France produced twice as many potatoes per hectare.[95]

Industrially, as can be expected, she was very far behind. In 1921 only 8.6% of the population lived from industrial work. In 1931 this had increased to 10.7%. This is an increase of only 2.1% versus a decrease in agricultural population of 4.5%.[96] These displaced people must have been going to the cities which meant that industry was not increasing at a rate to keep up with the increase in people in the cities looking for work. In fact, things were getting worse and a large group of hopeless poor was appearing. The problem has received more publicity in some of the other east european countries although Yugoslavia had a greater degree of this social problem. It certainly aggravated the other internal problems of the country. It was behind a good deal of the national question as well. The Croats were generally better off than the Serbs. Most of what industry there was in Yugoslavia was in prewar Croatia, particularly around Zagreb. The peasants generally were better off there since the land was richer and the landlords, who were mostly Germans, were more scientific in their methods. The rest of the country was much worse off. This was due to poor soil, ignorance of good methods as well as inability to sell in a glutted market. Generally holdings were too small to be efficiently managed and when land reform was instituted there was not enough land to change this picture. Landlordism was ended in the whole country during the 1920's. This was of little help to the average peasant since it affected less than 10% of the land. Due to the mountainous character of the country landlordism had never been widespread. It only existed in any large amount in limited areas where the character of the country made it more practical. Despite the end of landlordism, little happened to make the amount of land owned by each person more nearly equal. In 1931 67.8% of all holdings were under 5 hectares. In percentage of area of cultivated land, those of five hectares were only 28%. Most of the remaining 4.2% were in larger units.[97]

The political parties exhibited little interest in the plight of the peasants since they were dominated by intellectuals who, for the most part, were unconcerned with the peasant and his problems.[98] Pasić's Radical Party had been founded in Serbia long before World War I as a peasant party but had abandoned that orientation long before the war. Radić's Croatian Peasant party had been founded as a peasant party. After the war, however, this changed. It was largely because most Croatian intellectuals, particularly the young ones of a more radical turn, came into it. They began to dominate it and turned it to their interests which mainly had to do with the nationality problem rather than improving the lot of the peasant. The bulk of its membership continued to be peasants but it was dominated by the urban bourgeoisie.[99]

All of the foregoing means that the country had practically no surplus wealth. There was little chance to accumulate savings to build up industry or finance research or education to improve yield on the land.[100] What investment there was for industry came mostly from abroad. The government invested some but this was financed almost solely by foreign loans.[101] It is rather remarkable that any growth was registered when it is remembered how much damage the country suffered in World War I. In particular the industrial areas had suffered the worst damage. The loss of life was immense. Nearly the entire university youth of Serbia was killed in the war. Proportionally Serbia suffered the most loss of life of any belligerent in World War I.[102] She got very little back in reparations because Austria could not pay and Hungary would not. What little they did get came from Germany and took the form of railway equipment.[103]

The main factor, however, which contributed so much to the problem of Yugoslavia's independence was the direction of her foreign trade. The tragedy of her position was that her trade was tied to those very countries that most wanted to control or destroy her. The least trade was with her partners in the Balkan or Little Ententes. This, of course, was because they were all agricultural countries all trying to sell the same products. As for France and England, geography prevented the possibility of much trade. Goods for or from those countries had to come almost entirely by sea and then through Yugoslavia's poor harbors, negating the considerable advantage she had from very low labor costs. The lack of natural harbors and the rugged character of the country, making road or railroad construction extremely expensive, made American or Canadian wheat or fruit cheaper than Yugoslavia's for France and England. The only alternative markets were Italy, Germany and Austria.

Austria was her traditional market. She had taken advantage of this unmercifully making Serbia finally rebel in the so-called Pig War of 1907. In form it was a tariff war over her agricultural products. The result was a Serbian victory but still a considerable part of her trade remained in Austrian hands.[104] The hostility from that struggle remained and was increased by mounting evidence of Austrian manipulation of her trade during the 1920's. It is no surprise, then, that she regarded Anschluss with indifference from the point of view of trade.

Her most important trading partners were Germany and Italy. Transportation ease and cheapness were among the reasons. The Danube was the main route for Germany and the Adriatic for Italy. This was very important since Yugoslav exports were mainly bulk goods such as grain, cattle and minerals.[105] Furthermore, what Yugoslavia produced was just what those countries needed. German industry was very interested in her huge undeveloped supplies of copper, iron, chrome and aluminum. Her cheap agricultural products were also important considering their chronic shortages of food. Italy particularly took vast quantities of goods Yugoslavia could sell no where else. Italy would take great quantities of the soft wood which was her principle forest product. Other countries only wanted hard woods. She also found it difficult to sell her wheat and pigs elsewhere.[106] England was tied to the principal of free trade and so could not force her importers to buy from certain sources that the government might want to support for political reasons. The British government does not seem to have realized the importance of that idea and the capital Germany was making out of it. To Germany foreign trade was an important part of foreign policy. Thus, England could not switch trade partners or products to support her friends against German or Italian economic domination.[107] Yugoslavia was forced to sell her products to whomever would take them. Hitler wanted to capture the trade of this area to assure a food supply and raw materials for the war he was planning. This area in his backyard was the natural source.[108]

There follow some figures to show in a more concrete way the distribution of trade among her more important trading partners. The figures are in millions of dinars.

FIGURE 2[109]

TRADE

Country	Average, 1933-35 Exports to	Imports from	1936 Exports to	Imports from	1937 Exports to	Imports from
Italy	731.8	461.5	137.2	101.7	587.1	429.8
France	62.8	153.1	86.2	101.3	393.3	90.8
Great Britain	161.1	328.4	431.7	346.9	464.6	409.1
Germany	606.6	491.5	1039.1	1087.6	1361.3	1694.4

The figures for 1936 show an immense falling off of trade with Italy which was compensated for by an increase in trade with the other partners, although it was of a temporary nature. During this time, sanctions were applied against Italy because of her Ethiopian adventure. We will discuss that in more detail later.

Some figures on the value of all Yugoslavia's foreign trade could be added showing the effect of the depression on her trade and the bad state this caused in her financial position. The figures are in billions of dinars.

FIGURE 3[110]

FOREIGN TRADE

Year	Exports	Imports	Year	Exports	Imports
1926	7.8	7.6	1930	6.8	7.0
1927	6.4	7.3	1932	3.1	2.9
1928	6.4	7.8	1936	4.4	4.1
1929	7.9	7.6	1940	6.7	6.0

From these figures it can be seen that there was a drastic fall in the value of both exports and imports. At least it can be seen that most of the time a favorable balance of trade was maintained. Only in 1927, 1928 and 1930 was there an excess of imports over exports. Nonetheless, despite use of all the usual expedients, the value of the dinar fell by one third.

All of this was most tragic for the population at large. As we have seen, it lived a very marginal existence at best. The bulk of exports were agricultural products. If prices fell this affected the purchasing power of the greater part of the population. It is highly unlikely that such remedies as lower interest rates, public works or stimulus to building would have given much relief. It would probably not have even relieved the plight of the 35 to 40% of the agricultural population that was surplus.[111] The only alternative was to do everything possible to increase the country's agricultural exports. One attempt the government made was to make export of wheat a government monopoly while the price paid to the peasant was supported. They tried to maintain a price to the peasant of 160 dinars per 100 kilograms.[112] At the best of times the government barely made ends meet. Now with revenues falling they found maintainence of such a scheme impossible. This was the only major initiative they took during the 1930's. For the rest, they merely went whichever way their major customers told them. This meant most of the time doing what Germany told them to do.

Thus, as everything, went Germany was able to exercise increasing control over the Yugoslav economy. Slow and tortuous methods were used so that it is unlikely that many Yugoslavs knew what had happened when war broke out. The procedure used was to slowly increase trade by a series of steps far beyond the point where Yugoslav interests were served until such massive amounts of money were involved that it was impossible to end the situation. The Germans managed to do enough in return that there was always hope that they would fulfill the rest of the bargain. Always the major reason why this process could get started and why it was not broken off was that this was Yugoslavia's only opening for foreign trade.[113] A number of times they tried to break out of the ring, particularly by getting England to increase trade with them to a massive degree. They were told by the British that trade could not be forced in peacetime. Because of the high costs involved, it would have taken government pressure to make importers take Yugoslav products and none of the Conservative or coalition governments of the 1930's was prepared for such a move. The sacred principle of free trade would not allow it.[114] The only possible result was that Yugoslav trade fell more and more into the hands of Germany.

Of course, the major point as far as Yugoslavia was concerned was that this seemed the only way to serve her vital interests. She did receive actual concrete benefits. The Germans came into the country with technical experts opening and improving mines, building roads and railroads and constructing and improving processing facilities to put raw materials into a form more easily and cheaply transportable. Also, they built or modernized regular factories. All this meant more jobs for Yugoslavs and, even more, the buildup of her own technical plant and knowhow among her population so that in the future she could expect to be able to go ahead on her own. As far as the Yugoslav authorities were concerned, this was all to the good. This shows that to some degree the Yugoslavs walked into the lion's mouth with their eyes open.[115]

The whole scheme would never have worked without some advantages for Yugoslavia. The victim was persuaded to look on the bright side by the benefits he was getting while his economy was brought more and more under German control.

The scheme by which this was done has been credited to Hjalmar Schacht, Hitler's finance minister. His scheme made use of the bilateral clearing agreements used by most countries of Europe in the Depression to save what of their foreign trade still existed, while using none of their scarce gold or hard currency. Since 1931-32 Germany had clearing agreements with all the states of the Danube basin. When the Nazis came into power they immediately increased use of these agreements.[116] How much of this was due to Hitler's having to honor promises of full employment without money to finance the huge outlays necessary and how much to his dreams of empire is an open question.

Whatever the motive, large quantities of goods were purchased on credit. This built up a huge German endebtedness to those countries. This then encouraged the use of the already existing clearing agreements. These worked as follows. Germans would perhaps buy pigs from Yugoslavia. They would pay the purchase price in Reichsmarks into the clearing account in Germany. Instead of the German government then paying this in Reichsmarks, gold or scarce hard currency to Yugoslavia, the agreement provided that the Yugoslav government then paid the seller in dinars. From this, a huge credit was built up in Germany which could be used by Yugoslavia to buy manufactured goods. In this case it worked in the opposite way. The Yugoslav purchaser would pay into the account in Yugoslavia the purchase price in dinars. The German seller was compensated out of the mark account in Germany created by the purchase of pigs. Thus, it seemed to the benefit of all since no one had to pay for goods with nearly unobtainable gold or hard currency. It presupposes, however, that the trade would balance each other since it is a form of barter.[117]

Trade used some such system almost everywhere during the Depression. Its utility is obvious in a period when international trade has virtually come to a stop particularly from the disappearance of the gold and hard currency that was the lifeblood of trade. Central and East Europe particularly suffered at this time. The figures given before show the precarious state of the Yugoslav economy. The Depression made things considerably worse because there was no store of foreign exchange to tide the country over a bad period. The situation of the German economy when Hitler took over is well known. He made immediate efforts to create full employment and rebuild the military machine at the same time these problems were still present. It can be imagined what happened to the supplies of gold and foreign exchange under those conditions. What they had was needed to buy raw materials and machinery from the United States and Britain. They would only accept payment in gold or hard currency. Certain scarce raw materials had to be obtained from East Europe and the only way to pay for them was by such a barter system. The bad part was that, in fact, no effort was made to pay off the barter with goods to Yugoslavia. Germany got her purchases for free while at the same time politically tieing these countries to Germany. Before long such a sum had been built up to, say, Yugoslavia's credit, that her only hope of eventually evening it out was to maintain the trade even though the debt became more and more immense. Germany, though, could rebuild her economy and her military power and these semi willing customers would assure that Germany would not be starved out in a new war as she had been in 1918.[118] One of Hitler's greatest concerns in planning for his war was to make sure that could not happen. He realized there was little likelihood the public would support a war in which they suffered as they had in 1918 or that militarily such a war could succeed if the military were starved of their necessities.

In actuality this scheme worked out to the benefit of these countries in part and is a major reason why they walked into the whole thing with their eyes open more or less. Vast quantities of Polish, Hungarian and Roumanian wheat were purchased. They, however, were also encouraged to diversify their agriculture from the one crop. For instance, vegetable oil was very scarce. Not only was it a valuable food source, but it was an important ingredient in plastics, synthetic oil, explosives and the residue was a very valuable cattle feed. All kinds of German experts, machinery, seeds and so on were sent out to the East to stimulate production. It was greatly increased as a result.[119]

As shown before, Yugoslav trade, particularly in her agricultural products, fell to very low figures in the Depression. It seemed to all Yugoslavs that this new willingness of Germany to take their surplus was a godsend and a great act of friendship. Even more was the fact that Germany began to invest vast sums of money in the development of raw materials and processing plants. New mines were opened and old ones modernized. By 1937 Germany had invested 55 million dinars in Yugoslavia. The German conquest of Austria increased this to 820 million dinars and that of Czechoslovakia to 1,270 million dinars through Germanization of Czech holdings in Yugoslavia. In March 1936 Krupp got the contract to modernize the Zenica iron works in Bosnia into a very modern armaments plant and I. G. Farben bought several drug firms.[120]

One major reason why it all seemed so attractive was that Germany paid approximately 30% above the world price for what it bought.[121] Since, in effect, the whole thing worked out to Yugoslavia subsidizing the German war effort, this was no hardship on Germany. The Germans took care to work closely with the peasants in buying produce. This assured that later on there was a strong peasant lobby to assure that this state of affairs was continued despite its political result. One example may show this. In February 1937 German agents made an agreement with agricultural cooperatives to buy their entire output of plums. They would pay 2.30 dinars per kilogram which was far above the current price of 1.40 dinars. The difference between the two prices was then sent to Zbor, an ultranationalist, pro-German, pro-Orthodox, anti-Catholic organization headed by an extreme fanatic named Dimitrije Ljotić. As a result, in addition to all her other troubles, Yugoslavia found herself subsidizing a subversive organization whose aim was to destroy the state.[122]

Connected with the purchase of goods at higher than world prices was the overvaluation of the Reichsmark. It was kept artificially high in order to bring in more. Thus, these countries were forced to pay higher prices for what they bought and so the paper high prices they received were in effect aid by themselves.[123]

This sort of deal did not work out to Yugoslavia's advantage on the long run economic scale either. A large part of the goods purchased in this way were then dumped on the international market by Germany. Yugoslavia's non-German markets were then lost to her. The Germans were willing to accept any price at all to get hard foreign currency for her needs.[124] It did not matter to the Germans since they were not paying the Yugoslavs for their purchases anyway. By the end of 1935 blocked accounts in Germany amounted to 400 million dinars.[125] This resulted in a further problem. It soon became evident that if Yugoslav businessmen had to keep on waiting indefinitely for payment, they would soon be going bankrupt in wholesale lots. Therefore, the government had to step in and take over the debts. The government then had to pay the Yugoslav creditors of the German purchasers and then try to collect from Germany as one government to another. To pay for this they were forced to resort to a mild inflation which further decreased their international standing and credit so that long term payment deals became nearly impossible to get. Again, their only possible resort was Germany. They had become enmeshed in the first place because pre-Hitler Germany had a wonderful reputation for repaying her debts, even in the worst part of the

Weimar period. Everyone thought the same situation would prevail but they soon found their error.[126]

When the usefulness of this method began to run out the Germans were forced to give some kind of compensation. This usually involved the negotiation of some kind of barter deals offering goods in compensation for the huge debt built up. Quite commonly this was for arms. By 1936 most of Europe was getting started on a new arms race and so the small countries with a very small or non existent arms industry found themselves unable to purchase from their usual sources. Some historians give the erroneous impression that Germany already had in being in 1933 the prototypes of the weapons with which she fought World War II and the Nazis only had to start production. This is not true. There was much experimentation which resulted in the production of large quantities. These were often found faulty with prolonged use or they were displaced by more advanced models. In addition, there were the great stockpiles of old World War I equipment maintained sometimes secretly. All this had to be disposed of to make way for new equipment. Instead of merely transforming it into junk, it was discovered it could be foisted onto these eastern creditors.[127]

Another favorite scheme was to dump materials on these countries that could not be sold elsewhere. Large quantities of aspirin, fountain pens, typewriters, etc. were so dumped.[128]

Another method was to offer goods at very long term credit. As can be imagined, this would be valuable largely as a political weapon when conquest or control had been decided upon. It necessitated subsidizing by the German government initially. Most goods traded were sold normally on 3 months credit. Now they offered them at 1 or 2 years credit and with virtually no down payment.[129] A German maker of machinery would sell his product to Yugoslavia. This would be tied to an agreement that Germany could buy an equivalent amount of chrome. The German exporter of machinery could then be paid out of the proceeds of its sale. However, Yugoslavia was saddled with an ever increasing debt for the things it was buying. She could buy huge quantities immediately but it only delayed the reckoning and so tied her even more closely to her creditor.

The single event most responsible for achieving German control over the Yugoslav economy was the Italian attack on Ethiopia in 1936. Yugoslavia was one of those countries which most scrupulously imposed and maintained sanctions against Italy. Her scrupulousness in meeting her international obligations was probably more damaging to herself than to Italy. As cited previously, the average of her exports to Italy in 1933-35 were 731.8 million dinars. In 1936 they were 137.2 million dinars. Germany immediately stepped in to fill the void. Her trade jumped from an average in 1933-35 of 606.6 million dinars to 1039.1 million dinars. When the Ethiopian problem was settled Italy was never able to regain her controlling position.[130] The problem, however, was worse than the figures show. Trade to Italy, it must be remembered, contained items forming a large part of Yugoslav production that could not be sold elsewhere. Soft timber is the most important item of this sort. Thus, despite efforts by Czechoslovakia and Britain to increase their trade with Yugoslavia and help her over the crisis, her economy was considerably damaged. France gave her virtually no help so that by 1937 Italy had regained a substantial part of her old position. France made considerable purchases of wheat on a one time basis but Britain made virtually no gains over the long term. Germany was the real gainer. Exports to Germany rose by 31% and imports from her rose 56%.[131]

The effect was felt in another way as well. That was on the clearing balances. Trade with Italy always showed a substantial favorable balance so that there was always a good gain of solid international currencies. The sanctions ended that situation with no replacement available. Therefore, in June 1936 the government had to issue a list of commodities, only available from non-clearing countries, which would require a special government license to import. It covered about one third of the goods obtained from non-clearing countries. In 1937 and again in 1938 it had to be enlarged to take in some four-fifths of those things. This represented a new policy of rigid government control of foreign trade but even more it represented even closer economic ties to Germany. But, in the circumstances it was unavoidable.[132] It cannot be stressed too often how much the closeness of Germany geographically speaking and her insatiable need for raw materials made her increasingly the only possible customer. It was a question of turning to her or having no foreign trade at all.[133]

After the Anschluss with Austria there seems to have been some thought in Germany of moving right into the rest of the Danube basin. But, it was shown that this would arouse too much opposition and so instead there was an increasing attempt to accomplish the same thing by economic control. In October 1938 Dr. Walter Funk made a trip around the Balkans to promote this idea. Dr. Funk offered to buy 50% of Yugoslavia's exports and provide assistance for increasing ore production and building her industry on guided lines. In return Yugoslavia would buy more from Germany. He was met with a firm refusal because there was an increasing recognition of the danger these policies were creating in the East European countries. Later in the year von Neurath attempted to persuade Yugoslavia to sign a similar treaty with Germany. It was refused.[134] After late 1936 Yugoslavia made increasing efforts to diversify her trade. Although Britain was persuaded to buy more, this scarcely made a dent in the problem because Britain was not a natural trading partner for Yugoslavia. More important was the Italian Pact of 1937, which allowed her to reenter the Italian markets. Italy, also, in it gave Yugoslavia most favored nation status but, nevertheless, could not meet her requirements in manufactured goods. In addition, there seemed a deliberate hesitation on Italy's part that amounted to a withdrawal from Central Europe in Germany's favor. At any rate, Italy felt her political interests had more in common with Hungary and Austria at this time and so ignored Yugoslavia in their favor.

In 1938 Yugoslavia again tried to get Britain to do something to help her. This would have been for bulk purchases that would have required government subsidies. Therefore, the British government refused to do anything since this would have interfered with her usual laissez faire traditions. She had not yet grasped the importance of economics in modern warfare.[135] By 1939 there was no country left which could serve as an alternate market to Germany and Italy. Economic life was virtually paralyzed. In October 1939 a new agreement was signed granting still greater export quotas of nonferrous metals and foods. To honor this pact Yugoslavia had to limit the consumption by her own people of meat, fats and other essential foods. It became virtually impossible for her to import many essential commodities because Germany controlled the market in them. This was, of course, particularly the case with munitions to rebuild and modernize her army.[136]

This became even worse after the Italian declaration of war on France and Great Britain in June 1940. Her conquests in the west allowed Germany to take an even greater share of the Yugoslav economy by the seizure of French, Belgian and Dutch assets in foreign countries. In September 1940 Germany forced her to devalue her currency in relation to the mark from 14.80 dinars to 17.82. Altogether, these acts contributed to a rapid growth of inflation.[137]

In this chapter we have seen what was probably the most significant aspect of the German attempt to take control of the country. That is, through economic control which envisaged a Yugoslavia integrated into the German system as a producer of food, raw materials for industry and simple industrial products. She would retain her regular government, becoming a satellite much like Hungary and Rumania.

It must be remembered, however, that all of this was very unpopular with the vast bulk of the Yugoslav people. These were government policies which tied the country closer and closer to Germany and not attempts to meet popular pressure for such policies. The regent, Prince Paul, and Premier Stojadinović had great difficulty in implementing these ideas. The more political aspect of this will be discussed in the next chapter.

CHAPTER 3

INCREASING INVOLVEMENT OF GERMANY
IN YUGOSLAV AFFAIRS

Besides the political problems in the government and the difficulties with other countries, there was also the continuing difficulties between the nationalities. There was a period after the assassination of King Alexander when the nationality problem became quiet. Partly this was due to general disgust at the assassination and partly to harsh government repression that forced nearly all the opposition underground. Nevertheless, the fact that this problem was not settled was probably the most dangerous aspect of events of the time. Settlement of this problem would have gone a long way to cleaning up the political house. A greater national cohesiveness and strength might have contributed greatly to meeting foreign problems.

The assassination of King Alexander resulted in government by a regency council since the heir was a minor. The council was created by King Alexander in his will. The council was composed of his cousin, Prince Paul; Radenko Stanković, minister of education; and Ivan Perović, governor of Croatia. This council was to rule until the autumn of 1941 when Alexander's son, Peter, would come of age.[138] The composition meant that the council would be dominated by Prince Paul. All the other members were dependent on him. The difficulty was not in the prince's honesty, capability or selfless attitude to the job, but in his character and training. These simply did not fit him to be an autocrat. As we have seen, the government was set up as an autocracy now governed by the Regency Council, but with no one on it who was an autocrat. Failure of this group to govern meant that there was a power vacuum that must be filled from somewhere. The drift was toward a kind of Fuehrerstaat under the prime minister, Stojadinović.

Prince Paul's interests had made him devoted to art and to the life of a dilettante thus making him ill-suited to his new job. He had spent most of his life up to that time out of the country in England.

Therefore, his knowledge of conditions in the country and its political problems was very poor. He, furthermore, knew none of the politicians and had no one he could go to as an advisor. King Alexander had kept him from politics because Paul had not liked it and because the king was afraid the Prince's greater involvement in affairs would cause the jealousy of the politicians. That would lead to charges that the king was increasing his absolutist power by packing the government with his relatives.[139] In personality he was very different from Alexander in a way which did not meet the political situation. Alexander had a dominant and dynamic personality. In contrast, Prince Paul was an introspective man who believed compromise was the essence of government. On the good side, he was probably as much a Yugoslav in outlook as Alexander had been. He regarded the constant national quarrels as wasteful and harmful to the country. Domestically, he always spoke of his dislike of the harsh regime of the dictatorship; that is, its centralism, censorship and military control. His ultimate goal was to pacify the whole country by settling the Serb-Croat problem. He was, however, convinced he would have to do this through the 1931 constitution despite the fact it made the king a dictator and guaranteed Serb control of the country. He himself disliked this constitution very much but, when the subject of changing it was brought up, he reminded everyone that his was only a caretaker government. The new king would have to see to changing the constitution when he took the throne. To him the king was the only one who could change the constitution. Therefore, he was determined to resist all pressure for change.[140]

Perhaps the greatest pressures domestically at this time came from the extremes of the left and the right. On the left were groups favoring reform towards more democratic government and on the right were those who wanted a continuation of the dictatorship. Of course, on the farthest left was the tiny Communist Party. The Jevtić ministry could not see its way toward either extreme solution. When it called elections as a way out, its support fell considerably despite the fact that the elections were carefully managed. At least 40% of the voters voted for the opposition. When this was coupled with the way France handled the assassination crisis, the government was forced to resign.[141] In its place came Milan Stojadinović, a banker who had been minister of finance in the Jevtić government. Supposedly the new government was to introduce liberal reforms and ease political tensions. Stojadinović made a new political grouping of all those forces which were pro government. It was called the Jugoslovenska Radikalna Zajednica (Yugoslav Radical Union). Its executive committee was to be composed of Aca Stanojević, the head of the National Radical Party, Milan Stojadinović, also of that party, Father Korosec of the Slovene Populist Party, and Mehmed Spaho of the Yugoslav Moslem Organization. This was formed June 18, 1935. On June 23rd

Stojadinović was asked by the regents to form a government on the terms set out above.[142]

Stojadinović is a very controversial figure in modern Yugoslav history. Just what his relationship was to Fascism is a very open question. Among those who are beginning to study Fascism as a European movement of the 20th century, neither his movement nor any of the other brands of extreme right wing activity in Yugoslavia have been called a true form of Fascism.[143] We have already examined the Ustaša and seen how that resembled and yet differed from true Fascism (if there is such a thing). In the case of Stojadinović's Yugoslav Radical Union there was a great deal of copying especially from German National Socialism. The salute was copied as well as symbols, uniforms and titles. Stojadinović loved to be called by the Yugoslav form of the Nazi title, Fuehrer (Voda).[144] A true fascist movement should grow from strong roots within a country and use native forms rather than imported ones, according to the students of the subject. Stojadinović used very little that was native to the country. He received only a small amount of support from the people. Here again as with the Ustaša, membership was from a few disgruntled elements looking for a way to express their dissatisfaction or from downright criminal elements.[145]

Actually this movement did not find any wide support at all. Perhaps one major reason for this was the backwardness of the country. Fascism seems generally to be a movement of rather advanced countries that have developed a large middle class. Yugoslavia was, and is still, a country in a preindustrial and even a precapitalist stage. It is largely made up of peasants, as we have seen. Fascism certainly appeared in backward countries such as Hungary and Rumania. There it opposed the breakdown of authority of the old landowning classes. It was a product of the economic erosion of their position as cheap imports flooded into Europe from America and Australia. In Yugoslavia the last of landlordism was done away with by the land reforms of the 1920's. Except for parts of Croatia, it had virtually no middle class either except for a scattering of professional men and government officials. What trade existed internally was largely in the hands of small traders still in the old oriental bazaar tradition who kept a small shop or travelled over the country with a pack of trinkets on their back or on a mule. The studies carried out on the origins of the two classic forms of Fascism show that a large traditionally organized and motivated upper or middle class in the process of breakup and change due to the erosion of its position because of the growth of large scale capitalism, together with the growth of Socialism, are prerequisites for the appearance of Fascism. There simply was too little of this and so Fascism had little to work with.[146] What little appeal Stojadinović's form had was due to the example of Italy and Germany. It appealed to the frustrated national pride of many elements as a way for Yugoslavia to become as strong and powerful as those states.[147] Stojadinović's own ideas were formed in this way. He was educated in Germany, receiving a tremendous impression from the ideas and social movements rising there. He was particularly fascinated by the rise of the Nazis and by Schacht's economic policy for the development of East Europe. He himself was a banker and reputed to be an economic expert and financial wizard. Furthermore, the 1919 settlement of Europe appeared very shaky which may have caused him to believe that timely arrangements should be made before they were imposed from outside. To a Yugoslav with such ideas a settlement with Germany could appear to be the only likely solution. Germany had never had any ambitions in the Balkans while several states in or around the Balkans had spent the period since 1919 bemoaning their fate and attempting to revise the status quo. Therefore, to many, such as Prince Paul and perhaps the premier, it was a good idea to mollify Germany and get her to protect them before those who wanted to change the Versailles treaties destroyed Yugoslavia. This is a theme which comes up again and again. That is, that Germany had never been a threat. The preoccupation was altogether too much with the danger from Hungary, Bulgaria and especially Italy. Germany was seen as a possible protector, especially against Italy. This feeling was given a boost by the fact that war had nearly broken out several times between Germany and Italy over Austria. These things combined with Stojadinović's powerful personality and boundless ambition made him decide the German way was best and that he should make all efforts to make himself the Fuehrer of a fascist Yugoslavia.[148]

This approach to Germany went on as France's prestige decayed after the assassination of the king and Barthou in Marseilles. It was felt that France would not help them see that Italy and Hungary were punished by the world for promoting this kind of action. France's dilatoriness over the assassination seemed to confirm a feeling that had been growing throughout East Europe since the advent of Hitler that the two western powers were becoming too decadent to fulfill their obligations to the smaller countries. These small states were expected to tow the line when France or Great Britain required it but those countries would do nothing to protect the vital interests of these small states, especially when their own great power interests were not involved. Thus, a man like Prince Paul, who was definitely Anglophile, began to change.[149]

It seems to me, though, that a mistake is often made about him. He is linked in the writings of many opponents of the dictatorial regime with those who advocated friendship with the fascist powers for ideological reasons. Foreigners, however, with no ax to grind and who know the country are agreed that he was by training and nature an Anglophile. But the timid and vacillating policy of France and Great

Britain forced him to think that Yugoslavia would have to find her own salvation. He felt those two powers would not defend her. It would be impossible to look to Soviet Russia since Yugoslavia had opposed the Communist regime ever since the Revolution. Since she could not defend herself, she would have to make some kind of accommodation with her enemies. Stojadinović, in fact, had a hard job in moving the regent in this direction, not only because of his English sympathies, but because of his continuing dislike of the fascist leaders. He seems to have been very reluctant to follow Stojadinović in this direction.[150]

It must be remembered, though, that this change really began before the assassination. Alexander had gone to visit Barthou in France as part of Barthou's plan to reconcile Italy and Yugoslavia. Barthou's hope was to build a Mediterranean security system on the basis of France, Italy and Yugoslavia. He did not see how such a thing could work without both those states in it. It was to be based on pulling the small states back into France's orbit in a stronger way than previously. Her major alliances were at that time with Poland and the Little Entente. He hoped to strengthen the system into a real ring around Germany that would pen Hitler in. On the other side, he seems also to have looked for concessions that would bring Germany back into the community of nations so that she would no longer be a pariah.[151]

To Yugoslavia the idea was frankly suspect, however, because it seemed to be putting Yugoslavia under Italian control with cynical abandonment of them by France. There were enough indications that Mussolini was out to destroy Yugoslavia. These indications not only involved the old squabbles over Dalmatia and Fiume but the very existence of the state shown by Mussolini's support of the Croatian separatists and the consequent attempts on the king's life. Thus, the tendency, even before the assassination, was to look for another ally who was disinterested in the area but would protect them actively against Italy. This appeared more and more to be Germany.[152]

That Yugoslavia's interests appeared to conflict with those of France is, perhaps, one of the great tragedies of this period. Yugoslavia was so involved in her own problem of Italy that she failed to see the forest for the trees. Mussolini was, of course, no help. He failed as much as anyone else to read the situation. Everyone was so sure that Hitler could be used for their purposes while Hitler had no schemes of his own. Germany under the Nazis was being read too much in terms of the old policy of Imperial Germany. Serbia had seen only the danger of Austrian ambitions in the Balkans. It was thought that Germany had no desires in the Balkans but that she had involved herself there in World War I solely because of her ally, Austria. Many thought, therefore, because of this view of Imperial Germany, that she would continue the same attitude under Hitler and that her word was her bond. Certainly King Alexander saw the danger from Germany to some extent or he would not have responded to Barthou. Neither Prince Paul nor any of the politicians of the day saw what the rise of Hitler meant. They knew they were playing with fire but thought they could handle it in the good old Balkan fashion of playing one power against the other as they had done with Austria and Russia before World War I.

Alexander had been willing to recognize the reality of French fears. He did not want to hamper their search for security. But, he did insist that part of any agreement would have to be an Italian guarantee of the independence of the Balkan states.[153] Nothing came of it, however, because both Alexander and Barthou were assassinated on October 9, 1934.

The people of Yugoslavia immediately drew together in the face of this blow. The world, especially Italy, was amazed at the way all factions came together.[154] Even the vast bulk of the Croats were disgusted at what had been done supposedly in their name.[155] The new government immediately brought charges against Italy and Hungary in the League of Nations. They charged these nations with complicity in the murders by harboring the murderers who were known Croat terrorists. It was proved that the Ustaša maintained camps in those countries for the training of terrorists with the active support of the governments concerned. It was well known that Pavelić maintained a headquarters in Bologna, another office in Milan and camps for the training of terrorists in both Italy and Hungary.[156]

The Yugoslav government adopted the perhaps naive attitude that this was the sort of question for which the League of Nations had been designed. The whole case was brought forward. Proof was presented that the assassins had come from camps in Italy and Hungary. But, it proved impossible to do anything when both France and Great Britain intervened to prevent any embarrassment to Italy. Without the support of these powers it proved impossible to come to any conclusion and so the whole thing had to be dropped.[157]

This was done, of course, because of hopes in those countries that Mussolini could still be an important link in the anti-Hitler chain if he was kept happy. Barthou was immediately succeeded by Pierre Laval. As one writer has put it, the death of Barthou brought an end to all real attempts at a revival of French foreign policy.[158] At any rate, Laval had been a Socialist before World War I but was now to show a progressive movement to the right. One sign of this was his attitude towards the treaty with the Soviet Union which had been negotiated by Barthou. He did all he could to kill it, not by a definite program, but by inaction. It was only ratified after he fell from office in April 1936.[159]

Part of the reason here was not simply ideological or political but a very cold blooded respect for strength, and that alone. Truly

Germany had that strength and so he regarded any settlement of Europe as impossible without agreement with Hitler. He felt this could not happen without a united front of the other European powers. As always the fate of Austria was the key issue. Italian cooperation would be an absolute necessity in meeting this problem. For this Laval was willing to accept anything except what touched the vital interests of France. Of course, when it came to satisfying the outrage of Yugoslavia over her assassinated ruler or preserving Italy in the anti-Nazi front, the choice was obvious in Laval's eyes.[160]

Preservation of Italy in an anti-German front had assumed more importance in French eyes because of a shift in British policy in the last months of Ramsey MacDonald's premiership. This was heralded by the White Paper (Statement Relating to Defense) of 4 March 1935. This was a plea put out by a group of civil servants to persuade the government that, now that Hitler was rearming Germany, it was vital for England to begin a crash program of rearmament. They said it would not matter what the rest of Europe did. Once Germany was rearmed war would be automatic. Therefore, England must look after herself. This statement was accepted by the government and put out publicly with some modifications to mollify Hitler.[161] Its prime significance is that it signaled the end of collective security for England and a return to reliance on her own force. It had one other important effect because Hitler used it as the justification for restoring conscription in Germany on 16 March.[162]

There was one more effort at collective security. It resulted in the Stresa Front of England, France and Italy against breaches of the international order. As A. J. P. Taylor puts it, it was a pale reflection of the great meetings with which Lloyd George had once dazzled the world. It also presented a peculiar picture of a meeting headed by three renagade socialists to perserve the result of the war which two of them had opposed, and looked to convert Europe to democracy which one of them had destroyed in his own land.[163]

Mussolini's interest in an agreement with France and England was his desire to achieve two results. One was, of course, to prevent a German takeover in Austria, and the other was to get from Laval a free hand in Ethiopia. The Ethiopian problem came up at this time for a number of reasons. Perhaps the principal one, and the only one to concern our problem, was that Mussolini felt his prevention of a Nazi takeover in Austria had bottled up Hitler for at least a year. The conquest of Ethiopia should present no problems. It would be over in a year at the very latest so that his armies could be back in Europe ready to confront Hitler again when he would begin to act. This was a desirable conquest for several reasons. It would provide an invaluable training for his new army and force it into shape. Secondly, it would go a long way to solving several home problems. Italy was lacking in raw materials, particularly coal and iron. It was proved

that Ethiopia was particularly rich in these and they had never been
touched. At this Italy was dependent on England and Germany for
her supplies of these commodities. Also, Ethiopia was good for
European colonization as far as climate and terrain were concerned
and could go some way in solving the chronic agricultural over population while retaining the people under the Italian flag.[164]

This failure of her friends to join her in condemning Hungary and
Italy was greeted with dismay in Yugoslavia, as can be imagined.[165]
Since this had failed, their concern had to be to again find an alliance
to protect them from Italy. This took the traditional pattern of trying
to persuade France that an alliance with Yugoslavia was valuable.
If they succeeded then they might persuade France to urge Italy to
guarantee the borders of Yugoslavia. They made it clear to France
that if this was not done, they would join Poland and Germany against
Italy and France. Italy finally decided to follow the French-Yugoslav
line doing so in a general document calling on all states to guarantee
Austria's frontiers by guaranteeing all those of southeast Europe. It
met with a cool reception. Then Germany refused to go along as did
her adherents. When Austria refused a protectorate that ended the
plan.[166]

Nevertheless, the fact that the assassination had taken place on
French soil caused a feeling of coolness to develop in Yugoslavia
toward that country. Then this was coupled with the apparently dilatory
investigation of the murder, a definite anti-French attitude developed.
This lack of concern in France was contrasted in the popular mind
with the fact that Germany was the first country to send condolences.
Therefore, people began to say that if they had Germany as an ally,
Italy would never have dared to act.[167]

Public opinion over the assassination of the king coincided with
the worsening of the Ethiopian problem which affected Yugoslavia
badly economically. It will be remembered that Italy was Yugoslavia's
most important trading partner despite their political problems. The
result of the Ethiopian Problem was the breaking of this tie and the
substitution of Germany as her most important trading partner. This
was to be one of the most important European results of this
affair.[168]

In Yugoslavia a new government came into being with the regency
but it soon fell as did several successors. The major question which
brought all these changes was over the old dictatorship of King
Alexander. One party wanted a liberalization of the government while
the other wanted maintainance of the dictatorship. Finally, an election had to be called in May 1935 when the Jevtić government refused
to settle the question without a mandate from the country.[169]

All parties took part except the Slovene Populists.[170] Maček was
out of prison and headed a Serb-Croat coalition. This coalition was
purely an election maneuver and did not imply any future political

action together. Despite the usual hindrances to free elections, this group got 40% of the vote but because of the weighted system of allocating seats they only received 67 out of 373. Its members, therefore, again boycotted the parliament which soon fell apart even more when a Croat in the government accused Maček of secretly sympathizing with the murders at Marseilles. Three Croats and two Serbs promptly resigned, among whom was the finance minister, Milan Stojadinović.[171]

In early June the regent asked Stojadinović to survey the possibility of forming a new government. He found that all agreed the present one lacked public confidence. A new one must be formed that might even contain Maček. He felt a new political party should be organized combining all pro-government groups with the name of the Jugoslovenska Radikalna Zajednica (Yugoslav Radical Union). On June 23rd the regents officially asked Stojadinović to set about forming such a government. He was able to do so retaining for himself the office of foreign minister as well as premier. For a while the opposition neither opposed nor joined this new group.[172]

The new government went much further than England in condemning the actions of Italy in Ethiopia. They seem to have had no idea of England's wish to acquire Italy as an ally against Germany. They not only categorically refused to recognize Italy's action in Ethiopia but reaffirmed their ties to the Balkan and Little Ententes as well as with France.[173]

Since the primary desire of France in the whole affair was to bring Mussolini into an anti-Hitler coalition, the French did not let the crisis prevent them from holding military talks with Italy. In January 1935 an agreement was reached over mutual action in case of German aggression against Austria. Part of it envisaged a French army corps placed between the Italian and Yugoslav armies to prevent any trouble between them. The French urged the Yugoslavs to accept these ideas. As General Gamelin put it, Italy needed to expand and it was better she did so in Africa than in Europe.[174]

In government circles in Yugoslavia there began to be doubts about the wisdom of their course, even though Goering gave assurances of German support if Yugoslavia was attacked by Italy.[175] The French argument began to have influence as they saw that it was true that without Italy Yugoslavia would be the only state left in south central Europe interested in maintaining the status quo. The Yugoslav minister to France, Spalajković, argued in these terms and went further saying that it might be in the interest of both France and Yugoslavia if Mussolini could be given enough concessions to keep him busy in Africa for the next fifty years. This would mean peace in the Balkans. Thus, France and Yugoslavia should work together to bring England around to this point of view.[176]

Stojadinović also advocated giving concessions to Italy. The evident reluctance of Laval to take a strong stand combined with his feeling that Yugoslavia had rushed in with too strong an opinion without seeing where her interests lay made him think that she should sit back now and take a much more cautious position. He said that Yugoslavia alone could do nothing to effect the actions of Italy. When Ethiopia had been taken care of then who could tell where Mussolini's ambition might lead him. Therefore, the best position would be to give him concessions in Ethiopia rather than see him in the Balkans. As long as France had no clear policy it was suicide for Yugoslavia to commit herself before the great powers took a stand.[177]

As talk of sanctions increased among the small powers, the Yugoslav position began to change again. On October 3rd Italy invaded Ethiopia without declaration of war. On October 7th the League declared Italy an aggressor. On October 11th the League voted to impose sanctions. The same day the sanctions conference agreed to stop all arms exports to Italy and on the 14th agreed to withhold loans to Italian firms or the government. This sort of thing brought, of course, a great dilemma to many of the smaller states, particularly Yugoslavia. This was because Italy would impose restrictions on imports from those countries. Yugoslavia was threatened with a great loss of trade and, therefore, of jobs. Nevertheless, they did vote for sanctions, indeed, they took a lead in calling for them. This was because they saw their own security involved in this question. The application of Article XVI of the Covenant could be a means for preventing aggression against themselves or the rest of the Balkans.[178]

It was at this juncture that the Hoare-Laval Agreements became known. The result was the appearance of a large group in the British government for which Neville Chamberlain was the spokesman who held that there was now a very considerable danger of war in Europe. When this was coupled with the worsening situation in Asia caused by Japanese aggression, Britain found herself faced with the possibility of two wars at once, one in Europe and the other in Asia. In the state of her military forces this was an impossible burden. Therefore, Chamberlain said it would be wiser to try to localize the world's trouble spots. Thus, peace could be secured by local arrangements which could be guaranteed only by those nations vitally concerned. In agreement with this the British government raised the question of what Yugoslavia would do in the event of direct conflict between England and Italy. Yugoslavia pledged to uphold the covenant.[179] The publications of the Hoare-Laval proposals took the heart out of the small powers in their attempt to stop Mussolini by sanctions. Their disillusionment with the great powers, and especially with England because of her double policy, was complete.[180]

For Yugoslavia, thus, there was a great deal of merit in both points of view. It would be good to stop Mussolini as a lesson and especially as the League was actually doing what it was supposed to do; stop an aggressor. Thus, Yugoslavia could count on being protected herself in time of danger. On the other hand, it appeared equally good to let him go ahead. In this case his expansionist dreams would be satisfied and so he would stay out of the Balkans. Either way seemed to satisfy the interests of the country. The trouble with England was that she wanted to have her bread and eat it too by talking of stopping Mussolini but doing nothing effective to accomplish this.[181]

At this point the question of Yugoslavia's military position entered as stated by the general staff. Because of the overriding importance of military problems, their ideas were largely to decide the country's foreign policy until the country was conquered.[182]

England sent a note asking Yugoslavia to give them assurances that Yugoslavia would come to their aid militarily in case the question of sanctions resulted in an Italian attack on England. Also, they should take care to report their support of England to Rome. This would, of course, be a complete commitment and the feelings of the military on whether this could be carried out or not was of vital importance. Their answer was, however, very pessimistic.[183]

First off, their position was that no such commitment should be given because it would open Yugoslavia to the chance of overwhelming retaliation. Before such assurances could be given both the Balkan and Little Ententes would have to be consulted. None of the other members of those groups was in as exposed a position as was Yugoslavia, being the only one with a border on Italy. The others must be brought in because if Italy attacked Yugoslavia, certainly Hungary and Austria would attack and perhaps Bulgaria as well. Those first two bordered on the richest parts of the country. Such an attack would make almost the whole upper part of the country untenable and they would have to withdraw into the southern mountains, as they had done in World War I. A commitment by Czechoslovakia, Rumania and Greece to aid them would largely prevent this.[184]

However, the only real aid would be to get Laval to guarantee France's aid in such an eventuality. The French could easily make a show of force against the Italian frontier which would certainly cow Mussolini. Otherwise Yugoslavia was bound to bear the brunt of any fighting. England could do nothing to help them. All they had was the navy which could do little to help Yugoslavia considering that all sea routes were easily dominated by the large, powerful and very modern Italian navy. To help Yugoslavia would have required a large scale sea battle which might seriously damage the British fleet and leave it weakened for some time to come. Thus, without the Balkan and Little Ententes, and particularly France, the general staff felt Yugoslavia should not commit herself.[185]

A word or two should be said about the Yugoslav army since it was to play such a large role in events. It was quite large containing

about 1,500,000 as of January 1939. It was considerably helped by
geography. Except for the plains along the Danube in the north and
again in Macedonia in the south, the country was rugged and filled
with nearly impassable mountain chains in Serbia, Bosnia, Dalmatia,
Montenegro and most of Macedonia especially. The backwardness
of the country came to their aid as well. For instance, the almost unpro-
tected coastline seemed to offer a great chance for invasion. But, once
landings would have been made (which would have been difficult seeing the almost complete lack of natural landing places) there would
have been nowhere to go since there were virtually no roads of any
kind leading back from the coast. This wildness and the lack of drink-
ing water had always been one of the strongest defences of the area.
However, Italian plans looked to invasion from Trieste to the Danube
through Slovenia. This is easily passable for an army.[186] Yugoslavia's
army had, of course, a tremendous reputation gained in the Balkan
Wars and World War I. In such pretechnical wars it was certainly very
good. It was based on the peasant soldier, reared in a warlike tradition
and trained from childhood in the ageold guerilla tactics used against
the Turks. The fierceness, bravery and fanaticism of these soldiers
was famous throughout Europe. They were unfortunately little prepared for the wars of science and technology of the 20th century. Their
level of training and education for this was very low. For a modern,
technical war they were worse than the Greek or Italian armies.[187]

The poverty of the government had a great deal to do with this.
The whole artillery was mostly leftovers from World War I or even
earlier. They had a large store of shells for these guns but it was now
found that, because of poverty, the government had neglected to buy
fuses for them when World War I ended. To make it worse, these
had been made in countries now under German control. There was
virtually no armor and what existed was antiquated French material.
There was a large airforce, well trained but equipped with old French
planes and suffering also from French ideas on air strategy. The navy
was mostly a few small torpedo boats and coast guard craft.[188]

The army, therefore, was mostly a paper tiger. The true facts were
hardly known, however, outside of the country. It was to be as much
of a surprise to the world as the collapse of the French army when
the Yugoslav army fell so quickly. In 1941 Hitler, it is reported, felt
a considerable respect for this army and wanted it to be on his side.
That is certainly one of the reasons he courted Yugoslavia.[189]

The failure of the League to act with decision about the Hoare-Laval
proposals spelt the end of the League as an instrument of collective
security. The person who saw this most clearly was Adolf Hitler. His
attempt at domination of Europe was to begin very soon now that
it was obvious that nothing would be done to stop him.[190]

It was in the middle of the Ethiopian Problem that Hitler decided
to start the process of regaining those lands lost over the centuries.

The crisis had shown him that neither of the methods Europe had tried for maintaining her security would work. He saw no reason why they should work now against himself especially since they had failed against Mussolini.[191]

The problem involved both the Versailles and Locarno treaties. Articles 42, 43 and 44 of Versailles said that Germany could not have fortifications or military establishments on the left bank of the Rhine nor in a zone on the right bank for fifty kilometers east of the Rhine.[192] This was not so bad since most English and French opinion had formed the conclusion that Versailles was an imposed treaty and anyway the Germans had a perfect right to govern their own territory without interference.[193] The important treaty was the Locarno Treaty of 1925. Even Hitler had admitted that this treaty was one Germany had undertaken of her own free will. He had given a number of assurances that he would follow it religiously. It contained provisions which specifically guaranteed the demilitarized zone. Thus, what was resented in Europe was the flouting of a treaty which even Hitler admitted had been freely signed by the Germans.[194]

The excuse for this action was the Franco-Soviet Pact signed by Laval in May 1935 but still not ratified in January 1936. The main credit for it goes, however, to Louis Barthou, the assassinated foreign minister. His idea in getting this treaty was to achieve a kind of eastern Locarno. This project failed, however, on the refusal of Poland to go along. It also involved bringing the Soviet Union into the League of Nations. Both were, of course, extremely unpalatable to Hitler. Recognition of this by Hitler would involve the very thing on which most of his support was based. Most Germans at the time had a general hatred and contempt for the Slavs based particularly on the loss of so much territory to the Poles. An eastern Locarno would have blocked all chances for getting those territories back. Hitler's foreign policy was, of course, based on a return of all lost territories.[195]

He went about remilitarizing the Rhineland by what became his classic method. Propaganda took great care to play on the theme that this was only rectifying another of the terrible injustices of Versailles. Also, that Germany was merely exercising her due sovereignty in her own country. Who could object to that? This was his standard theme and it certainly worked very well. Much of world opinion may not have favored him but there was this idea of a man fighting for justice for his country. That could not very well be approved of for France and not for Germany. Thus, much of the hostility to Hitler was frustrated because they could not very well condemn him for this. Such an attitude was increased when he took great pains to say this was not a move in a plan to invade France but that he wanted peace with France and would do all he could to achieve it.[196]

The actual move also came on a Saturday, March 7, 1936. This again became standard procedure. His hope was to be finished over a long weekend before there could be a reaction against him. At the time most governments all but closed down over the weekend and the officials were scattered to country homes or on trips. Also, nearly all newspapers at the time published no Sunday editions. Thus, nothing could be coordinated until it was too late to act. By then Hitler had consolidated himself in his new position.[197]

France and Belgium were the nations most concerned and had quite enough authority under existing treaties to act by themselves. They certainly had the military power to do so. France still had the largest, best equipped and best trained army in Europe. They had, however, already been considerably hypnotized by German claims of how much the armed forces had been rebuilt.[198] Therefore, the French government was convinced that any move to prevent German remilitarization by force would mean a long, drawnout and very costly war. Nothing could be done without a general mobilization. This ran into a constitutional problem as this was just when a French general election had to be carried out. The politicians were afraid of their political lives if they seemed to be moving in the direction of a new war with Germany.[199]

For these reasons, France and Belgium tried to get the League to back them up. Russia and the Little Entente urged them to use force as the last hope of preserving European peace.[200] England, on the other hand, urged caution. They felt that taking a legalistic stand was perhaps the best way of bringing about that war everyone feared so much. They felt that negotiation was the best approach to the problem. Eden admits that Hitler could not be trusted. But, an agreement would at least buy some time. England was only barely starting her rearmament and so was in no position to help France. The Germans were reasonable people and so something temporary could be got out of them to prevent war at this moment. They certainly could not want a war either.[201]

This refusal by the British to support France in a military move was then used by the French as an excuse for no action. Just what would have happened if they had acted seems to be something of a mystery. It used to be assumed that Hitler would have been forced to back down because he simply did not have enough force. After the war documents were discovered that purported to show that the army units had orders to proceed with great caution and even to turn back for home if there was the slightest hint of French counter action to the remilitarization of the Rhineland.[202] More recently other material has come to light which seems to show that, on the contrary, the army was merely to move back to better positions.[203] Thus, the question has been opened up again.

French fear of a new holocaust on the lines of World War I had the result of cutting her off from her allies in the east and giving her no chance to effect events in Central or Eastern Europe. The rapid construction of the Siegfried Line opposite the Maginot Line made it soon apparent that, despite her great strength, France could no longer effect events. The West was now cut off from the areas where Hitler was most ambitious to move. M. Flandin, French foreign minister, put the position as the French saw it when he said that Frence would have to make the best terms she could with Hitler and leave the East to its fate.[204]

All that appeared to give any likelihood of stopping Hitler was again a policy of sanctions. Yugoslavia, for one, was against them because they had not worked against Italy but had badly effected Yugoslavia's economy. Germany was, by now, pretty much their best customer. There was no other country capable of taking her place. New sanctions against Germany would have really wrecked things and without any good purpose being served as far as they could see. If it was done on the same terms as the sanctions against Italy, Germany would not be stopped or seriously inconvenienced while Yugoslavia's economy would be wrecked. If Germany attacked France over this question though, Yugoslavia was bound to come to France's aid.[205]

At this time Austria followed Germany's example and went over to an army based on conscription. For Yugoslavia this little effected her direct safety. At the same time there was a rise in pro-Habsburg feeling.[206] The next move would undoubtedly be Hungary also going over to conscription. If this happened, Yugoslavia would be facing a ring of suddenly powerful states all with long standing desires to see her destroyed. The trouble was, of course, that France now would not and, indeed, could not come to her aid. She was all alone. At this point (June 1936) Hjalmar Schacht came with an offer of aid against Italy from Goering. Yugoslavia greeted this, of course, with a deep sense of relief. Yugoslavia could now be seen to be swinging toward Germany.[207]

By October 1936 Germany had taken on the task of supporting Yugoslavia against Italy and Hungary. Hitler urged that Italy must reach a solid understanding with Yugoslavia and that Italy must press the Hungarians to direct their irredentism against Czechoslovakia. Hitler told him that this would serve two purposes. 1) It would have inestimable propaganda value against the Communists. 2) It would lure the Hungarians from the influence of the British. Perhaps Yugoslavia could even be enticed away from the Little Entente.[208]

By now the Little Entente had broken up in fact if not in name. In 1935 the Czechs had signed a treaty with the Soviet Union. This flatly contradicted the treaties which bound the Little Entente nations together. It was stated that no member state could sign a treaty of a political nature with a non-member without the express approval of all the members. Yugoslavia flatly refused to recognize the Soviet regime while Rumania had swung in a circle from once wanting an alliance with Russia to now opposing it. Rumania's swing in opinion was motivated by German pressure and the growing recognition that great power involvement in the area could only mean the small states would be taken over by one or the other of them. No longer was there then the focus of a common defense against a common foe.[209]

France tried to mend her fences but it was too late. All her credit was gone. This attempt involved a mutual assistance pact. Yugoslavia had pressed this for years but France had refused on the grounds that it would bar a reconciliation with Italy. In June 1936 M. Titulescu of Rumania raised it again in the form of Barthou's plan for a mutual assistance pact between France, Germany and the Little Entente. By then it was highly unlikely Germany would have accepted. But France still refused to consider it on the same grounds it had given Yugoslavia earlier.[210]

But, by November France had a change of heart. They admitted that it was largely the Czechs who were responsible for that. On November 2 and 13 two démarches were handed to the Yugoslav government. France said she would enter into mutual assistance pacts with each of the governments of the Little Entente if in return they would broaden the scope of their concern. As of that time the alliance existed for defense against Hungary and Bulgaria. It should be expanded for defense against attack from any quarter.[211]

Yugoslavia refused to agree to this because they no longer trusted France or, at least, her ability to fulfill her obligations. In the meantime, as we have seen, the situation was opening in other directions. Therefore, without turning the French offer down precipitously, they waited to see what sort of deal their new friends in Berlin could push the Italians into giving them. Thus, a new phase in Yugoslav foreign policy begins. Instead of tieing themselves to some big power or international organization to be saved they decided to strike out on their own. This would mean making no new commitments to any power or alliance system until a settlement had been achieved with Italy. Even then no commitments could be made that might jeopardize that. This was all important.[212]

Thus, Yugoslav policy began to gravitate toward neutrality. Indeed, their policy from now until the signing of the Anti-Comintern Pact in 1941 attempted to play one side off against the other.[213] Italy also began to realize that a policy of friendship might be of benefit. The change began as early as the murder of Chancellor Dollfuss of Austria on July 25, 1934. Ciano began to fear the rising power of Germany. His wish was to build up an Italian sphere which could balance Germany. He saw the inevitability of an Anschluss and wished to prevent further German expansion toward the southeast.[214]

The new conditions were shown by a series of treaties between the two countries. In September 1936 a financial and economic agreement was signed. In November Mussolini made a speech calling for efforts toward more cordial relations. The Yugoslavs immediately responded that they hoped for the same thing while letting him know that he would have to do something about his support of the Ustaša and Hungarian irredentism.[215]

In March 1937 there was finally an Italian-Yugoslav treaty. In it Italy made many concessions. They tried to insert a provision that neither could make further treaties with third parties without consulting the other. This was dropped after Yugoslav insistence because they said that this would even prevent them from signing trade treaties and would also interfere with treaties made earlier.[216]

Another sore point was the status of Pavelić and the other members of the Ustaša in Italy. Yugoslavia asserted that they had proof that even with negotiations being carried on these members of the Ustaša had complete freedom to travel and were being subsidized by the Italian government. They wanted Italy to allow Yugoslav police officials access in order to assure that the Ustaša was being kept muzzled. Italy refused to allow this for some time but tried to make the whole thing a matter of Italian assurances. Finally a police official from Yugoslavia was allowed access.[217]

The last major point was Albania. Yugoslavia felt it was becoming an Italian knife poised at the south side of the country. Its control by Italy would place the country in a very bad position militarily since an invasion could come simultaneously from north and south. Thus, it seemed a matter of vital national security to see that Italy did not exert complete control but was only one of an international group. Italy remained adament here, however, saying that Yugoslavia must trust them or no lessening of tension could result. Yugoslavia had to finally give up on this point because Italy would brook no interference in Albania.[218]

On the whole, Italy conceded much to Yugoslavia. They agreed to respect the territorial integrity of Yugoslavia and not to allow on Italian territory any activity against the existing order in Yugoslavia. They agreed to remain neutral if the other were attacked by a third power and they recognized Yugoslavia's attachment to the Little and Balkan Ententes and the League of Nations. We have already seen the concessions on the terrorists and Albania.

On the economic question, Italy agreed to import more from Yugoslavia. Also they agreed to give her most favored nation treatment in trade.[219]

Ciano obviously felt the treaty with Yugoslavia was fundamental to Italian foreign policy. He also stated that nothing here was done without the approbation of Germany.[220] It seems strange when the agreement was designed to take the worst sting out of Anschluss by blocking Germany from expansion to the south. However, to my mind, it merely shows what I stated before. That is, that Hitler had no desire to expand in that direction at that time. If he could control the economies of the eastern states, being able to get all the raw materials he needed, that was all he wanted. He also wanted to know that they would not join coalitions hostile to him. As usual he let Mussolini have the appearance of glory while he had the fact. Ciano had a personal liking for Stojadinović. He found him, "strong, sanguine, with a resounding laugh and a vigorous handshake. He is a man who inspires confidence."[221] In their conversations Stojadinović told Ciano much that showed him as an admirer of the fascist system. He seems to have had complete sympathy for the domestic ideals of the system but he opposed their foreign policy. He liked the idea of being a strong man himself but did not want his own country to be a victim of expansionist fascism.[222]

Ciano probably had as much knowledge of him as anyone. He regarded him as a Fascist although not by an open declaration of party loyalty. He wrote later, "He is certainly one by virtue of his conception of authority, of the state and of life."[223] Ciano thought of him as already the primary political figure in Yugoslavia because Prince Paul had unlimited confidence in him and let him do as he wished.[224]

Stojadinović certainly had all the marks of the strong man. He had unlimited confidence in himself and his luck. He imported into the country as many of the marks of Fascism as he could. This was as far as he dared to go at the moment since even that roused a storm of protest not only from the other parties but from the mass of the people.[225] Even though the South Slavs saw the only decent life for a man as that of war, they saw war as a horrible necessity of life to which a man must steel himself as a crusader. Thus, the individual hero has been glorified but not the war chieftain as such.

Another reason, of course, was the nature of political life in the country. So many of the parties (and certainly the more vigorous ones) were based on nationality. Thus, there were many fascisms as among the German Slovenes or Italians in the northwest or the Ustaša of Croatia but it was virtually impossible to unite them. Each area developed a purely local fascism based partly on hatred for other kinds of Yugoslavs and that real Yugoslav Fascism was an impossibility. It illustrated the basic fact of disunion because of hostile brands of nationalism.

Thus, his attempt to set up such a movement in Yugoslavia met a distinctly hostile reception and any support was a distinctly minority affair.

Prince Paul, the regent, was also distinctly anti-fascist. As stated before, his training had been English and he admired their way of life and attitudes. He certainly admired the power and new vigor which Fascism had given to the countries where it was found but this was an admiration which produced fear rather than the desire to emulate those countries. He went along with them as far as he felt he had to.[226]

He disliked the growing fascist tendency of the premier. As time went on, he would have liked to get rid of him but did not dare in the international situation. Finally, as we shall see, he was able to. This was not from any failure of foreign policy or any more pro-fascist attitude there but because he feared the growing fascist trend internally. The attempt to put down the Croats and allow them no position in the government finally caused Stojadinović's downfall.[227]

The last two chapters have, thus, shown the country in increasingly difficult straits. At first some attempt was made to put the country on a better footing especially as regards the relations of the government to the Croats; a bad feeling caused by the inauguration of the royal dictatorship. This failed due to the assassination of King Alexander and because the following regime had to be an essentially weak one since it was a regency.

The king's death also, produced a crisis in foreign policy since it appears to have been directly engineered by Italy and Hungary, Yugoslavia's worst enemies. But, as the crisis worsened, she appeared to be helped by a friendly Nazi Germany. Germany took the opportunity to gain greater and greater control over the economy until by wartime she had a stranglehold on it.

In foreign affairs France and Great Britain increasingly showed themselves ineffectual in meeting the challenge of Germany with the result that Yugoslavia found herself adrift with no friends she could count on to help her. Germany cleverly stepped in. Thus, we have seen a policy of neutrality evolve which involved a nice balancing act between all her enemies. It was felt by many influential Yugoslavs that Germany, at least, had no direct involvement or wishes in the Balkans. The conflict between Italy and Germany for control of the Danube could be used to get Germany to protect them against Italy. It was well realized that this is a dangerous game and might backfire at any moment. What else was there to do? The Little Entente was not designed to protect Yugoslavia against the enemies she now had and France obviously could not. All they could do was follow this policy and hope things would change favorably before either one gobbled them up. Instead, the two were to get together and destroy her with ease. The rest of the story is that of the gradual erosion of this position and the final conquest.

Stojadinović completed his round of efforts at a general settlement begun with the Italian treaties by a trip to Berlin in mid-January 1938. The Germans were obviously very interested in wooing him. To greet him at the station were Goering, Neurath and five ministers of state. His visit was filled with pomp and all sorts of very flattering ceremonies.

On January 17th Stojadinović had a conversation with Hitler and summed up Yugoslavia's position in one sentence. Yugoslavia would never enter any grouping hostile to Germany. Hitler said that he also hoped that the two countries would never again face each other as enemies. In fact, he went on to say that a strong Yugoslavia was something he was very much in favor of. The murder of the king had distinctly worried him, he said, but he hoped for a Yugoslav-Hungarian rapprochement. Germany's ambitions were confined to the north and the Baltic Sea stopping at the Brenner Pass. The Adriatic was not part of Germany's interest. He assured Stojadinović, "In the Balkans we want nothing more than an open door for our economy."

Stojadinović, on the other hand, assured Hitler that Yugoslavia considered the Austrian question as a purely German matter. The Hungarian question was at the heart of the Little Entente and would have to be solved within its framework. He assured Hitler that Yugoslavia relied on the word of the Fuehrer. He acknowledged that he had learned much in Germany and was particularly eager to win over the youth of his country as Hitler had done in Germany. They must start to think of themselves as Yugoslavs and not as Serbs, Croats or Slovenes.[228]

It is obvious that Stojadinović said in Italy and Germany what would most please each side regarding Austria. His main interest was in completing King Alexander's policy of easing the Italian problem. Austria could work itself out when the time came. It is obvious that he had two things in mind in what he did here. One was to achieve the

understanding with Italy, and the other was to keep Germany happy
and available as a counter-foil to Italy.[229]

Germany's policies in Yugoslavia were now along the lines Hitler
set out to Stojadinović. That is, towards economic control of the country by Germany. [230] Yugoslavia's trade with her allies was negligible
while Germany was capturing it at the expense of Italy.[231] The new
trade treaty giving Italy most favored nation status made little difference in the loss of Italian trade. Italy simply did not make the manufactured goods Yugoslavia needed.[232]

The government of Yugoslavia increasingly recognized the problem
this was creating for them. From late 1936 to 1939 they tried to get
out of this net but with no real success. One of the major examples
of the German effort was their attempt to get the same sort of most
favored nation treatment as Italy. In October 1938 Dr. Walter Funk,
Reichsminister for Economic Affairs, made a trip to Belgrade in hopes
of achieving this. He offered to buy from Yugoslavia 50% of its
exports and give technical and financial assistance in increasing ore
production. In return Yugoslavia, of course, was to buy more from
Germany. They completely refused.[233]

That they would do so should have been more obvious to the
Germans. It was to the deputy director of Germany's economic policy
department, a man named Clodius. He wrote in January 1938 cau-
tioning against trying to push Yugoslavia into closer relations. He
showed how unpopular such relations were in the country and that
Stojadinović's position might suffer if he had to champion such an
unpopular policy. Their current policy was already achieving everything Germany could hope for, i.e., the withdrawal of the country
from anti-German groupings in the Danube region. Too much identifi-
cation of these economic moves with political closeness might have
the effect of cancelling what good had already been done. This statement was ignored when Funk made his trip.[234]

The way the Germans ignored their sensibilities plus the evolution
of the Italian treaty made the Yugoslavs very wary. It became obvious
as time went on that Italy was slowly withdrawing its commitments
from Central Europe in favor of Germany. They, thus, saw themselves
rapidly becoming, perforce, an economic satellite of Germany with
no freedom of movement.[235]

They made frantic efforts to find alternative markets. The need,
of course, was for trade on credit or by clearing agreements. They
simply did not have hard, international currency. The need was to
unload large bulk purchases of her raw materials, the proceeds from
which could then be used for purchase of munitions, airplanes and
antiaircraft guns. This sort of thing required massive subsidizing by
the governments concerned since Yugoslavia wanted delivery on credit
and pay by clearing agreements. France could not do this and Britain
was unwilling to do so.[236]

In 1936 Eden was successfully approached on increasing British purchases. Over the next few months there was a considerable increase in British purchases but nowhere near enough to overtake Germany's lead.[237] In the latter part of 1938 Prince Paul went to London to try again. He pointed out how the German trade policy was strangling the country and how political this was. The Board of Trade promised to do all it could but pointed out that it was not the custom in England for the government to interfere in the freedom of trade. This was particularly hampering because of the necessity for subsidies for trade of this nature. Laissez-faire would not permit this.[238]

Several times high British officials made speeches deploring the hold Germany was getting on the Balkans by these methods but failing to carry it to the step of workable solutions. They did not seem to realize that in this case politics and economics were tied together or, perhaps more likely, not wanting to sink to such methods themselves. Their philosophy was for profit for the individual as the prime consideration while to Germany it was all subordinated to profit for the state.[239]

Again in May 1939 Ivan Subbotić approached Lord Halifax at Geneva. He showed him how Germany had absorbed 50% of Yugoslavia's trade. These materials were going directly into German war industry. Yugoslavia needed an immediate increase of trade with England before she was totally captured.

To this Lord Halifax replied that it was England's custom to let her people trade where they wanted without government regulations. Subbotic replied that because of the political situation Britain should do something to keep them out of the hands of the Germans. This was not a purely economic problem and should not be treated as one. They must be assured of bulk purchases of raw materials by Britain before it was too late.[240]

This was, however, on the eve of the war and the British government felt itself too involved elsewhere to try to save what they regarded as a lost cause anyway. By then Germany did have a stranglehold on Yugoslavia's foreign trade since she was the only possible buyer left. Italy by then had ceased to have any real importance in Yugoslavia's trade.[241] Nevertheless, Yugoslavia looked on this as a very bad thing by 1939. What could they possibly do to change the situation was the question, however.

Stojadinović had come to the conclusion that the only way to end the Croat Problem was to crush Maček and the Croat Peasant Party. This he could legally do because of some obscure provisions in the constitution. This kind of thing was what moved Prince Paul to decide to get rid of him before it was too late. That point was fast approaching with the coming constitutional end of the regency. When King Peter came of age it was likely that Stojadinović would retain his position and be impossible to remove under the young and inexperienced king.[242]

It was really strange that this should be so because Stojadinović, it must be remembered, had come to office in the first place because his predecessor, Jevtić, had been unable to come to terms with Maček. Now Stojadinović had also failed and was about to meet the same fate. The first contact of Prince Paul and Maček occurred shortly after the death of King Alexander. This was when Maček was interned. At this time he is reported to have said that Croatia could only exist as part of Yugoslavia. He, also, said that he favored the setting up of the dictatorship by King Alexander. But, he said, he disliked the particular men who came into the government that afternoon.[243] Maček's own account of the affair mentions only condolences for the king's death.[244]

Maček was released from prison in December 1934. In June, at the time of the Jevtić crisis, he was called to meet with Prince Paul as head of the opposition. Maček requested as a solution that the constitution be set aside and that new elections for a consitutional convention be held. Prince Paul rejected this and empowered Stojadinović to form a cabinet. Throughout 1937 and 1938 the situation did not change. There were meetings between Maček and the Prince but neither could change the other's mind.[245]

The new prime minister, Cvetković, had begun to make his political connections with the Croats as far back as 1928. He took part as a Radical Party delegate in negotiations to form a coalition government. The venture never even got started particularly since this was the middle of Radić's accusations that the Serbs were attempting to impose their hegemony on the Croats. But Cvetković never allowed this to affect himself. Therefore, when efforts at a settlement with the Croats began under Stojadinović but at the insistence of the Prince, it was natural that Cvetković would be able to use his contacts among the Croats. Actually he had been secretly at work on this for over a year. By late summer 1937 he was able to report that contact had been made with two of Maček's lieutenants, Ivan Pernar and August Kosutić, and had convinced them that the time was now ripe for Maček to work energetically for agreement.[246]

Maček himself seems to have had his own ideas on how to get his program accepted. At the end of January 1938, Cvetković heard from Pernar and Kosutić again. This was about three months after Maček and the three opposition parties agreed to work together to get a new constitution. They told Cvetković that Maček thought the agreement of the three parties had failed in its goal and that only he and Prince Paul could settle the problem. As the guest of the opposition, Maček proceeded to visit Belgrade in August 1938. An estimated 100,000 people greeted him. This visit seems to have been Maček's own idea done over the protests of his colleagues. They thought this would only redound to the benefit of the opposition. Cvetković kept pushing at Pernar that the time was very ripe for an agreement and that a protocol should be drawn up and signed by both groups. This would assure the opposition that, even under the present constitution, their demands would be met through cooperation in parliament.[247]

The December 1938 elections were a disappointment to Maček. As a result he became more amenable to an accommodation with the government. Nevertheless, immediately after the election Stojadinović called a meeting of all the Serbs in the government to work out a means for negating Maček's vast strength at the polls. This was the situation when the government of Stojadinović fell. This left Cvetković in a commanding position because of his closeness to the Croats. He was one of the few left able to contact them and make progress. This was to make him premier.[248]

All of this was bound to appear unpalatable to the Germans and Italians since they had achieved a good relationship with Stojadinović. Cvetković had to act immediately to reassure them of his good-will. At a meeting on 11 February 1939, he assured the German minister, Viktor von Heeren, of his personal sympathy and his country's friendship for Germany and said that he would work, as he had in the past, for Germany-Yugoslav friendship. "The line of Yugoslav foreign policy with respect to Germany naturally remained unchanged. This was guaranteed not only by the appointment of the minister to Berlin as Foreign Minister but, above all, by the fact that the Prince Regent alone was and would remain authoritative in this matter."[249]

Heeren himself deplored the fall of Stojadinović. To him it meant the end of any kind of government in which Germany could have confidence. He felt that Stojadinović was the only man who had a real sympathy for Germany's form of government. Heeren foresaw the rise of a democratic government now that would contain a considerable number of Croats and Serbian leftists. In such circumstances, it might be to Germany's advantage to cultivate the Croats because of their fear of Italy.[250]

Italy regarded the change with misgivings. They knew the official policy would not change but they feared for the Albanian project. Cvetković was an entirely unknown quantity here. Mussolini and Ciano agreed that if Cvetković went along with the old plan for the partitioning of Albania between Italy and Yugoslavia, well and good. If not, they would occupy it all without and, if necessary, in spite of Yugoslavia. They then moved fast to prevent any further contacts of Yugoslavia with the democracies by deciding to move the date for the invasion of Albania to Easter week, 1939. Part of the reason for this haste was also the growing belief that the Germans had perhaps engineered this coup as an anti-Italian maneuver so as to keep them away from the Croats.[251]

The evidence shows, however, that if anyone engineered the coup, it was the Yugoslavs themselves because Stojadinović was too closely identified with the Axis. Thus, the coup could be seen as a reaffirmation of neutrality. The international situation had by now deteriorated to the point where all the small states of Europe could only hope to preserve themselves by staying out of these great power squabbles. It took great political agility and frequent changes of tack to do so. For Yugoslavia, this tended to aggravate the internal political problems of the country and so increased the danger that a great power would intervene. Thus, the next period was to be a highly dangerous one, in which no one seemed able to find a way out of the impasse.[252]

The Croats thought of the separatist agitation in Czechoslovakia as similar to what was going on in their own country. Now, when it seemed that the claims of the Slovaks might be granted by the Germans, there began to be more and more agitation for a settlement of the long standing Croat cry for autonomy or, at least, the implementation of the equality promised in the constitution.[253]

All the Croatian deputies to parliament held a meeting at Zagreb on January 15, 1939. In a resolution they urged that the great powers intervene to assure the Croats liberty of choice and destiny. They stated that the history of the country since 1918 proved that the Yugoslav idea was a failure. Claiming to speak for all the Croatian people they declared all acts of the Yugoslav government null and void, particularly the treaties concluded with foreign powers.[254] This was reinforced in mid-March when Maček's lieutenant, August Kosutić, went to Prague for "personal reasons." Belgrade was sure that his real purpose was to learn how to turn Croatia into a German protectorate. Other followers of Maček also tried to see Goering in Berlin. He refused to see them on the grounds that, if they were to hold discussions with foreign governments, it should be with Italy rather than Germany.[255]

Despite all this Germany stepped up its activity among the Croats. This, of course, worried the Yugoslavs and made the Italians frantic. Mussolini was already sullen over Germany's successes in Austria and Czechoslovakia and now began to fear that he must put off his Albanian project. This was because he was afraid that this would give Germany the excuse to bring Croatia under their protection or for Maček to proclaim an independent Croatia that would be closely allied with Germany. Mussolini would not tolerate the swastika flying over the Adriatic, his lake.[256]

Ciano thereupon called in Hans von Mackensen, the German ambassador, and made plain his feelings over these events. He strongly implied that Germany was behind the whole thing. Italy, he said, considered maintenance of the status quo in Yugoslavia a fundamental factor in preserving peace in East Europe. Mackensen protested his government's disinterest in the whole thing and said that the Fuehrer would substantiate all this.[257] This proved true. On March 25 Ribbentrop notified all German foreign missions that the policy of the Reich was to support Italy's claims in the Mediterranean without question. In the future German missions would have no contact with Croat organizations or other minority groups.[258]

Now begins a period that sounds like one of Oppenheimer's spy novels of the late 19th century. It was brought on by Ciano's fears of the dangers to Italian interests of a civil war in Yugoslavia. If, as seemed likely, Yugoslavia should disintegrate in such a civil war, Italy must be ready to take her share of the spoils. The result was a search for suitable instruments to carry out such a policy with a blossoming of all sorts of plots, counterplots and spies, enough to make James Bond sound like a small child.[259]

The first of these plots involved a Croatian landowner, the Marquis de Bombelles. Ciano and Bombelles met at a hunting party organized by Prince Paul. Later Bombelles presented himself to Ciano as a spokesman for the Ustaša. He went on at great length about the bad conditions under which the Croats lived. Without asking for money, he tried to warn Ciano of Serb hostility and begged for introductions into the Ustaša organization in Italy. This was done.[260] Bombelles came to be regarded as the best avenue of approach to Maček and was asked for advice and his opinion on all Italian plans for Croatia. He continually urged Ciano to intervene militarily before Germany could do so and Ciano actually contemplated this for a while. This all blew up when Pavelić relayed to him German information that Bombelles was an agent working for Belgrade. The Germans had found out the deception from an agent they had been able to plant in Yugoslav military headquarters.[261]

The role of Maček in this affair is still unsettled. He reports a meeting with Bombelles that parallels Ciano's report.[262] It is shown by another affair, that of one Carnelutti. He was an Italian but professed himself a friend of the Croats and was a member of the Croatian Peasant Party. He was well connected in the Italian government, having a brother in the diplomatic service and being related to Propaganda Minister Alfieri, or so he said. Ciano reports Carnelutti as having told him that the Croats were anti-German but that if nothing was done to help them, they would be forced to turn to the Germans for help. Therefore, Italy should make overtures to Yugoslavia to treat the Croats better. If this failed the Croats were sure to revolt and ask Italy for aid. Italy could count on the fact that they would ultimately unite with her. When Mussolini was told of this, he ordered Ciano to support this.[263]

In the meantime Maček and Cvetković were negotiating over the Croat problem. These talks broke down.[264] According to Ciano, Carnelutti then came to him telling him that Maček would continue his movement but would need a loan of 20 million dinars. This would be used to finance a revolt in the Fall.[265] The two met later to draw up an agreement that specified the amount of money and when the revolt would break out. Once the revolt was under way, Maček then undertook to call in Italian troops to aid in the restoration of order. Croatia would then proclaim itself a republic in confederation with Italy, the two having common ministries of foreign affairs and national defense. Mussolini signed this and payments began, subject to signature by Maček.[266]

On being presented with this agreement, Maček refused to have a thing to do with it.[267] It is certainly evident, though, that Maček would do almost anything to protect Croatia. He would prefer autonomy within Yugoslavia if he could get it but would get the same result by other means if he had to. Therefore, the incident as protrayed by Ciano could be true. It seems more likely, though, that Maček was sounding Italy out in order to protect himself if negotiations with Belgrade broke down completely. It does not seem likely in such circumstances that he would want to have this in writing or done by anyone official (witness the use of someone like Carnelutti). Thus, Carnelutti probably went too far even though he certainly was an emissary between the two men. Things had been done in such a way that he could be repudiated if the need arose.

England appeared in the picture at this time. They learned from an informant in Italy early in March 1939 that the Italians planned to invade Yugoslavia. This would be accompanied by a landing in Albania around April 1. On March 12 Lord Halifax sent this information to Prince Paul in the greatest secrecy.[268]

The Prince was sure that this information was out of date since he had received a communication from Mussolini urging him to make a settlement with the Croats. He believed, though, that Mussolini possibly had his eye on Slovenia as a block to German expansion to the Adriatic.[269]

At the same time Ciano told the Yugoslav minister to Rome, Hristić, that Italy had no designs at all on Croatia but he refused to make a similar declaration about Albania. He warned Hristić that they intended to move soon against that country but wanted to get assurance first that Belgrade would not interfere. Hristić presented no objections to this except that Italy should not use Albania as a base to attack Yugoslavia.[270]

Despite the most vehement assurances to Hristić, they had a very hard time convincing him of Italy's good intentions toward Yugoslavia. Hristić asked them to take no action without first informing Belgrade and to preserve the existence of the Albanian state as a matter of form. To assure him, Ciano went over all their plans for Albania. Ciano says that Hristić took the whole thing with resignation remarking as he left that King Zog was coming to the same end as Beneš.[271]

The Italian army landed on the Albanian coast on Good Friday, April 7, 1939. There was little if anything Yugoslavia could do in the situation. Expecially when it was found that Ciano had arranged for Hungary to have six divisions mobilized and on the frontier to intimidate the Serbs. The best they could hope for was that the Italian occupation would only be temporary, that they would not establish a protectorate, and that they would be generous enough to recognize Yugoslavia's desiderata.[272] At the same time the new foreign minister, Cincar-Marković, took steps to assure the goodwill of Germany. He asked them to make an open assurance of Germany's interest in a strong and united Yugoslavia. In return Yugoslavia would promise not to become involved in any combination hostile to the Axis.[273] In fact, he told Ciano that all that was keeping them from joining the Axis was hostile public opinion.[274]

Everyone agreed to this as the best policy at the moment. When Ciano reported these facts to Ribbentrop they both agreed that it was necessary to preserve the status quo in Yugoslavia. If the country fell apart, however, Italy would take charge.[275] So that both were reacting to their declaration of neutrality almost as though it were due them. They were already getting an inflated idea of their power. England also accepted it as necessary in their exposed position and even that it was in Anglo-French interests. At the proper moment, when the back of the Axis had been broken, they could pour in fresh forces and decide the issue. England had an overinflated opinion of the Yugoslav army which was not deserved and was making an attempt to put the best face on what was an obvious loss for the Allies.[276]

May 31 to June 8, 1939 Prince Paul went on a visit to Berlin. He had a formal meeting with Hitler and Ribbentrop June 5. It left him with the feeling that war was inevitable. The effort they made to sway him to the Axis side was truly massive. Over 30 million marks were spent on decorating Berlin. Some 30,000 storm troopers had been brought to Berlin for security duty. The propaganda service filled all public media with nothing but laudatory material on the prince. More to the point, there were the usual parades of German military might.[277]

The Fuehrer made every effort to bring the Prince into his camp. He insisted that Yugoslavia make some unmistakable gesture of friendship for the Axis. It was suggested that this take the form of withdrawal from the League of Nations. Cincar-Marković displayed great reluctance ending by saying he would think about it.

Ribbentrop then suggested that Yugoslavia join the anti-Comintern Pact. Cincar-Marković said this was impossible. Yugoslavia had sentimental ties of common slavic blood with Russia which bound them together. Hitler repeated that it was necessary for Yugoslavia to give some sign of solidarity with the Axis. This would be an advantage for Yugoslavia in two ways. For one, when the Slovene and Croat separatists realized that the Axis supported the status quo in Yugoslavia and, therefore, that they could get no support from the Axis, they would have to stop their efforts. Similarly, it would get rid of the Italian problem. Mussolini must know whether they were to be his friends or foes.

The conversations were a great disappointment to the Fuehrer. As he left the last meeting, he made no effort to hide his anger.[278] To the Yugoslavs it showed what the Germans might demand. It also had an educational value. They got a practical glimpse of what German military power was really like. They not only saw it on parade but were able to get some estimates of its fighting strength. The Germans seemed quite willing for them to get this as a lesson.[279]

Prince Paul came to some conclusions on the international situation from his visit. The principal one was that war was inevitable. Germany would never back down on the public demand for Danzig and neither England nor France could back down on the promise to prevent it. Danzig now had become a matter on which neither side could back down from their public position because prestige was too much involved. Hitler, however, did not believe this. He was convinced he could do virtually anything and those two powers would back down. Prince Paul became convinced on this trip too that Hitler was taking out insurance to prevent Russia from acting because Hitler refused to answer him when he asked what Hitler thought Russia would do.[280]

He found that the Allies did not regard war as inevitable either. In July he dispatched General Peter Pesić to London and Paris for consultations with their military leaders. This man was chosen because King Alexander had often said that he was his choice to lead the army if war should come. He reported that Paris believed Yugoslavia would have to enter any war. They would be forced to choose sides by Axis demands that would make them join the Allies. If this did not work, The Allies planned to occupy Salonica immediately to prevent it falling into Italian hands. If the worst came to the worst, a stand could be made there for eventual reconquest as had happened in World War I. Anyway, they thought the quality of the German army was well below that of 1914. It lacked sufficient trained reserves and good officers. The morale was reported as so low that the French believed their might even be a revolution if war broke out. Therefore, they expected some caution on Germany's part and that threats were sheer bluff since Hitler must certainly know the state of feeling in his country.[281]

It was, thus, obvious from both sides that, if there were war, Yugoslavia would be dragged into it whether they liked it or not. Therefore, Cvetković and the cabinet decided that the rearmament and fortification program had to be speeded up. Even more important was the necessity for ending the internal strife in the country. The Croats must be brought into the government. If this meant that the internal political structure had to be completely overhauled then, so be it.[282] Cvetković told parliament on March 10, 1939 that the settlement of the Croatian Problem was the most urgent task facing the country. The central government had to face the fact that the Croats had, because of geography and cultural contacts, developed differently from the rest of the country. The government, therefore, must find means for people of differing development to live a normal common life in one Yugoslavia.[283]

Actually Cvetković and Maček had been negotiating since December 1938. This had been going on despite the efforts of Stojadinović to stop them. Now that he had political power, Cvetković picked these conversations up again in March.[284]

There was agreement by the two men on many fundamental points. These included the fusing of Croatia, Dalmatia and parts of Bosnia into one administrative unit; on dissolving parliament and holding new elections for a constituent assembly; on placing responsibility for the army and foreign affairs in the hands of the central government; on leaving to the constituent assembly the decision about what ministries would remain under the central government and which would go to the units; and of a complete reorganization of the state.[285]

Once this had been done, Maček sent representatives to Belgrade to meet with the Serbian parties which had joined the United Opposition. They were asked to assent to the agreement and to authorize Maček to sign on their behalf. This they refused to do. The main argument was that it would weaken the country at the very time when it should be strong and present a united front to its enemies. The Italian landings in the Balkans made this particularly imperative.[286]

Another hitch was that Prince Paul refused to go along with the document. It would appear that he was under pressure from the Serbian politicians who were afraid it would mean a lessening of their power. The Prince only approved the amalgamation of Croatia and Dalmatia and the town and county of Dubrovnik.[287]

As soon as he heard of this, Maček issued a statement putting all blame for failure of the negotiations upon the Prince. He then called a meeting of the Croat National Assembly which gave him full authority to represent the Croat nation.[288] According to Count Csaky, the Hungarian foreign minister, Maček was indirectly requesting Germany, Italy and Hungary to support him with propaganda. Both Germany and Hungary agreed not to interfere. It was to their interest that the situation in Yugoslavia be allowed to cool down.[289]

Soon thereafter, Ivan Subasić, one of Maček's advisers, received an urgent call to see Prince Paul. The result was that negotiations were resumed. Cvetković and Maček agreed to salvage those parts of the agreement on which all agreed, at least, and to postpone discussion on the rest. Maček abandoned his insistence on personal union and only insisted on decentralization of the administration.[290]

Each named three experts to work out the details. All was fine until they got to the question of the gendarmerie. At that time it was under the joint jurisdiction of the Ministries of the Interior and War. To the Croats this was one of the prime instruments of Serbian oppression. Therefore, they wanted it placed under the control of the Ban of Croatia. The central government refused to yield on this point and once more the negotiations broke down.[291]

Maček's reaction was to threaten secession. If Belgrade could not bring order, Germany could, he told the foreign press. He saw the Croats and the Czechs in a similar situation.[292]

This threat of foreign interference reinforced the danger already apprehended from growing German power. The Pact of Steel signed by Germany and Italy on May 22, 1939, plus the rumor that negotiations for a non-aggression pact between Germany and Russia were in the offing, brought both parties back to the conference table. Their own fears plus a public opinion more and more insistent on agreement to strengthen the state in such times kept them at it. Maček, also, at this time became convinced that war was inevitable and liable to break out at any moment and that his party should not have to bear blame for weakening the country under such critical conditions. Therefore, agreement was soon reached. On August 23, 1939 the Sporazum (Agreement) was signed and on August 26 the new government was formed, including Maček as vice-premier.[293]

The main provisions had to do with giving the Croats a measure of autonomy. Croatia, Dalmatia and seven adjoining districts where Croats predominated were combined into one administrative unit. It was to have its own legislature in Zagreb and a separate budget. Its governor would serve at the pleasure of the crown. Crown and legislature would share in making the laws. The central government would retain control over foreign affairs, defense, foreign trade, commerce, transport, public security, religion, mining and education.[294]

Only 5 days before World War II broke out the new government began its work. In its way, it was perhaps as felicitous an arrangement as could have been obtained at the time. In particular, the personalities of the two leaders somewhat complemented each other. Maček was almost entirely concerned with internal problems. These, however, were of such a nature that their effect upon the international scene could destroy the country. This was the great weakness of the time and was part of the reason for the final collapse of the country in 1941.[295]

Cvetković, on the other hand, was far more interested in foreign affairs. Perhaps he devoted himself too much to this side of things. He tended to view internal problems too lightly. Thus, the internal problems were largely left in the old hands which had always made such a mess of them in the past. Nevertheless, each was a man of integrity and so Maček's mistakes tended to be balanced by Cvetković's greater concern and knowledge and vice versa. It is highly doubtful if more able men could have been found with as much integrity as those two.[296]

Now that the nationality problem seemed on its way to being solved, the main concern of the government was to prepare the country for a possible war. This involved economic and financial measures as well as strengthening the armed forces and using the existing treaty arrangements to assure the neutrality of the other Balkan states.[297]

One of the first measures was to assure the safety of the gold supply. The German Foreign Ministry learned in July that a large part of the country's gold reserves had been shipped to England. Later a large amount was to go to New York. Minister Heeren was requested to make urgent inquiries in Belgrade. They wondered if this, plus a rumored recent visit to London by Prince Paul, reflected the success of anti-Axis propaganda. The minister to Rome was also less friendly than usual.[298] It took Heeren some time to get any confirmation of the gold matter, finally learning that some had been shipped to London as a result of the Czech crisis. This had come from a "reliable source." He was able to report, also, that there was no anti-Axis feeling. The country, he told his superiors, did not intend to become involved in a war of the Great Powers. They would remain neutral in such a conflict selling their goods to those who had been their best customers before the conflict. It would avoid any open breach of neutrality.[299]

At the same time economic and financial measures were begun whose sole purpose was the obtaining of funds to buy arms. The government hastened to take such measures as setting up a system of war bonds, authorization was given for the army to make exceptional purchases abroad, the principles of a requisitioning system were laid down, and a system for compensating and easing the financial plight of reservists called up was instituted.[300]

In December 1938 Stojadinović had raised the question of the army's defense capability with Minister of War, Nedić. The resulting report is filled with a rather odd optimism as regards the country's capability for defense. Virtually all the armaments to make up deficiencies or to plug holes in existing supplies were to be obtained from the Axis. He was certain he could obtain 100 antiaircraft guns from Italy by August 1939, and 500 more from Czechoslovakia by 1940. A factory to make gasmasks had been started and would be finished by 1941. Krupp had agreed to build a new steel mill at Zenica for steel to make shells and guns. This was regarded as particularly good because by this time there were several million Reichsmarks to Yugoslavia's credit in the clearing account in Germany. There were 750,000 artillery shells left over from World War I. These, together with

180,000 new shells would be ample for a while. All that was needed to make them ready were the right fuses which could be obtained from Czechoslovakia.[301]

At the beginning of 1939 the airforce consisted of 50 reconnaissance planes, 50 fighters and 50 bombers. General Dušan Simović recommended that 150 new planes be bought. These would be 50 Hawker Hind reconnaissance planes, 50 Messerschmidt fighters and 50 Dornier bombers. This satisfied Stojadinović who thought an airforce of 300 planes would give Yugoslavia the most powerful airforce in the Balkans.[302]

Implementing these plans proved difficult. Krupp demanded that the German government give a total guarantee on the price for the order. This amounted to 100 million Reichsmarks. Secondly, the army was bitterly opposed to buying goods from Germany. They had always bought from Czechoslovakia and wanted to continue to do so. Stojadinović had to fire two generals before he could get his ideas accepted. Finally, when Stojadinović was dismissed, General Neuhausen, Goering's agent on the spot, recommended the final decision be postponed until the situation was clarified.

Finally, the whole matter became a test case in the constant power struggle in the higher echelons of the Nazi movement. This was between Goering's Ministry of Economics and Ribbentrop's Foreign Ministry. Ribbentrop insisted that his ministry should have the entire control over foreign affairs and that included economic and trade policy. This battle slowed down the procedure so much that the Yugoslav minister in Berlin, Ivo Andrić, had to warn the foreign ministry that if Yugoslavia could not satisfy her needs in Germany she would go elsewhere, perhaps Sweden.[303]

It was not until the negotiations had been underway for four months that an agreement came about. The protocol was finally signed in July perhaps because there were rumors that France had offered to supply arms. By it, Yugoslavia would receive an unspecified amount that would be decided on later. This was to serve as a valuable lever to exert pressure on Yugoslavia.[304]

The Fuehrer himself intervened to stop supplying antiaircraft guns and planes. Finally he did despatch a number of Heinkels and Messerschmidts because the Yugoslavs were becoming so uneasy. By now Germany's raw material supply was becoming tight. It was decided to tie future deliveries of armamants to deliveries of Yugoslav minerals. In return for her entire output of copper and substantial shipments of lead, zinc, tin and hemp, Germany would give her 100 Messerschmidts, 120 Skoda antiaircraft guns and 250 Skoda antitank guns.

This gave Germany the entire output of the French owned Bor copper mines and the British owned lead and zinc mines. It was not such a catastrophe for the Allies as this may sound, however. Almost all their output had gone to Germany up to now anyway. The Yugoslavs had to confiscate the mines to conform to these demands. The gesture satisfied the Germans because it indicated to them that Yugoslavia was practicing "benevolent neutrality."[305] The Yugoslavs found all other avenues of supply for armaments closed to them no matter how much in principle the other countries wanted to help them. British and French factories were already going at capacity to try to get over the long gap during which Germany had feverishly rearmed while they did virtually nothing. They approached America but found that the manufacturers there were totally committed to French and British orders and that America was starting to think of her own rearmament. They could only promise the start of delivery in 18 months after receipt of the order. Fulfillment would require expensive retooling and involve them in the risk that the crisis might blow over in a short time leaving them with all that expensive and now useless plant. They insisted on a large amount down to prove good faith and immediate payment in cash on the barrelhead on delivery. This was something Yugoslavia could not do.[306] President Roosevelt was approached but could only offer words of goodwill. In the isolationist mood of the country he could not venture to give a government loan or any large scale government aid.[307]

For the rest, the Yugoslav army was substantial and had a fine reputation from the First World War. However, its officer corps was not very good. Discipline was very severe, destroying personal initiative. Most officers were Serbs (of 165 generals, 161 were Serbs) regarding the army as their preserve and the only institution left dedicated to turning Yugoslavia into a Serbian empire.[308] This, therefore, made it an instrument for increasing national quarrels rather than healing them. As the nationality problem increased many of these Serb officers came to regard soldiers from Croatia or Slovenia as, at the very least, potential traitors.[309]

Furthermore, nearly all senior officers were veterans of World War I. Their training was prewar. Most were very poorly educated, particularly in military matters. Most regarded trench warfare as the epitome of the military art beyond which it could not advance. Only the younger officers were very well trained, many having gone for advanced training to Germany, England or France.

The events of 1938-39 shocked the military badly. The agitation resulting in the Sporazum convinced many of the older officers that Croats were German or Italian agents. They began to organize a special military force called the Cetnik Ordredi (chetnik detachments) to check on, report and possibly control the political activities of Croatian civilians and soldiers. The result was a catastrophic fall in the discipline and morale of the army. The fissures dividing the nationalities got wider and wider.[310]

The Balkan Entente was another instrument for aid in this direction. At the February 1939 meeting in Bucharest, Gafencu of Rumania, speaking to the German minister, Fabricius, assured him that the Little Entente was dead. Further, the Balkan Entente would never be used against Germany. The four countries agreed that Germany's drive to the east was "a natural phenomenon which would increase in strength." They said that for them this was a fact of life and that they would have to cooperate closely with Germany particularly in the economic sphere.[311]

Bulgaria was not mentioned in this exchange. Indeed it could be said that the major reason why the Entente had been unable hitherto to repulse Axis intervention in the area was lack of Bulgarian participation in Balkan defense. Thus, Bulgaria's constant reiteration of her territorial demands against the members of the Entente dating back to 1878 had become a matter of Great Power politics. She would only participate in area defense to the degree that the members satisfied her territorial claims.[312]

Yugoslavia took the first step toward settling the differences between Bulgaria and the Entente by a treaty of friendship signed on January 24, 1937. This was followed by an agreement between Bulgaria and all the states of the Entente by which they agreed to renounce force in relations among themselves, allowed Bulgaria to increase the size of her army and opened machinery for a further discussion to revise the Thracian frontier.[313]

This agreement did not satisfy the Bulgarians. They insisted on specific, detailed revisions before they would even consider mutual defense. For them the Dobrudja Question with Rumania was particularly pressing. They took this so seriously that they told the Germans they would be willing to cooperate politically and economically with them if Germany would back their territorial demands.[314]

Although the Germans bent their efforts to get the Yugoslavs out of the Entente, they tried hard to get Bulgaria to join some such organization.[315] On July 4th, Cincar-Marković and Bulgarian minister-president, Kiesseivanov, met in Belgrade. Their discussion revolved around the question of the continued existence of the Balkan Entente and what they would do if it ceased to exist. They also discussed the question of their neutrality against pressure from both the West and the Axis and how long this could be maintained. They agreed that if neutrality had to be abandoned each would join the same side. They then discussed possibilities for political, economic and military cooperation, even to the point of a military alliance. They found they were in perfect agreement on the whole thing.[316]

A few days later Kiesseivanov found himself less happy than he had been over the entire situation. Yugoslavia refused to denounce the Balkan League stating that it was better to remain in it in order to influence it. Furthermore, he had to tell the Germans that he could get no answer on what Yugoslavia would do if Turkey attacked Bulgaria nor did he think Prince Paul's visit to London could do Bulgaria any good.[317]

In London Prince Paul was not too sanguine in talks with Lord Halifax. He said he would like to see the Dobrudja matter settled but he was opposed to Bulgaria obtaining a port on the Aegean Sea. This would only give Italy another door into the Balkans.[318]

Soon after the invasion of Poland Cincar-Marković and Gafencu met to discuss ways to strengthen the Entente and settle the Bulgarian problem. They decided on three conditions that would have to be met before they would consider certain territorial claims of the Bulgarians.

1. Bulgaria must join the Balkan Entente and take up all the obligations of membership.

2. Each member state of the Entente must contribute territory with which to satisfy Bulgaria.

3. Bulgaria must put down all agitators who would increase tensions among the states of the Entente.[319]

In mid-February 1940 the Kiesseivanov government fell and was replaced by one much more sensitive to the demands of both Germany and the Soviet Union. Russia had at one time supported the Entente states in resisting Bulgarian revisionism. Now they supported the Bulgarians in their territorial demands. They told the Germans that the Southern Dobrudja was a minimum demand. They would resist all offers of the Entente until this was granted. They said they would be able to realize their demands only when they stood side by side with Germany.[320]

Thus, by apparently pushing Bulgaria into joining the Entente, Germany and the Soviet Union had succeeded in assuring that she would not join. They had by this prevented a unified defense of the Balkans. This is undoubtedly what they were after from the beginning.

Hitler was none too happy with Yugoslavia in the first months after the start of the war. The dismissal of Stojadinović, Prince Paul's apparently close ties with the British, their failure to leave the League of Nations, their refusal to let the germans control the Balkan Entente and Prince Paul's refusal to make an unequivocal statement in support of the Axis all combined to make Hitler look upon Yugoslavia as an uncertain neutral. He felt this only meant that they would remain neutral until the Allies were clearly winning. Then they would come out openly on their side. At this time, he pointed out to Ciano, the Yugoslavs were in a position to adversely effect events. Therefore, Italy should liquidate Yugoslavia. Earlier Ribbentrop said the same to him stressing that the present time of turmoil presented a golden opportunity to liquidate Yugoslavia without danger to interference.[321] Ciano was quite disgusted since he was opposed to Italian entry into the war under any terms. Ciano told Mussolini that the Germans were liars and cheats upon whose word Italy could never rely. At first Mussolini agreed with this but then the lure of empire was too much for him. His desire for loot, a place of honor for Italy as a nation of warriors was rationalized to the point where he concluded that his honor demanded war.[322] He immediately, therefore, ordered Marshall Badoglio to prepare for an attack on Greece and Yugoslavia.

Like Ciano, Badoglio was not eager for Italy to enter the war. He had a number of questions that bothered him which needed an answer before he felt he could act. What help could he expect from the Hungarians and Bulgarians? Could he use the Drava Valley which would mean swinging wide next to the Hungarian border? Mussolini wrote in reply that neither Hungary nor Bulgaria would oppose them and would come in on their side later. He cautioned Badoglio, however, to forget about the Drava Valley for the moment. Apparently he was afraid that using this route would offend the Germans by coming too close to their sphere of influence.[323]

The very day Mussolini's letter was sent to Badoglio the non-aggression pact between Germany and Russia was signed. This put a whole new light on Italy's position. Ciano felt that this made it more imperative than ever for Italy to avoid war. Italy should bide its time preparing to reward itself at some future date in Croatia and Dalmatia. To do this Italy could do two things. It could build up a special army designed for a strike there at Italy's own good time. Also, they could do all possible to work with dissident groups in the area.[324]

Mussolini was convinced of the wisdom of that stand.[325] He suddenly saw how dependent they were on Germany for all the sinews of war.[326] Although he was extremely eager for war he begged Hitler to let him out of his obligations because of Italy's real lack of supplies and his own fears. When he got it he was humilated but relieved. The realities of the situation had to be recognized, though, and so Yugoslavia was spared once more.[327]

For Yugoslavia, a neutral Italy meant a neutral Yugoslavia. Prince Paul assured Lord Halifax that she would defend herself if attacked. This would only mean her eventual destruction. Much would depend on Great Britain and her reaction to the eventual involvement of Italy in the war. The fate of the Balkans was at stake. If Britain allowed Italy to build her force until she could operate from a position of strength in Albania, said Prince Paul, then Britain would be responsible for allowing a process of rot to develop that would engulf the entire Balkans and eventually destroy Turkey as well. Each state would be driven to make what terms they could with Germany. The English regarded this as hysterical thinking. Yugoslavia could easily dispose of the Italian army under any circumstances.[328] The Germans were also informed of the feelings of the Yugoslav government about this situation. They were told that if Italy entered the war and advanced on Salonica (which they could only do through Yugoslav territory) Yugoslavia would defend herself.[329] They said that they expected the Axis might attack them next after the defeat of Poland. To counter this 500,000 men were mobilized and two armies were deployed along the northern frontier from the Adriatic to Rumania.[330]

The period from September 1939 to May 1940 saw a slow abandonment of neutrality as Yugoslavia moved closer and closer to France. In September 1939 Prince Paul began stressing the importance of Salonica to the Allies as well as to Yugoslavia. He said the Allies should occupy Salonica with or without Italy's consent.[331] Yugoslavia would be able to maintain her neutrality as long as Salonica was open and not controlled by the Italians. Eventually they would be able to join the Allies in the war.[332]

The French recognized the importance of Salonica as much as did the Yugoslavs. Nevertheless, they had to report that nothing could be done about organizing an expeditionary force for at least three months.[333]

As the war went on General Weygand expressed his willingness to occupy Salonica with a crops from the Levant but only if the Greeks agreed and neutral Italy did not object.[334] The British were quite bitterly opposed to the whole thing. The first meeting of the Supreme War Council at Abbéville took up the matter. Mr. Chamberlain said that Salonica was not a suitable base of operations. Further, the Allies must do nothing that would give Italy the excuse to abandon her neutrality. Also, Chamberlain said he thought the Allies could not supply another base with their poor supply position.[335] At the December 9 meeting this was thrashed out again with the added warning from Chamberlain that action in the Balkans would prevent action in Norway.[336]

Eventually the French and British were able to agree on the necessity for such a move. On 18 April 1940 the British cabinet instructed the Chiefs of Staff to make plans for a possible Italian attack on Yugoslavia. Plans were prepared for the occupation of Crete, but only if the Italians attacked Greece.[337] The Yugoslavs were all for this. Prince Paul asked if a Yugoslav military mission could go to Paris to participate in the planning. In return for agreeing to this, Weygand asked to send an air force officer to Belgrade to maintain very discrete contacts throughout the Balkans without involving the British.[338]

The plan for occupation of Salonica did not come to fruition since Britain soon had to retreat from Norway and in June the French had to surrender to the Germans. This did not put an end to the scheme, however. As long as the policy of Italy was so nebulous some scheme had to be there to counter her actions. Allied occupation of Salonica seemed the only thing possible. Prince Paul bluntly told the German ambassador that there was no truth in Italy's word and that he had nothing but distrust for Germany's friends, the Italians.[339]

Italy was certainly eager to grab the country. As Ciano put it, Mussolini's hands fairly itched to grab Croatia, Dalmatia and the islands of the Adriatic. He believed, according to Ciano, that neither Britain nor France would do a thing to stop him.[340] In fact Churchill has written that he opposed an automatic declaration of war against Italy. He would prefer to wait and see if the attack was just to seize bases or was, indeed, an attack for conquest.[341]

Actually, Mussolini was to be prevented from attacking by two factors. One occurred in March 1940 when he received a flat order from Berlin to keep his hands off the Balkans.[342] The second was the sheer inability of Italy to go to war with anybody. They simply did not have the materiel nor the trained manpower. Furthermore, there was not the industrial base to supply an army.[343]

Toward the end of April Mussolini was again gripped by his dreams of conquest. He said he must have Yugoslavia because of the raw materials to be obtained there. He would move offensively against Yugoslavia and defensively against France. Again the army dashed his hopes showing him that, in their present shape, they could do nothing.[344]

As Germany moved from conquest to conquest and Italy got nothing, hopes began to revive. Mussolini and Ciano began to think more and more of the usefulness of Pavelić. He could be put at the head of a Croat army that could be made up from Croatian exiles in Italy. Also they began to fear that if they did not act Germany would get the same idea.[345]

The Yugoslav government learned of this possible revolt led by Pavelić. The question was how to get out of this increasingly dangerous situation without being dragged into the war. Given the state of public feeling and the traditions of the country it would be impossible to align the country with Germany. France and Britain could not be counted on. France did not have the strength and Britain considered Italian neutrality as sacrosanct. The conditions put into the Balkan League at Greek insistence made it unreliable. There was only one power left, then, with the power to stop Italy and Germany. That was the Soviet Union. But a pact with the Soviet Union would involve the reversal of a policy 23 years old.[346]

Yugoslavia had refused to recognize the Soviet government after the revolution and had become a center for anti-Soviet activity. They welcomed with open arms the refugees of Wrangel's and Denikin's armies. A special military school was set up for their sons and a girl's school for their daughters in the tsarist tradition. The Serbs had particularly close feelings for these Russians. The long years were remembered when Russia had helped the country gain its independence and the years of sacrifice in the First World War. These Russians contributed a great deal to their new country. They were able to greatly increase the supply of doctors, forestry and agricultural experts, engineers, etc. Thus, it is not too strange that the Imperial Russian Government maintained an embassy in Belgrade down to 1939. A former councillor in the pre-revolutionary embassy maintained it in a building across the street from the royal palace and the old imperial flag with its double eagle continued to fly from it.[347]

In some ways, though, Yugoslavia had been forced to recognize the existence of the Soviet Union. In 1934 Czechoslovakia had gotten them to agree not to block Soviet entry into the League of Nations. After 1935 they had to recognize that it was only a matter of time until they would have to grant full recognition. But, they would do so only under certain conditions. Prince Paul said it was necessary to procrastinate as long as possible. Then it should come about only when absolutely necessary and only when conditions in Yugoslavia became completely quiet and orderly. He said it is absolutely necessary to keep in mind the fact that the Soviet minister would be bound to become the nucleus for all the dissatisfied elements in the country.[348]

Despite all the dangers, it seemed desirable to approach the Soviet Union by the Fall of 1939. The Sporazum seemed to have settled the internal situation. It was remarked by all that Prince Paul held close talks with Mr. Strandtman, the tsarist representative. Not long thereafter Strandtman let it be known that he would no longer function as a diplomat for a government which no longer existed.

It still seemed advisable to go slowly. Since Russia was involved in the Finnish War it seemed inadvisable to get France and Britain upset by negotiating now. It was not until the end of March 1940, when the rumors from Italy about invasion or a revolt by the Ustaša began to fly about, that is was imperative to act. Then Cincar-Marković instructed the minister in Ankara to approach his Soviet counterpart, Terentiev, with the proposal that the two countries establish economic relations. At the same time he was to impress on the Russians the expansionist tendencies of Italy and that it seemed to Yugoslavia to be contrary to the national interest of Russia to allow her to succeed. Moscow answered that she firmly opposed Italy's aspirations in the Balkans and was emphatically committed to maintaining the status quo. They closed by saying that Russia was ready to start economic talks.[349]

The result was the signing of three documents on May 11: a treaty of commerce and navigation, a protocol covering the method of payment for goods, and an agreement covering commercial delegations in Belgrade and Moscow.[350]

In the negotiations the Soviet Commissar of Foreign Affairs, V. M. Molotov, took care to see that the Yugoslavs would understand

Russia's position. He repeated the following ideas three times. He never said flatly that Russia would oppose German or Italian penetration into the Balkans but then he never said they would not. The Yugoslavs were left with the impression that it was more likely than not that Russia would openly oppose Axis expansion in the Balkans. If so, it could do nothing but help their defense efforts.[351] Finally, on June 24, 1940 in Ankara, the two powers signed a treaty establishing diplomatic relations. The first ambassador was sent off by Yugoslavia to impress on the Russians the dangers surrounding Yugoslavia and the Balkans, to obtain armaments, and to secure the help of the Red Army if the country was attacked. Due to circumstances he was never able to fulfill his mission.[352]

Neither Axis power looked on this with any favor. Both were convinced that there was a military alliance back of all this. They became more convinced when a military attache was attached to the Yugoslav embassy.[353]

Before the ambassador left for Moscow, he had a long talk with the German ambassador to Yugoslavia, Heeren, who minced no words at all. He told Gavrilović that Berlin flatly opposed his appointment, mainly because of his reputation as a liberal and democrat as well as his pro-British and French orientation. He was told that the Germans felt that his only purpose was to injure Russo-German relations and that they would oppose any such attempts with all their means. Gavrilović said he was flattered by such compliments on his abilities as the representative of such a small, weak country. On the contrary, he was going to place Yugoslavia's interests within the framework of present agreements. His countrymen liked Russia despite the regime. They had a long historical association in which Russia had done a great deal and made heavy sacrifices to help the Yugoslavs. How could they now do something against a policy the Russians had accepted? Heeren then ushered him out with no comment.[354]

Any doubts the Axis may have had were dissolved when Russia delivered her ultimatum to Rumania on June 26 soon followed by seizure of Bessarabia and the northern Bukovina.

Molotov followed this up by telling the Germans that Sir Stafford Cripps believed it was Russia's mission to unify the Balkans and maintain the status quo there. The Soviet Union had no desire for such a mission although it was interested in the area.[355]

Ciano soon began to report back to Mussolini that he sensed a growing and marked distrust of Russia in Berlin. He said the Germans saw the policy of Russia as exploitation of Germany in order to push forward herself using Bulgaria and Yugoslavia to go as far as the Straits, the Aegean and even the Adriatic.[356] This was soon followed by Hitler's forceable awarding of further Rumanian territory to Hungary and Bulgaria.[357]

On November 12 Molotov went to Berlin to try to clarify the situation. The Germans tried to get the Russians out of Europe and interested in Persia. Molotov insisted on raising the question of the Balkans by seeking to learn what the Axis intended doing about the future of Poland and about Rumania, Greece, Yugoslavia and Bulgaria. The German government never replied to these questions.[358]

None of these negotiations meant much to Hitler, of course, since he had been planning war with the Soviet Union ever since July of 1940. Their importance lies in the use Hitler made of the negotiations in finding an excuse for war which the German people could accept and, hopefully, the world. Also, he was able to use this series of discussions and the Rumanian affair to convince many in the army and the government of the need for war against Russia. A large part of the upper echelons of the officer corps as well as the foreign ministry believed that Russia could be kept neutral by astute diplomacy and that war was not needed. Russia's conduct was used to convince them that Russia was preparing for war and that she was out to encircle Germany with a line of buffer states which would keep Germany from her legitimate Lebensraum.[359]

For Yugoslavia the policy was to backfire. The original idea of using recognition of the Soviet Union to restore the balance of power in the Balkans had been logical. There had appeared to be a balance of power on the western front when the negotiations began. But, by the time the agreement was signed, the western front had disappeared and the Axis now had the preponderance of power. Therefore, the Yugoslavs could not use Russia to balance the Axis. Russia was now alone so that her old idea of a balance between the Axis and the West in which she could supply the leverage could not work. She now had to assume a defensive role everywhere, including the Balkans.[360]

The last open door left to Yugoslavia was the fact that Italy was not yet in the war at the beginning of 1940. Every intimation that they were about to enter the war terrified the Yugoslavs. Ciano tried to reassure them by saying that Italy would fight only the great powers.[361] In fact, Mussolini had to reassure Hitler as well. The Balkans were the only source left on the continent for supplies vitally necessary to Germany that had once been obtained elsewhere but which were now blocked.[362]

On June 10, 1940 Mussolini announced to his blackshirts that Italy was in the war on the side of the Axis. He insisted that Italy did not want to drag any other state into the war, especially those with which she shared land frontiers. He urged Yugoslavia especially to note what he said. Only the actions of Yugoslavia could cause him to change his mind.[363]

At this juncture Hitler had a change of heart toward Yugoslavia. This was occassioned partly by discovery of the so-called Gamelin Papers. Hitler told Alsieri, Italian ambassador to the Vatican, that in them he had found evidence of Yugoslav hostility toward Italy. Ribbentrop echoed this and Himmler said the Yugoslavs were corrupt and perfidious.[364]

This, together with the Soviet efforts in Yugoslavia, prompted Hitler to merely channel Mussolini's anger without trying to end it. Ciano, at a meeting with Hitler on July 7, urged the liquidation of Yugoslavia. Hitler expressed himself as now willing to see Italy destroy Yugoslavia but only at a time good for the Axis. He pointed out that precipitate action would bring the whole Balkans into the war and probably the Soviet Union as well. This would probably do more than anything else to unite England and Russia in opposing the Axis. Hitler advised him to look for some other outbreak in the Balkans which could serve as an excuse for Italian action in Yugoslavia. At any rate, they agreed to exclude Yugoslavia from citizenship in the new Europe they were creating.[365]

All through August Germany kept pressure up to prevent Mussolini's projected attack in September. Ribbentrop believed that all efforts by the entire Axis had to be concentrated against Britain if they were to defeat her. The Balkans, he acknowledged, was in the Italian sphere of influence but it must take a back seat. It was especially important that Russia be given no excuse to intervene.[366] Ciano noted on August 17 that they would have to abandon their plans for Yugoslavia and Greece for the moment.[367]

In these circumstances it began to be felt that Stojadinović might be used to bring about internal turmoil by German and Italian agents as well as Yugoslavs who shared his political outlook. His continued presence, even worse, was an invitation for the Axis to apply pressure for his reinstatement as premier. At the end of 1940 Stojadinović applied for a passport to go to Switzerland. Cvetković refused this but offered one for Greece. Stojadinović refused. On March 15, 1941 Cvetković asked the British if they would admit Stojadinović to British territory and keep him there if he was expelled from Yugoslavia. The British agreed and on March 20 he was taken to the Greek border where he was picked up by the British. He was subsequently interned on the island of Mauritius.[368]

Mussolini, though, was becoming more and more disgruntled at German successes with nothing to show for Italy. He felt he must do something entirely on his own which the Germans could do nothing about. This feeling probably reached its height in October. This was after the Germans got control of Rumania. It can be seen from the fact that he set October 28th as the date for the invasion of Greece.[369]

Ciano agreed with Mussolini on this while the general staff was bitterly opposed, pointing out Italy's inability to fight a great war. She did not have enough trained men. The most serious shortages were in equipment and munitions with no industrial base capable of supplying them. Furthermore, her raw material position was very poor. Italy not only had no deposits of industrial coal, she had done nothing to build up a stockpile. She totally lacked resources in oil. She was entirely dependent on imports for these things as well as minerals and rare metals. Practically all her sources of these things were under German control. Since Germany was very short of these things herself she was in no position to supply Italy. Thus, the generals reasoned that war now would be suicidal for Italy. Instead she should wait until one side or the other was clearly winning so that she could join that side and claim the rights of a victor. Italy then could realize her colonial dreams with very little risk.[370]

Ciano thought the moment was right to act as far as the situation in the world was concerned. France had no longer to be reckoned with while Britain was fighting now for her very life and so was in no position to intervene. Russia would not want to fight far from home and all alone. Neither Turkey nor Yugoslavia would make a move while Bulgaria would undoubtedly join Italy.

He was wrong, however, on at least one count, that of the Yugoslav attitude to an Italian conquest of Salonica. This was still Yugoslavia's main outlet to the sea. Immediately on receipt of the news of the Italian invasion, a meeting of the crown council took place. They could not agree on what to do although all were at least agreed that Italy must not have Salonia. Prince Paul urged immediate mobilization near the southern frontier. Cvetković expressed agreement but wanted nothing hasty in the way of mobilization. He was afraid that this would mean war with both Italy and Germany. The country could not face that. Nedić argued that they should wait to see what Germany was going to do. Mobilization would cut off Yugoslavia's options and force her to a single course of action. Prince Paul finished by stating that Greece would be better off with Salonica in Yugoslav hands rather than Italian.

The following day Minister of Court Antić instructed Nedić to telegraph Colonel Vauhnik, military attache in Berlin, to query the German military leaders on their reaction to a Yugoslav takeover of Salonica. Yugoslavia in the meantime would send troops down to concentrate around the Greek border.

This all seemed odd to Vauhnik. It was signed directly by Minister of War, Nedić, instead of his superiors, the general staff. From what he could discover, the general staff knew nothing at all of what was going on. He decided to obey his orders but in such a way that the government would get the credit and not Nedić.

Accordingly, he asked for an appointment with the political representative of the German high command. He was received by the chief of political intelligence, General Quentzsch, and by Colonel von Mellethin, liaison officer with foreign military attaches. He opened immediately by referring to the Italian invasion of Greece. He said that Yugoslavia was very interested in Salonica and that she feared Italy would occupy that port. It would be in the interest of peace if

Germany would warn the Italian government of this fact and counsel moderation. It was important to realize that all Yugoslavia was united in this feeling and were prepared to intervene if Italy attempted to occupy the city.

General Quentzsch expressed surprise saying that he had not sufficiently thought over the consequences of a Greek-Italian war. So far as he knew the High Command knew nothing of any plans regarding Salonica. The only thing possible was for him to raise the question with the Foreign Ministry which could then inform the High Command of the political implications. It was clear to Vauhnik that this would result in the German Foreign Ministry relaying a summary of these conversations to Rome. This was just what he wanted.

However, the government at home was on tenterhooks and kept pressing him for an answer. This he was unable to get. The Germans kept telling him to be patient. Finally, he persuaded the Greek military attache to tell General Marras, Italian military attache in Berlin, that he had heard from Ankara that Yugoslavia was thinking of intervening if Italy did not withdraw its troops from Greek territory. By this time the Greek counter-offensive was well underway. Marras immediately became very friendly to Vauhnik. He confided that Italy was only doing this to prevent Germany from establishing itself in the Mediterranean.

To his consternation, Vauhnik received a telegram at this time ordering him home. He was on the point of doing so when he received another one from minister Antić informing him the Prince Paul had dismissed Nedić. He thereupon cancelled his plans to go home. His work had evidently produced some results.[371]

On November 5 Nedić had submitted a memorandum to his government:

> "The war has reached a point where Yugoslavia is forced to align herself with one side or the other. France is defeated. Great Britain is not strong enough even to defend her own colonial empire, let alone carry on a successful war on the continent or to assist smaller nations ... its failure to overcome the resistance of Finland's small army is indicative of the impotence of the Soviet army ... it is unlikely that the United States will enter the war. Even if she did, she will need so much time to get ready, that the war will be over in the meantime.
>
> Germany and Italy, on the other hand, are at the summit of their power; they are the lords of Europe and well along on the road to victory which will end the war.
>
> "Yugoslavia should join the Axis powers as soon as possible and forthwith occupy Salonica with the explanation that this is necessary to prevent the landing of British troops and their penetration deeper into the Balkan peninsula. In reality, the reason for the occupation would be to reach the port before the Italians."[372]

The same day as well as the next, Italian planes bombed the town of Bitelj (Monastir), a town very near the Greek-Yugoslav frontier but well within Yugoslavia. When Prince Paul asked General Nedić why he did not send Yugoslav planes to protect the town, Nedić replied in the same terms. However, he went further saying that Yugoslavia could no longer shilly-shally but must state its position. If Yugoslavia ceded a small piece of territory to Germany, the Axis would spare the rest.

Prince Paul replied that this was preposterous seeing that Germany had never shown the slightest interest in Yugoslav territory and Yugoslavia would under no circumstances give her any. With surprising candor, Nedić then said that if Yugoslavia had a clever diplomatic policy it would have no need for an army. Upon that Prince Paul asked for his resignation.[373]

This attempt by Antić and Nedić had failed but Antić was not discouraged from trying again. Although he viewed Germany as the major power in Europe, he did not discount using Italy to lessen or avoid pressure from Germany. Cincar-Marković on the other hand, felt that they had to come to a total agreement with Germany because she was the only power capable of guaranteeing Yugoslavia's neutrality. He isisted that she would never ask Yugoslavia to sign the Tripartite Pact.

Antic acted entirely on his own. He sent a Belgrade lawyer named Stakić to see Ciano. This was a really secret mission since knowledge of it was kept from Cvetković, the Allies and Berlin. Stakić was specifically to ask Ciano whether or not Italy still regarded the Belgrade agreement of 1937 as valid.

Ciano said yes, that he was still completely loyal to the accord. He said he believed a strong and independent Yugoslavia was necessary to Italy's future and that Italy entirely respected Yugoslavia's rights and territorial integrity. Then he came to the crux of the matter. He said he would like to see the agreement of 1937 broadened to an alliance in the widest sense of the word. He stressed in his remarks that Yugoslavia had nothing to fear from Italy since her ambition was for territory south of Albania. He said that Italy did not want to occupy Salonica either temporarily or permanently.

Ciano then prepared a new Italo-Yugoslav agreement. Yugoslavia could prove its friendship by demilitarizing the Adriatic coast. Stakić then asked what power this alliance would be against. Ciano replied that, since he knew the feelings of Prince Paul, he would not say Great Britain but was not the Soviet Union also a good candidate for such a position? Stakić then interjected that perhaps someday it would also be useful against Germany. Ciano is reported to have said yes with a smile.[374]

Belgrade rejected the whole thing. Prince Paul thought it would rob Yugoslavia of its sovereignty and she would get nothing in exchange.[375]

In fact, from now on the policy of Italy was to make little difference in the fate of Yugoslavia. Mussolini had lost the initiative in southern Europe entirely and now Hitler would have to get his chestnuts out of the fire for him. As will be seen, Hitler seems to have seen Yugoslavia as having an important role to play in the Mediterranean power structure, especially in getting the British out of that area. This seems to be particularly illustrative of Hitler's basic character as a great power politician. That is, the way the war rapidly got out of his control, if he ever did control it. As I have attempted to show, Germany under Hitler appears to have had no real policy as regards Yugoslavia. At first his idea was to control Yugoslavia economically to assure that her food and raw materials would go only to the Axis. As long as Yugoslavia fulfilled this economic function and did nothing against Germany he let her go her own way. Necessarily the result would be that, despite the feelings of the people, the Allies could do nothing. Two things were to effect this situation at the same time. One was the policy of Italy which also did two things. First was the damage the Greek war was doing to the prestige of the Axis. Second was the fact that that had brought Britain into the Balkans in the shape of an expeditionary force to help the Greeks. This had entirely changed the picture of the Balkans and made it imperative to get them out.

The second major point was a change in strategy which Hitler formulated to get Britain out of the war. This Hitler came to after the failure to overwhelm British power during the defeat of France. Then came the failure to destroy British airpower which made any effort by Germany to invade Britain impossible. Therefore, something different had to be tried.

The new idea was to bring most of the rest of Europe into the Tripartite Pact thus showing the British that they would have to face facts and get out of the war. The first steps were a change in policy toward the Vichy regime in France to get them into the Axis. They promised Spain that, on their joining, they would help them obtain Gibraltar. This was to be an utter failure about which Hitler could do nothing.[376]

In a letter to Stalin of October 13, 1940, Ribbentrop pointed out the gains which both parties had made as a result of the Molotov-Ribbentrop Pact of 1939. He hinted in his letter at the advantage of a closer relationship between Russia and the Pact powers and suggested that Molotov come to Berlin to formulate a common policy.[377]

Stalin agreed to the visit which Molotov made on November 12 and 13.[378] Hitler had high hopes despite an unyielding attitude displayed by Molotov.[379] Hitler hoped that Stalin would yield on reflection. Nevertheless, on November 18 Hitler complained to Ciano that the Italian reverses in Greece were having psychological repercussions on his efforts to make a grand coalition. Bulgaria was less inclined than ever to join, Russia had just showed at the talks a considerable interest of her own in the Balkans and Turkey could be expected to move after these Italian reverses.[280]

On the evening of November 25, 1940 Molotov gave the German ambassador to Moscow Stalin's answer. He stated that he was not averse to closer relations with the powers of the Tripartite Pact, with certain reservations:

1. Provided that the German troops are immediately withdrawn from Finland which, under the compact of 1939, belongs to the Soviet sphere of influence. At the same time the Soviet Union undertakes to ensure peaceful relations with Finland and to protect German economic interests in Finland (export of lumber and nickel).

2. Provided that within the next few months the security of the Soviet Union in the Straits is assured by the conclusion of a mutual assistance pact between the Soviet Union and Bulgaria, which is situated inside the security zone of the Soviet Union, and by the establishment of a base for land and naval forces of the U.S.S.R. within range of the Bosphorus and the Dardenelles by means of a long term lease.

3. Provided that the area south of Batum and Baku in the general direction of the Persian Gulf is recognized as the centre of the aspirations of the Soviet Union.

4. Provided that Japan (renounces) her rights to concessions for coal and oil in northern Sakhalin.[381]

This was too much for Hitler. He had already in the summer put into operation the planning for ''Barbarossa,'' the name for the invasion of Russia. Since that time, relations with Russia had been deteriorating. This document did not seem to hold out any hope for a basic change that would preclude war. The result was scrapping the attempt to woo Russia into the Tripartite Pact and plans went all out for war sometime in the spring as soon as the weather was right.[382]

Despite this defection and the failure to bring Spain in, the policy did work in the rest of the continent. Certainly this European unanimity would scare the United States off and convince Britain that their resistance was useless. By this time there was only one state in the Balkans which had not joined, outside of Greece, of course. This was Yugoslavia. Their adherence might force the Greeks to expel the British and offer Mussolini facesaving terms.[383]

From this point began the German efforts to bring Yugoslavia into the Tripartite Pact. It now became increasingly obvious that efforts to play Italy and Germany against each other could no longer work. They had identical interests now. From now on the only question was how Yugoslavia would be brought into the Pact. Would it be voluntarily or by conquest?

The Italian invasion of Greece had changed the entire situation for Yugoslavia. If Germany had not had to come to Italy's aid in Greece, it does not seem likely Yugoslavia would have been pushed as hard as it was to join. There would have been no need as was the case with Sweden and Switzerland. However, the need to rescue Mussolini and to deny the British a foothold on the continent made the settlement of Yugoslavia's relations with the Pact imperative.

The effort to bring Yugoslavia into the Tripartite Pact began when Ciano went to see Hitler at Fuschl on November 12. He was there to ask Hitler for aid in Greece. He found that, for Hitler, the key to the situation was Yugoslavia. The situation there was already bad and if Mussolini intended to make it worse the situation was indeed black. He visibly brightened when Ciano told him that secret talks were already being held with Belgrade. He asked if Mussolini would be prepared to make a pact guaranteeing the frontiers of Yugoslavia and ceding her Salonica in exchange for the demilitarization of the Adriatic coast. Ciano said he believed this was possible.[384]

Hitler then wrote to Mussolini to seal this. He warned that a threatening demeanour was worse than useless since a military campaign against the country was impossible before March at the earliest. This, of course, was because of the terrible communications which were virtually wiped out by the snow and mud every winter. Thus, threats would only backfire by being unenforceable and, thereby, give the Yugoslavs time to prepare themselves at leisure long before a blow could fall. "Therefore, Yugoslavia must be won, if at all possible, by other ways and means."[385]

Mussolini hastened to reply. He agreed that Yugoslavia was indeed a trump card in the war on Greece. He was ready to guarantee Yugoslavia's present borders and under specific conditions to recognize Salonica as belonging to Yugoslavia. The Yugoslavs must adhere to the Tripartite Pact, demilitarize the Adriatic coast, and put troops into the war only after the Italian forces had given Greece a "shock."[386] Hitler was eager to get things started. On November 20 at the ceremony of the signing of the Pact by Hungary he told Ciano he planned to invite Prince Paul to Berlin and propose the alliance.[387]

Already on the 19th the German authorities had invited Gregorić, the Belgrade journalist, to come for talks. He spoke with Ribbentrop on the 23rd and 24th.[388] Immediately after this Ribbentrop ordered the German minister in Belgrade to invite Cincar-Marković to Germany. He left Belgrade on the 26th. Utmost secrecy was important. Therefore, he told Heeren before he left that he would go only part way by train, transferring to an automobile to actually cross the frontier.[389] This worked so well that the Yugoslav minister in Berlin only learned of his visit two days later from an inadvertant leak in the German Foreign Ministry.[390]

After a talk first presumably with Ribbentrop at Fuschl on the 27th,[391] he was received by Hitler at Berchtesgaden on the 28th. Hitler began by recounting his plans for a world wide coalition from Yokohama to Spain and for the consolidation of Europe. Every European state must now take a position on the matter. He went on to state that Germany had no ambitions in the Balkans but that Italy did. He showed that this was a golden but fleeting moment to reach a settlement on this problem. Because of what had happened in Greece and Albania Mussolini was willing to make an agreement and, once it was made, Germany would insist on its observance. After dismissing the likelihood of Bulgarian or Hungarian claims, he assured Cincar-Marković that, "Germany did not ask for anything, not even the right of passage for troops." Finally, he suggested that Yugoslavia might receive Salonica.

"In summary, the Fuehrer stated that Yugoslavia could now obtain a secure position in Europe. Between Italy and Germany on the one hand, a nonaggression pact could be concluded; in certain conditions one could go even further in order to consolidate Yugoslav security. In addition, Yugoslavia would obtain an outlet to the Aegean Sea. In this way the Yugoslav problem would be settled permanently."

While he remained noncommittal, Cincar-Marković insisted that he understood these terms. He would immediately return to Yugoslavia and present them to Prince Paul.[392]

Prince Paul, Cvetković, Maček, Cincar-Marković and Anton Korosec, minister of public instruction, conferred about this on December 5. A written answer was given to Heeren two days later. It stated that the Yugoslav government was willing to discuss a non-aggression pact based on the Italo-Yugoslav agreement of March 25, 1937.[393] As Hitler wrote to Mussolini later, the two powers had carefully said nothing about guarantees to Yugoslavia. Thus, Hungary and Bulgaria were not committed to withhold their claims nor would Germany and Italy be committed to helping Yugoslavia.[394]

Mussolini had also changed his view. By this time the Greeks had not only driven the Italians from their country, they were invading Albania. Italy must have something which would change the situation. Mussolini was convinced that the only thing was a firm adherence of Yugoslavia to the Tripartite Pact. On December 8 Alfieri, the Italian ambassador, informed Hitler that:

> The Duce had instructed him to ask the Fuehrer to hasten the accession of Yugoslavia to the Tripartite Pact. This would, in the opinion of the Duce, produce great unrest in the Balkans and be a serious warning to Greece. Greece would then be compelled to rush some units to the Yugoslav border, as a result of which the pressure on the Albanian front would be immediately lessened ... his (the ambassador's) real, specific mission was to request the Fuehrer to bring about a speedy accession of Yugoslavia to the Tripartite Pact.[395]

Thus, the simple non-aggression pact was no longer adequate. On December 21 Ribbentrop told Heeren to inform Cincar-Marković that such an agreement still left the question of Yugoslav adherence to the Tripartite Pact open.[396] Cincar-Marković countered in a conversation the next day with the complaint that Hitler had brought up the subject of the non-aggression pact himself. Therefore, he had thought the whole question of the Tripartite Pact had been put off to sometime in the future.[397]

On the other hand, the very factors which made Mussolini push for Yugoslav adherence to the pact made it less attractive to the Yugoslavs. Now that the Italians were pushed back, the threat to Salonica was automatically removed. On December 6 a German request for transit of a thousand trucks to the Italians in Albania was politely rejected.[398] In a letter to Mussolini of December 31 Hitler drew the appropriate conclusions. He said the policy of Yugoslavia was evidently one of watchful waiting. She wants non-aggression pacts under certain circumstances but does not under any circumstances

wish to join the Tripartite Pact. Hitler went on to say that he could
see no way to improve the situation except by a change of the psychological climate.[399] What he was evidently implying was a series of
Italian military successes. As he had already said to Mussolini in his
letter of November 20, there was no chance of German military
involvement before March. Therefore, Germany could do nothing
to help Italy in her difficulties at this juncture.[400]

Thus, the situation had worsened for Yugoslavia in her relations
with Germany. Up to the summer of 1940 these relations had been
based on political and economic questions, as far as Germany was
concerned. Now for three reasons the military had come to dominate
them completely. One was the use of the Tripartite Pact to convince
Britain she was defeated. Another was to assure that Russia would
have no influence in the Balkans. This would make certain that in
the forthcoming attack on Russia by Germany, Russia could open no
second front on Germany's southern flank. Third was the necessity
of rescuing Mussolini from his fiasco in Greece. Italian defeat was
too damaging to the prestige of the Axis while at the same time, it
left a festering sore on the flank just at the time when Hitler wanted
all his resources concentrated for the attack on Russia. Lastly was
the question of Solonica. It would appear that Yugoslavia's insistence
on this point opened Hitler's eyes for the first time to the uses Germany
could make of a foothold there. It could be the key point to eventual
German control of the eastern Mediterranean and certainly, for the
present, in applying pressure on Turkey about the Russian war.[401]

Despite the dangers of the situation, the Yugoslav government was
very loath to leave their onetime allies, the Greeks, to their fate. Not
only did Prince Paul want them saved but the country shared his
wish.[402]

The Prince could not act directly. Shortly after the start of the Italian
invasion Milorad Djordjević, former minister of finance, called on
Nikola Stanković, owner of the Vistad armament works. For a while
Djordjević railed against the government's refusal to come to the aid
of the Greeks. Even the Prince's reasonable pleas had failed to move
them. Stanković was sympathetic to the Greeks and so asked
Djordjević to ask the Prince to authorize him to manufacture and ship
to Greece at his own risk needed war materials. The Prince received
this idea with enthusiasm and then worked out procedure with the
Greeks.

It was done through the Turkish government. The goods were
addressed to a Turkish businessman in Istanbul. He then sent them
to Salonica falsely declared as ordinary merchandise. In two weeks
after receiving an order he was able to ship 200,000 hand grenades
to the Greeks in this fashion.[403]

The government did all it could to help. The Greek government
asked to organize a supply depot on Yugoslav territory. They readily

agreed. Hundreds of thousands of tons of material was shipped into Greece in this way. They were particularly grateful for such efforts as those of Vistad because these were the sort of things obtained up to then from Germany and Hungary. Their artillery would have been almost unusable without Yugoslav artillery fuses to replace those formerly obtained from Germany. Also, the Greek cavalry bought all the horses it needed in Yugoslavia. They felt that, without this help, they would not have been able to defeat the Italians in Albania.[404] At the same time, all this did not pass unnoticed by the Germans. When it was considered along with the refusal of the Yugoslavs to allow shipments of German goods through the country to the Italians, it was felt they had to be taught a lesson. Ribbentrop cut off German deliveries of aviation materials to Yugoslavia. It was now obvious that Yugoslavia could no longer count on Germany as a supplier of arms.[405]

Internally the government was also having its problems. A crisis was developing out of the Sporazum of August 1939. Maček had said publicly that if a banovina were created out of those parts of Bosnia and Herzegovina not given to Croatia under the 1939 agreement, he would make no territorial demands. However, if they instead were incorporated into Serbia, he would demand compensation. He maintained that no one had objected to this either publicly or privately.[406]

Apparently, though, Cvetković considered it more prudent to say nothing in the face of this ultimatum. However, trouble which he could not ignore came from another minority source. The leader of the Moslem Party, Mehmed Spaho, had died. His place had been taken by Dzaferbeg Kulenović. It appeared he was ending his party's support for the government by boycotting the meetings of its inner council. He, therefore, assigned Korosec to find out if he could still count on their support.

Korosec found Kulenović sulky and angry. He complained about rumors that the name of the government party was to be changed from the Yugoslav Radical Union to the Yugoslav Radical Party. This, he said, smacked of domination by the Serbs over the whole country. In such a case the Moslems could no longer cooperate with Cvetković. He went on to complain about the treatment he, his party and his co-religionists seemed to be getting. He said they were not getting their fair share of political patronage. He complained about the enlargement of Croatia by including large slices of Bosnia and Herzegovina with their large moslem populations. Furthermore, large banovinas were to be established for the Serbs and Slovenes with the same rights of home rule given the Croats. He demanded a fourth banovina to include the remainder of Bosnia and Herzegovina together with the large Moslem population of the Sandzak.[407]

It seems that the first complaint had some reason behind it. Cvetković was trying to build a political apparatus of his own in Serbia and make his government one of national union. Such an effort was doomed, however, from the beginning and for the same reason that King Alexander had set up his dictatorship. That was the self centered and vindictive nature of the other political leaders. One example is the attitude of the Serbian Democratic Party. After agitating for twenty years for an accord with the Croats, they suddenly reversed themselves in January 1940. Instead, they accused Cvetković of oppressing the Serbs who lived in Croatia. They opposed the holding of general elections until the 1931 constitution was replaced by one more liberal. Maček tried to pacify them by promising to work for a new electoral law before the elections. When Maček sided with Cvetković it only enraged the Democrats the more.[408]

To make things worse, the old-line radicals under Milos Trifunović and the Democrats led by Milan Grol refused to enter the Cvetković government. Both the leaders were highly ambitious men, Trifunović wanting to be premier and Grol, foreign minister.

It seems hardly believable that they could have thought that Cvetković would resign in their favor or dismiss a highly experienced and knowledgeable man like Cincar-Marković for a man with no experience or foreign contacts. It also seemed that Prince Paul liked neither one for personal and security reasons. They were known for their loose tongues in all the coffee houses. Also, the Prince was sure they would scrap the Sporazum if they were in power.[409]

Maček looked on all this as a Serbian problem which hardly concerned him. He already had what he wanted; all the Croats in one body under him. He had worked with these two and did not trust them. Maček, therefore, supported Cvetković.[410]

Cvetković did his best to form a national government by bringing in the followers of Trifunović and Grol but without them. He failed despite all his efforts. Thus, the national cohesion the country desperately needed versus her enemies was not forthcoming.[411]

In the midst of these problems Prince Paul began to seriously consider resigning as regent. He was all too conscious of his own shortcomings. He had accepted the office of regent in the first place from a sense of duty and the troubles of the years since had weighed heavily on him. Maček and other politicians were trying hard to persuade him to remain as regent beyond the constitutional date of 1944 and had even prepared a constitutional amendment to that effect. The Prince rejected the idea.

His letter of resignation was actually drafted. He wrote that his principal goal had been to settle the internal quarrels and make Yugoslavia's borders safe. He had always attempted to act before the world in order to foster the country's best interests and preserve her dignity. He believed he should remain as regent only as long as he could be useful to his country. He was convinced that that was no longer the case as he had not succeeded in his task. The fault, he said, was his alone. He had not been able to infuse confidence in himself in those who should have been his closest collaborators. The future of the country lay only in the brotherhood and understanding of the Serbs, Croats and Slovenes working in harmony and accord around the king. Few others shared this ideal with him. When news of this draft of his resignation reached his councillors, they spent hours trying to get him to change his mind. Eventually they did by stressing how he was leaving the young and inexperienced king in the worst sort of situation. If men of ripe years and great experience had not been able to cope with all these problems how could a boy of seventeen?[412]

In the meantime, in January 1941 the situation became much more dangerous for Yugoslavia. During the first week of the month German troops poured into Rumania. On January 4 the Bulgarian prime minister called on Hitler at Berchtesgaden and on the 18th Mussolini and Ciano paid a similar visit. On the 9th an official of the Yugoslav foreign ministry told the American Minister, Arthur Bliss Lane, that he considered the Balkan situation as being in a very difficult phase. German policy had completely changed so that she was prepared to strike the moment her vital interests in the Balkans were being jeopardized. In reply to a question, he said that Yugoslavia had received no assurances from Germany in more than a month.[413]

In a conversation with Heeren, Cincar-Marković was visibly tense listening with skepticism to Heeren's assurances that Germany only meant to establish peace and order in the Balkans. Cincar-Marković expressed fears over the domestic situation in Bulgaria. Heeren assured him that if anything happened Germany would take action similar to that just taken in Rumania. Yugoslavia could count on the fact that Germany would dissipate any trouble the Bulgarians might cause.

Heeren reported all this back to Berlin stressing that Yugoslavia contemplated no action against Bulgaria. New instructions were sent to him that he should stress that the occupation of Rumania was a political and not a military move, and that he could assume that this was not directed against Yugoslavia.[414]

None of this changed the fact that these moves were ultimately designed to make it possible for Germany to link her forces up with those of Italy for the purpose of defeating Greece. The question remained as to what Yugoslavia's security position would be if Germany invaded Bulgaria or Bulgaria unconditionally joined the Axis.[415]

This brings up the question of just what was at stake here. German plans called for use of the Struma Valley in Bulgaria which contains a road connecting Rumania and Greece. Yugoslavia's neutrality was vital for Germany to protect this road. This accounts for much of Hitler's friendly attitude at this time. It also happens that there is a more direct route through the Monastir and Vardar Gaps. These are, however, on Yugoslav territory. Only an invasion would give a right of way over these. The last thing Hitler wanted at this juncture of his plans for Russia was another war. It is likely he remembered the long hard struggle of the World War to defeat the Serbs and wanted no such thing again that might tie down troops for years in those mountains who were desperately needed in Russia. At any rate, even if the Yugoslavs were quickly defeated, it would only mean a new occupation eating up troops and in a country that was used to massive, long term, hopeless resistance. On the other hand, if Yugoslavia allowed and cooperated in this plan, she would be encircled by her enemies. Italy and Germany would now encircle the country and would be cooperating in a venture. Hope of continuing her policy of division would no longer be possible. She would be faced with only the choice of fighting or joining the Axis.[416]

Without giving in to the Axis, it was apparently decided by Cvetković and Cincar-Marković that some exploration was needed. Thus, on January 30 Gregoricc wrote a letter to the press chief of German foreign ministry. In it he admitted that the visit of Cincar-Marković to Fuschl and Berchtesgaden had not produced a complete solution. This was mainly because of Italy's succession of failures and the efforts of anti-Axis people such as the minister of justice. He thought it all could be settled by a meeting of Ribbentrop and Cvetković. The prime minister would certainly accept an invitation immediately.[417]

This was all done with greater secrecy than previously. The letter was given to a German press agency representative in Belgrade who then gave it to a Gestapo agent for personal transmission to Berlin where it arrived on January 25. Hitler read the letter two or three days later and agreed to invite Cvetković to Berchtesgaden.[418]

Hitler was to remain in Berlin for a week or two more. Therefore, Gregorić was invited to Germany in the meantime.[419] He spoke with the press chief on February 4 and with Ribbentrop the next day. The press chief asked him for his personal opinion as to how matters could develop.

At this question he became very cautious. He claimed not to have asked Cvetković directly regarding the question of Yugoslavia's accession to the Tripartite Pact. He stressed several times that all actions that signified a support of, or concession to, Italy were exceedingly unpopular in Yugoslavia in the present situation. Accession to the Tripartite Pact with the political statements resulting from it could easily make Yugoslav policy unpopular at the same time. This could be remedied, however, if the national successes deriving from accession "I am thinking of Salonica, for example," added Gregorić, should appear immediately after the accession.[420]

Gregorić envisaged this as taking some time. There would be discussions between Ribbentrop and Cincar-Marković, a decision by Cvetković, presumably after discussions in the government in Belgrade, a decision by the Prince Regent and, finally, a meeting between Prince Paul and Hitler.[421]

Meanwhile, Stakić went to Italy. It was hoped that settlement with Italy would lighten the pressure from Germany. Minister of Court, Antić, briefed him to say that Yugoslavia had not accepted Italy's earlier proposal for talks about a new treaty because accepting would have looked as though they were giving in to political blackmail. Even now, Yugoslavia was not ready to negotiate a new treaty. Instead, Stakić was to ask Ciano if such a treaty with Italy would satisfy the Germans so that they would not be forced to sign the Tripartite Pact.

On February 4 Stakić talked with Mussolini. The Duce said he was willing for Yugoslavia to have Salonica in return for a pact between the two countries. He, also, offered to exchange the Yugoslav minority in Italy for the Italian one in Kosovo. He agreed to take up these questions with Hitler although he said he regarded them as strictly Italo-Yugoslav matters.[422]

On February 9 he reported back to Prince Paul. While the Prince was happy to learn that the Axis would not demand transit rights for their troops or territorial concessions, Prince Paul refused to accept the offer of Salonica. This was the property of a people fighting for their lives and freedom. He would make no alliance with the Italians while they were attacking the Greeks. Nor did he favor transferring whole populations. Istria had been the home of Yugoslavs for more than a thousand years and he would not abandon them to the Italians.[423]

All this would have come to little anyway. The Germans did not like the idea of a new Italo-Yugoslav pact. Weizsacker in effect told the Italians the German negotiations had priority over their efforts to get an agreement.[424]

Meanwhile, the Germans asked Cvetković and Cincar-Marković to come for talks. They were held first at Fuschl with Ribbentrop and then at Berchtesgaden with Hitler on February 14. Both first gave lengthy assurances of German invincibility and stressed the hopeless situation of Britain. Ribbentrop urged adherence to the Tripartite Pact stating that it had the aim of preventing the spread of the war and did not represent a treaty of alliance against Britain. The Pact should facilitate the restoration of peace, which was in the interest of all countries, including the enemies of the Axis. Technically this was correct since article three of the pact required the signees to come to each others aid only if attacked by a power not then engaged in the European war or the Sino-Japanese war. Both men also dwelt at great length on the Soviet Menace to the Balkans.

Cvetković suggested neutral mediation of the Greek-Italian conflict and called for the formation of a neutral Balkan bloc aimed at preventing British bases or penetration. As Cincar-Marković stressed, "The condition, however, was that Germany, too, would not march into the Balkans."

Both Hitler and Ribbentrop thought mediation a matter which only Mussolini could accept or reject. They thought the only way to get the British out was by force, and that such countries as Turkey would never join an anti-British coalition. Hitler went on to say that Yugoslavia was at an historic moment. She now must be clear on her attitude to the new order in Europe and that from her own interest. That means that she must take her place in the new order envisaged by Germany and Italy by immediately joining the Tripartite Pact. Thus, the whole idea of a Balkan bloc died before it could come to anything. Also, Hitler would promise a German-Italian guarantee of Yugoslavia only when she adhered to the Tripartite Pact.

At the end of the meeting, the Yugoslav representatives said that all they could do was to report to the prince regent. The point was raised that perhaps direct talks between the Prince and Hitler would be useful. The Yugoslavs agreed but asked Hitler to send the invitation through Heeren in Belgrade rather than have them take it back. This was agreed to.

During these talks, both Cvetković and Cincar-Marković refused to make any decisions but referred them to Prince Paul. They left the impression that they were not really interested in Salonica but were willing to act as mediators in the Italian-Greek war. Hitler believed Mussolini might accept this and referred the matter to Rome.[425]

The British had also begun to move in Yugoslavia. While the Axis had been stressing the fact of its power, the British used the desirability of cooperation with Turkey, the emotional involvement of Prince Paul with Britain through his family and education, and the promise of future aid from the arsenal of the United States.

At the suggestion of the British, the Turkish minister in Belgrade submitted a proposal to the Yugoslav foreign office on January 19th. He noted that, now that the German army was in Rumania, it could move against the Soviet Union, or any other Balkan country, let alone Greece. He suggested that Yugoslavia and Turkey lay out a plan for common action. The Yugoslavs refused believing Turkey had no concrete plans and that their army was unprepared for war. The Turks had already refused to enter the war, together with Yugoslavia, on the side of Greece.[426]

Shortly after Colonel William Donovan, an emissary of President Roosevelt, arrived in Belgrade. He was sent as an agent to further the British aim of establishing a Balkan front. He remained in Belgrade from January 23 to 25 treating with the prince regent and government officials. The regent told him that Bulgaria would undoubtedly yield to German pressure and that Yugoslavia might fight if the Germans occupied Bulgaria, although he was doubtful about it. Donovan replied with a threat. If the Yugoslav government did not intervene when German troops crossed the frontier, the United States would not intervene for Yugoslavia at the peace conference. Cvetković assured him that attempts by Germany to enter Yugoslav territory would mean war. Although Donovan got no committment from Yugoslavia to go to war making his mission seem a failure, yet it had one important effect. Many in Yugoslavia believed that he had also given a moral committment from the United States to supply arms as soon as they attacked Italy.[427]

When Cvetković and Cincar-Marković returned, Prince Paul had to decide on whether he should refuse to sign the pact outright and risk war or should possibly open the door to the Germans anyway by signing. Before signing, he decided to sound out the British. Ronald Campbell, British minister, was asked about the extent of British aid if Yugoslavia were attacked by Germany. He asked if British troops on their way to Greece would be able to remain there as long as needed. He got no reply. All Campbell could say was that the Balkan states could resist Hitler if they got together. He promised that if they did so Britain would support them to the full extent of her ability. He reminded Prince Paul that Britain had already given considerable amounts of military equipment to Turkey and Greece.[426]

The Yugoslavs made one last effort to use Italy against Germany. Again Stakić went to Rome. His orders from Antić again were to tell Mussolini that Yugoslavia could not accept the Tripartite Pact. He was to request from Mussolini some gesture that would ease the tensions building up in Yugoslavia caused particularly by fear of Italy.

Stakić had a meeting with Mussolini on February 24th. The Duce expressed himself as annoyed that Yugoslavia should have had so many talks with the Germans but showed so little interest in an agreement with Italy. Stakić then showed him the extent of German demands. He asked if it was still possible for Yugoslavia to avoid the Pact while retaining their relationship under the Belgrade accord of 1937.

Mussolini rejected the idea out of hand. Since Germany had brought up the question of the Tripartite Pact, they could no longer ignore it, said Mussolini. The international situation had changed too much since 1937 for that to be the basis of their relations anymore. Only by signing a new accord with Italy could the Yugoslavs take German pressure off them. Bulgaria was about to sign the Pact and Yugoslavia would have to act soon. Only by signing a new agreement with Italy could they avoid the Tripartite Pact which, of course, would not then be needed.

To Prince Paul this was only a means of forcing him into a position where he could no longer oppose the Italian conquest of Greece.
He rejected the idea.[429]

From now on Yugoslavia had no visible alternatives. A week later
the Italian minister in Belgrade was ordered to cease negotiations and
leave the field to the Germans.[430] No longer could they play the
Germans off the Italians or vice versa. Neutrality was from now on
a nearly impossible dream for Yugoslavia.

There was one hope left, though. That was the Allies. They had
been a broken reed before but, as we have seen, the British were starting to realize the importance of Yugoslavia, especially now for Greece.
The neutrality Yugoslavia had struggled to maintain up to now was
unsatisfactory to Churchill and Roosevelt as well as to the Axis.
Churchill wished now to strengthen Greece as the first line of defense
and also set up a Balkan defense system of Yugoslavia, Greece and
Turkey.[431]

As a result, Foreign Secretary Anthony Eden went to Cairo for talks
with Greek and Turkish representatives on February 12th. He proposed to the others that a first step towards their goal had to be to
find out the intentions of the Yugoslavs. That is, whether they intended
to enter the war or not and on whose side if they did. They had to
call Prince Paul's attention to the importance of Salonica. If will be
remembered that only a couple of days before the prince had put a
similar question to Campbell and had received a discouraging reply.
Therefore, the prince's answer was uncommunicative, to say the
least.[432]

The United States also tried to get some action. After long delays,
Ambassador Lane finally saw the Prince on February 18th and again
on the 22nd. The Prince assured the ambassador that they would fight
if directly attacked. He was more restrained about an attack by the
Germans on Bulgaria. He pointed out bitterly that, despite goodwill,
the British could do nothing to help them in their present state. Also,
the United States was so far away that her wealth and power would
take months to get to Yugoslavia and by then the issues would have
been decided. He wound up by expressing a deep pessimism on the
future of Europe under German domination. He did express a conviction in ultimate victory by the British although that seemed to him
to lie decades, if not centuries, in the future.[433]

Thus, the Allies could get no committment from the Prince that
Yugoslavia would do much of anything to help the Allied cause. The
Prince seemed, like so many before and after, fascinated and captured by his own impending doom and to think it certain. The efforts
of the Germans had, as usual, convinced the victim of their overwhelming power and the futility of resistance.

Finally the blow fell which the Germans expected would bring the
Yugoslavs in to the Pact. On March 1 the Bulgars signed the Pact

unconditionally. Immediately the German government notified
Belgrade that the army was about to move into Bulgaria. On March
2nd a German army crossed the frontier and moved on Sofia. There
was no reaction of any kind from Belgrade, a fact which worried the
Germans greatly. They had to have assurances that the Yugoslav army
would not move before they dared to move to the Greek-Bulgarian
frontier since that would leave the Germans completely open to a flank
attack by Yugoslavia. It would appear that Hitler had no desire for
a war with Yugoslavia but wanted to solve the problem as he just
had with Bulgaria. That is, by a peaceful settlement which would bring
penetration and control. Not only was it safer for him, but was more
in line with Germany's interests.[434]

Yugoslavia was now confronted with very little, if any, choice.
Cvetković and Konstantinović, Yugoslav minister of justice, drew up
a series of solutions as they saw it. Assuming that Germany would
certainly not ask for anything which did not advance its own interests,
they listed the various demands they could expect.

1. The demand for immediate passage of German troops through
the country. To submit would be to commit national suicide. It must
be answered as completely unacceptable.

2. Signing the Tripartite Pact. Again this would necessitate acquies-
cence in the passage of troops and, indeed, collaboration. It would
be incompatible with their obligations to Greece and Turkey and, so,
again could not be signed.

3. A tripartite pact of non-aggression. This would be dangerous
for the rest of the Balkans and they already had enough treaties of
that kind with Italy and did not need another.

4. A pact of friendship and non-aggression with Germany. This
would have the same dangers as the Tripartite Pact. If forced to sign
such a document, they would ask the Germans to guarantee their independence and integrity.

5. Yugoslavia might offer to serve as an intermediary in ending
the Greek-Italian war, preliminary to the negotiation of an understanding with Germany in which the Balkan states would guarantee not
to let their territory be used by a foreign power for military operations. Cvetković did not believe that Germany would accept this
because of their position in Bulgaria. They might insist on the right
to control and supervise this which would convert the Balkans into
a protectorate of Germany. But, this solution did seem to offer the
only hope of avoiding the immediate danger.

There seemed to be no clear solution to the problem. It was clear,
though, that Germany's shortest route to Greece lay through Yugoslavia. For that reason, Yugoslavia must not allow Salonica to fall
into German hands. If it did, they would be slowly strangled. Even
though resistance seemed hopeless, they must resist this. At least honor
would be saved and that would be important at the end of the war.

This document was sent to Prince Paul and he agreed with their ideas. This document became the basis of discussions in the cabinet in the weeks of turmoil that followed.[435] It was decided that Prince Paul must see Hitler at once. He went to Berchtesgaden on March 4.

Both Hitler and the Prince seem to have been anxious to preserve secrecy. The Prince again went to the border by auto and then by train hinting to the Germans that he hoped the affair would not be leaked this time.[436] The surviving summary of the meeting was taken by Ribbentrop himself. This seems to mean there was no interpreter present nor any formal minutes. Thus, probably there were only three people present; The Prince Regent, Hitler and Ribbentrop.

As usual Hitler began with a tirade against Britain and the "fact" that they had lost the war. He went on to say that for many reasons Germany needed a strong Yugoslavia. But, Germany would not remain forever in the Balkans. What would happen to Yugoslavia then if she had no protection from her enemies? She now had a unique opportunity which would not be there forever. German troops would occupy Salonica. If Yugoslavia did not stake her claim by showing Germany friendship, that port would be handed over to Bulgaria or Italy.

Ribbentrop wrote that the Prince Regent seemed to be visibly impressed by these remarks. However, he went on to recount the difficulties in the way of such a step. He concluded, nonetheless, by saying that he thought a further agreement with Italy a possible first step on the course suggested by Hitler. In reply, Hitler assured him that Germany did not require that Yugoslavia take part in the war. She was merely to accede to the Tripartite Pact. In return they would get Salonica after the war. The Prince went on to express his fears about such a course. He said that if he did all that was suggested, the internal state of the country was such that he would not be around in six months. On his departure he insisted on reserving his decision. Ribbentrop concluded his summary by saying that Germany must now wait to see how Yugoslav policy would develop. In conclusion, he ordered Heeren to do everything possible to hasten the accession of Yugoslavia.[437]

The Prince returned home depressed and uncertain. Would Hitler demand immediate signing of the Pact? Would he declare war or would he allow diplomacy to continue? To help him, he called a meeting of the crown council on March 6th. The end result was that all who voted (Prince Paul did not) agreed that the Pact must be signed but not before certain guarantees were given by Germany in writing.[438]

On March 7 Heeren was called in by Cincar-Marković. He was told that the signing of the Pact was regarded as a serious matter by the crown council. This was especially so in light of the strong anti-Axis feeling in the country. They were, also, concerned about Bulgaria's revisionism. After hours of discussion they had come to the conclusion that they must have reassurance on three points before they would make a final decision.

1. The sovereignty and territorial integrity of Yugoslavia will be respected.

2. No military assistance will be requested of Yugoslavia and also no passage or transportation of troops through the country during the war.

3. Yugoslavia's interests in free outlet to the Aegean Sea through Salonica will be taken into account in the reorganization of Europe.

Cincar-Marković said he had received the impression that Germany was ready to grant these demands. Ribbentrop had offered a written guarantee on these three points. Nonetheless, he was requesting Heeren to get a specific answer on these three points in order to be fully clear on the situation. "If it was in the affirmative, it would extraordinarily facilitate the policy desired by the government."[439]

Ribbentrop immediately consulted Hitler about a written guarantee. The next day he told the ambassador in Italy to inform Mussolini and tell him the Fuehrer thought it should be granted.[440] The same day Heeren informed Cincar-Marković that all three points were answered affirmatively by both Germany and Italy.[441]

On March 9th Ribbentrop wired Heeren that point two of the guarantee actually involved two points. "In the first place, the question of passage and transportation of troops through the country and in the second place, the question of military assistance." Germany was willing, he said, to give a written promise that she would not request the passage of troops. Assistance in the Greek war was specifically ruled out by the terms of the Tripartite Pact. But, Berlin could not formally release Yugoslavia from the obligation to render assistance in the case of attack by a power not now involved in the war. Such a thing would cancel the effect of Yugoslavia's accession. As a last resort, Ribbentrop was willing to allow the insertion of a strictly secret provision by which Yugoslavia was to be promised access to the Aegean through Salonica. This was to remain strictly secret.[442]

On March 10 Heeren had a meeting with Cincar-Marković. In the conversation the point that seemed to be holding things up was this very question of how much military help Yugoslavia would be required to give under the provisions of the Pact. Heeren never mentioned that this might be waived altogether but tried his best to convince him that he could not think of throwing out the most important provision of the Pact. Cincar-Marković kept stressing that Yugoslavia could not be expected to go to war for something which might not touch her national interests at all.[443]

The next day Heeren returned to the attack, as per Ribbentrop's telephoned instructions. Cincar-Marković said he fully understood the arguments but he expected difficulties in getting the country to accede to them. Heeren reported that, "In conclusion, the Foreign Minister expressed his firm hope that there would never be any conflict between Germany and Yugoslavia."[444] In a second wire that evening, Heeren warned Ribbentrop that there were growing efforts by the British and the United States to stiffen Yugoslav resistance to the Pact. Also, resistance was growing in the army. Thus, the government would undoubtedly try to accede to the Pact in such a way as to remove the odium of having done so. They would try to avoid a clear decision.[445]

Even before the second report was sent by Heeren, it would appear that Hitler and Ribbentrop decided to give in on the demand and agree that Yugoslavia would not be called on for military assistance under any circumstances. Probably that evening Heeren received another telegram stating this. At any rate, he presented it to Cincar-Marković the next day. It said:

"Germany and Italy assure the Yugoslav government that they will not, of their own accord, make any demand for military assistance. If the Yugoslav Government should at any time consider it to be in its own interest to participate in military operations in accord with the Tripartite Pact, it will be left to the Yugoslav Government to make the necessary military arrangements for this with the Powers of the Tripartite Pact."

This could not be published although the Yugoslav government begged to be allowed to do so. They said it was absolutely necessary to do so in order to quiet the agitation sweeping the country. Heeren also urged this saying it might otherwise delay actual Yugoslav accession to the Pact. Now the crown council would have to meet to make a final decision once it had Ribbentrop's reply.[446]

His answer came on March 14th. He showed a great deal of exasperation in his reply. He said that disclosure of Germany's final concession publicly would only be an excuse for Germany's enemies to heap ridicule on her. Anyway, they had made so many concessions that they could see no reason for more. The way it was, the Pact was worth practically nothing especially if all the other signers saw these concessions and demanded the same. He would, because he could see its special significance for Yugoslavia, allow them to publish a special note. But, in no circumstances could they allow the publications of the fact that Germany would not require military assistance from them. Instead when they signed the Pact he would put that, as well as the assurance of free access to the Aegean Sea, in a secret note to them.[447] Ribbentrop, also, presented all this to Mussolini who agreed with it completely.[448]

As the days went by, it became increasingly obvious that the Yugoslavs were dragging their feet. Heeren took the view, though, that the leaders had made up their minds to sign. Indeed, he was right since by now their only alternative to signing was war. After all the concessions Hitler had made, he was bound to insist absolutely on signing the document as it was.[449]

There was one bit of news that gave the Yugoslav government some hope and seems to have been the main reason for the delays. This is that they managed to learn of the impending German attack on Russia. If they could delay long enough, this new war would begin and Germany would have little if any excess energy to waste in the Balkans.

The information was gathered bit by bit by Colonel Vauhnik. The bits began with the revelations by Goering that he would have by Spring 200 air divisions. Why would he need so much air power? Against Britain he needed only 50, in Africa not more than 6. The vast bulk were, thus, unaccounted for. Another bit was supplied by the Slovak military attache who told him they had been asked for two divisions to attack Russia.

Others confirmed this information and added new parts. He was particularly helped by a friend, Willy Pabst. He had earlier been a major on the German General Staff but had resigned and was now in business. During the second week of March he informed Vauhnik that preparations for the attack were in full swing and it might come any time soon.

The next day another friend told him it would take place the second half of May with some 200 divisions. Through the Swedes he passed this information on to the British who passed it to the Russians. He himself later passed it on to the Russian military attache who had already had the information from other sources. Of course, He passed it on to his own government, but, as is well known, the Russian government refused to believe any of this information. When he received no acknowledgement, he tried to send it directly to Cincar-Marković. I do not know what happened to that, but it would appear Cincar-Marković knew of the impending attack and was hoping it would affect the position of Yugoslavia favorably.[450]

It would seem the government was facing the inevitable as early as the 14th. That evening the U.S. Treasury was informed that Yugoslavia wanted to sell them the gold already transported there for safekeeping and transport the proceeds to Brazil. Obviously that was to keep their assets from being frozen by the United States in retaliation for a pro-Axis move by Belgrade.[451]

The institution of General Ion Antonescu's dictatorship in Rumania seems to have frightened them also. It was feared that Germany might be planning on using Stojadinović in Yugoslavia the same way. As stated before, he was handed over to the British in Greece who interned him far away.[452]

On March 17 a formal reply was handed to the Germans. It said that the crown council had decided in principle in favor of accession to the Pact. The decision was stated again that the Axis would not demand the passage of troops or supplies through Yugoslav territory. They, also, accepted the form of a secret addition to the Pact that Yugoslavia would not be called upon to give military assistance to the Axis, as Ribbentrop had stated. The reply concluded with a request for the Germans to set up a time and place for signing.[453]

The rest of the government knew nothing of the decision to sign now arrived at by the Regent. Only Foreign Minister Cincar-Marković and perhaps Court Minister Antić knew all the details. Even Prime Minister Cvetković probably did not know all the details of the negotiations. Accordingly, a meeting of the crown council was called for March 19th.

Present at the meeting were Prince Paul and the other two regents, Radenko Stanković and Ivan Perović, the Slovene leader Fran Kulovec, Maček, Cvetković, Cincar-Marković, Antić and the minister of war, General Pesić. First Prince Paul told of the German demands showing how they must be met by signing the Pact. Hitler had allowed for no alternative and pressed for immediate decision. The Prince said that all his personal and family feelings were for Britain but he could see no solution but to sign. War would be suicidal with all her frontiers except the Greek giving on an Axis state. He went on to chronicle the compromises Hitler was willing to make.

Cincar-Marković said there were only two alternatives left; sign or immediate war. General Pesić went on to show that war was impossible given the state of the armed forces. They lacked modern arms or even spare parts or ammunition for those they had. Her traditional supplier was the Skoda Works and other companies now in areas controlled by Germany. Neither Britain nor the United States was in a position to supply her needs.

Stanković seemed to agree that Yugoslavia's position was hopeless as things stood. But, to yield without a fight was not in the Yugoslav tradition. He advocated a policy of "token" resistance. Then as many units as possible should withdraw to Greece. The general said he had never heard of such a concept and stressed again that the country could offer no effective resistance. Maček agreed with him and so the council finally voted to accept the German demands.[454]

On either the evening of the 20th or the morning of the 21st the cabinet was convened to be told of the decision. When informed of the crown council decision, three ministers resigned in protest although one later withdrew his resignation. That evening Heeren was told of this development and that it might take several days to replace them.

Only then could the decision, which was already a majority one without them, be carried out.[455]

German pride was now at stake and so they moved quickly. This haste was increased by the fact that a Japanese delegation was arriving in a few days and this delay would be very damaging in their eyes.[456] On the 22nd Ribbentrop told Heeren to deliver to the Yugoslav foreign office a note to the effect that they had until midnight of the 23rd to reply as to whether or not they would sign the Pact and whether or not the 25th was acceptable as the date for signing.[457]

In the meantime Cvetković was busy trying to find replacements for the resigned cabinet ministers. In the middle of this he received bad news. Prince Paul told him and other officials that he had had a call from General Simović, commander of the air force. He gave the Prince a warning which he had expressed several times before. This was that if the Pact was signed, he could not guarantee that his officers would not immediately revolt and overthrow the regime. The Prince asked for their opinion on this development. No one would venture an opinion until they heard from General Pesić. When he finally came he said that he knew Simović well and thought that his warning should be taken seriously. He said he would call Simović early in the morning and reprimand him. Maček has confessed that he did not take the warning seriously because, he says, he never heard of a coup that was announced in advance and then actually carried out.[458]

At midnight of March 23, Cincar-Marković informed Heeren that the Yugoslav government would sign the Tripartite Pact. An hour later he telephoned Berlin to inform them that a seven member delegation would leave for Vienna on the 24th.

Opposition to this decision began to appear immediately. Its effect internally was, of course, the most important aspect. It, however, also resulted in action by the Allies. Britain, aided by the United States, did all it could to persuade them by mere words against the raw power of Hitler's panzers.

Ever since the end of 1940 the British had been trying to persuade general John Metaxas, the Greek Prime Minister, to allow them to start building airfields and bases for eventual use by a large British airforce. They stressed that this might not be possible later on when the planes would be vitally needed for combat. The general, though, was afraid this would provoke a German attack. The British, he said, should only land forces when they could immediately be in sufficient strength to beat off any attack. In a note of January 18, 1941 the Greeks rejected the idea except if Germany entered Bulgaria.[459]

Metaxas died on January 29. The Greeks were beginning to wonder if they could hold the Italians back indefinitely alone. Accordingly, on February 9, they formally enquired if the offer was still open. General Wavell had just taken Benghazi and it looked as though the

British would be able to maintain the initiative in North Africa for some time. Therefore, it seemed as though they could spare the four divisions needed to aid the Greeks.[460]

Anthony Eden, the foreign secretary, was sent out to Athens to arrange the matter. In the process he asked Prince Paul for his intentions. Prince Paul replied that Yugoslavia would defend herself and would not allow the passage of foreign troops but his government had not yet decided what they would do if Germany attacked Greece through Bulgaria.[461]

Meanwhile the British government was having second thoughts. Churchill questioned whether it was wise to encourage Greece to resist Germany when Britain could actually offer very little help. They might be encouraged to resist and then find Britain could do practically nothing for them. What then?[462]

Both Eden and Sir John Dill, Chief of Staff, replied that it did not really matter what Britain was going to do. The Greeks were determined on resisting, if necessary all alone. Before this was received, the war cabinet decided to go along with the recommendations of the men on the spot. Thus, the fate of both Greece and Yugoslavia was sealed by this decision.[463]

On March 10 Churchill informed Roosevelt of this decision. He told him there was no telling what outcome would result if the Yugoslavs could be persuaded to fall on the Italian rear in Albania as the British force and Greeks fell on them from the front. He finished by calling for concerted action by the British and American ambassadors in Turkey, Russia and above all, in Yugoslavia, to bring this about and bring Turkey into the war.[464]

U.S. Ambassador Lane spoke to Prince Paul on March 16th and then had dinner with him on March 20th. The regent stressed that rejection of the German guarantee would mean that the Croats and Slovenes would not support the government in the conflict. But, if the Germans attacked later in violation of the guarantee, the whole country would be united. Lane tried to argue that if the invasion was inevitable, then why not reject the Pact now and save the country's honor and reputation abroad. Lane felt after this that the Regent wanted to avoid war at any cost and was merely using the Croat-Slovene disaffection as an excuse. He said he thought the Regent possessed the qualities of a good diplomat rather than those of a statesman. He was too weak to form a goal and stick to it if he was right no matter what the consequences.[465]

In Washington the next day Sumner Welles, acting secretary of state, spoke with Yugoslav minister Fotić. He told him officially that if Yugoslavia made any agreement with Germany which limited or ended her sovereignty, facilitated in any way a German attack on the Greeks or the British forces in the Mediterranean, or assisted them in any way in a military or naval sense the United States would freeze all

Yugoslav funds in the United States and would refuse to consider any subsequent pleas for aid. The United States might understand an agreement which was solely and purely a non-aggression pact. However, any agreement which allowed Germany military facilities would end all hope of friendship between the two countries.[466]

Of course, there was some hope of fitting the actual agreement into this frame but the Prince was not allowed to do so by the Germans. Internal opposition, though, was the real problem for the government. As soon as the rumor began to spread that Hitler was making demands, a flood of pressure was brought to bear on the government by individuals, groups and patriotic societies. Even some threats were made to the Prince Regent. When news got out that the Pact was to be signed many groups came to Belgrade and demonstrated in the streets.[467]

General Simović was very outspoken in warning the Prince about uneasiness prevailing among the officers because of the government's wavering attitude and the Prince's irresolution. He argued that Hitler would ultimately attack Russia and would fail. He warned about the danger if the Axis cut Yugoslavia's communications to Salonica. Yugoslavia would then be enclosed in a ring from which it would be impossible to break. The Prince asked him if a defense was possible. The general replied that the only defense would be guerilla warfare by a portion of the army left in the mountains and on the enemy's communications. This would be in the expectation of the formation of a Salonica front.[468]

It was at this time that the whole matter was presented to the cabinet. As will be remembered, three members resigned. Ribbentrop on March 22 informed Heeren that he understood the difficult internal situation for the government. Nevertheless, Heeren was to push for an immediate answer. The Japanese minister would be arriving in Berlin on the 26th. He would, therefore, be busy with other matters after that date. A Yugoslav accession after that date would be pointless. On the 22nd Heeren presented those arguments to Prince Paul, Cvetković, Cincar-Marković and the Slovene leader, Kulovec. Heeren received the impression of a firm decision to sign and that they would be able to meet the deadline given by Ribbentrop. On the 23rd they were presented with Ribbentrop's final word. He must receive a final yes or no by midnight of the same day.[469]

At 6:00 P.M. that day Lane had his last conversation with the Prince. He informed the ambassador of the necessity for a final answer by midnight that day. Lane reported to Washington that he had never seen the Prince so upset. He seemed to have entirely lost his self control and said, "I am out of my mind; I wish I were dead." He went on to condemn Bulgarian perfidy, British stupidity and the opposition of the Croats. Nevertheless, he refused to consider the possibility of not signing the Pact.[470]

At 8:10 that night, General Simović received a call to come to the palace. The Prince asked him if he still thought Britain would win the war, to which Simović replied that she would. He said that she always loses all the battles but the last. He admitted that she was in a critical situation but the worst of this had passed by the autumn of 1940. Now the United States will join her and Russia soon will be forced to enter the war. The Prince stated that the minister of war, chief of staff and Belgrade garrison commander did not agree with him. The general replied that these were all jealous of their places and were old and senile, unable to cope with the situation.

The general set forth the consequences if Yugoslavia did sign the Pact. The future would be compromised since they could expect nothing at the end of the war when Britain and the United States would have won. Why should they pay any attention to the desires of a state that had deserted them in their most difficult hour? On the other hand, if Germany won she would tolerate no independence from her slaves in the empire meant to last 1000 years.

Most importantly, Yugoslavia would not be spared the horrors of war. Her losses and damages might be worse than if she actually fought. Hitler could not leave her with her army intact. He would spread dissent until revolution occurred. He has already given a sample of what Yugoslavia could expect in his treatment of Rumania. Revolution would lead to armed German intervention. Then Yugoslav youth would be drafted to fight Germany's battles for her.

The Prince went on to say that they could not hope to resist. The general admitted that if France could not stop the Germans, even from behind the Maginot Line, Yugoslavia could not do much. He argued, though, for the establishment of a Salonica front and the sending of men to the mountains. Conditions were such in a mountainous country like Yugoslavia that the armored columns of the German army could not operate off the narrow, twisting Yugoslav roads. They could not hope to conquer, let alone dominate, the country.

Most importantly he warned the Prince on the state of public feeling. Tension and indignation were so great, he said, that revolution might break out if the pact were signed. He said that he himself would have trouble restraining the airforce from, perhaps, bombing the various centers of army command in Belgrade as well as the Prince's palace. He intended to discuss this with the various army leaders tomorrow. The Prince demanded that he do it that evening. In Subsequent talks the minister of war categorically denied that there was any such danger. He said all reports from his subordinates showed the country tranquil.

It would appear that nothing more came of General Simović's warning. They would rather believe the statements of General Pesić. Those intimations of internal trouble given to both Hitler and Ribbentrop would appear to have been only part of the maneuvres to avoid signing the Pact. No one believed that a serious coup d'etat would be announced in advance like that. The Prince was worried but when General Pešić completely discounted the whole thing and finished by saying he would reprimand Simović in the morning, the whole thing was regarded as finished.[471]

On the morning of March 24 Cvetković and Cincar-Marković left for Vienna. The signing ceremony was held in the Belvedere Palace the next day, March 25. Present in the conference room were Cvetković, Cincar-Marković, Ribbentrop, Ciano, General Hiroshi Oshima (Japanese ambassador to Berlin), and the representatives of Hungary, Rumania, Slovakia and Bulgaria.[472]

After the signing Hitler appeared. The two Yugoslavs plus Hitler and Ribbentrop then returned to the Hotel Imperial where the Yugoslavs were staying. Hitler proceeded to reiterate how fortunate they were in getting in on the ground floor as claimants in the future remaking of Europe.[473] That evening the German radio broadcast that Yugoslavia had signed the Pact and said that assurances had been given that Germany and Italy would respect the sovereignty and territorial integrity of Yugoslavia and would not request the passage of troops or war materiel during the war.[474] Also on the 25th Ribbentrop and Ciano gave Cvetković four formal noted confirming the promises made earlier; the last two were to be kept secret.

On the occasion of Yugoslavia's accession to the Tripartite Pact this day the German (Italian) Government confirms its decision to respect at all times the sovereignty and the territorial integrity of Yugoslavia.

With reference to the discussions which have taken place on the occasion of Yugoslavia's accession to the Tripartite Pact today, I have the honor to confirm to your excellency herewith in the name of the Reich (Italian) Government the agreement between the Governments of the Axis Powers and the Royal Yugoslav Government that during the war the Government of the Axis Powers will not address the demand to Yugoslavia that she permit the passage or transportation of troops through Yugoslav territory.

Germany and Italy, taking into account the military situation assure the Yugoslav government that they will not, of their own accord, make any demand for military assistance. Should the Yugoslav Government at any time consider it to be in its own interest to participate in the mulitary operations of the Powers of the Tripartite Pact, it will be left up to the Yugoslav Government to make the necessary military agreements for this with the Powers of the Tripartite Pact.

In the new settlement of the frontiers of the Balkans the interests of Yugoslavia in a territorial connection with the Aegean Sea, through the extension of her sovereignty to the city and harbor of Salonica, are to be taken into account.[475]

In a formal note of the same date, Cvetković promised that his government would keep all written communications from the Axis governments strictly secret. Except for the territorial guarantee and the statement regarding the passage of troops, they would publish them only in agreement with the governments of the Axis Powers.[476] In actual fact, Yugoslavia had given practically nothing away. On the other hand the Axis had demanded very little. Probably General Simović could have objected to nothing beyond the mere signing of the treaty. The trouble with it was that no one really knew exactly what had happened except Cvetković and Prince Paul, if each actually knew as much as the other. Two days after the coup, Lane reported to Washington that Momcilo Ninčić, who had replaced Cincar-Marković as foreign minister, was not able to find out all the secret committments.[477] The German minister, Heeren, later blamed the coup on:

> violent aversion to the "foreigner" Prince Paul and the "gypsy" Cvetković, by whom fanatical Serbian patriots believed they had been betrayed in Vienna. Enemy propaganda had circulated reports that secret clauses had been signed in Vienna, in which Yugoslavia had had to humble herself before Germany and, even worse, before Italy.[478]

Even though British agents from Hugh Dalton's Special Operations Executive had begun to operate in Yugoslavia early in 1940, they were actually to have little effect. Churchill had come to the conclusion that early that the regency government was not going to fight Hitler and, so, set out to get rid of it. A group under Tom S. Masterson had gone in during the summer of 1940. He was sent in as temporary secretary to the British Legation in Belgrade for economic warfare. His job was to organize and finance anti-regency elements to make them an organized and tangible political force. When news came that Yugoslavia had signed the Pact, Dalton cabled Masterson to do all he could to start a revolution. They were very confident of success because they had been working so long among the opposition politicians. In fact, they had been so quiet that General Bora Mirković, leader of the revolt, only heard of the British role when in exile.[479]

All this was unnecessary, however, since they merely worked within a situation all ready to blow up.[480] As I have tried to show, Yugoslavia was filled with all sorts of groups and tendencies ready to explode over the situation of the country. It was only a question of which would blow up first. We have seen the nationality problem, the problem with Italy and now that with Germany. Since it was the Serbs who traditionally hated the Germans, it was they who were to lead and carry on this revolt.

The tradition of revolt has always occupied an important place in Serbian history. This was led by the officers of the army. The country in the 19th century was particularly turbulent. In the years 1804 to 1941 the country had nine rulers. Of these, two died on the throne, one abdicated, one went into exile, one was denied his throne by a communist revolution. Four kings were murdered: two by political rivals, one by international conspirators, and one by army officers.[481]

After the murder of King Alexander I and his wife in 1903, the country was virtually run by the assassins under King Peter I. They were the leaders of the Black Hand Society which was deeply associated with the army. The army in turn controlled the throne. King Alexander II did all he could to end this situation when he became regent in 1914. He finally succeeded at the Salonica trial of 1917. Colonel Apis, leader of the Black Hand, chief of the Serbian intelligence service and one of the leading men in the plot to kill Alexander I and his wife, was the leading defendant. These men were generally disdainful of civilian rule, party government and the rule of law. They were extremely chauvinistic about Serbia. They believed that, when Yugoslavia would be formed, it should be completely centralized under Serbian control. They believed they should be the guardians of the purity of the state after the war, checking the beliefs and credentials of those who would return. Thus, the real question at the trial was who would rule; the king and his ministers or the Black Hand.[482]

After the execution of Apis, the army became completely docile to the king but their old dreams were still there. Also, they had a precedent of what to do if they felt the king had violated their heroic code or the national honor.

They could accept the actions of King Alexander against them because he had been raised a soldier. They always thought of him as one of themselves. Thus, his actions against the regicides could be accepted as a cleaning of house by one of themselves. Further, the establishment of the dictatorship meant the imposition of police and military rule. From 1929 to 1934 the army was in control although definitely under the king's control and authority. Never after 1917 while he was in control did it try to go its own way. The first premier under the dictatorship was General Peter Zivković, himself a veteran of 1903.[483]

Under Prince Paul things were very different. New forces and new faces appeared to give a new direction to its internal policy and, to some extent, its foreign policy. The regency slowly eliminated the Zivković group from the government, and released members of the imprisoned opposition. Gradually many powerful Serbian officers were forced out of the government and army into retirement. They probably would have accepted this from Alexander. Since Paul had spent most of his time abroad before becoming regent, he was almost a foreigner. Even worse, he was a civilian and had never had an interest in the army. Thus, he was not regarded with favor by them.[484] Also, as we have seen earlier, the politicians had not been pleased by the changes. Parliamentary government in Yugoslavia up to 1929 was virtually in chaos. National groups insisted on separation and their own rights. Corruption was rife. Hardly anyone would cooperate with anyone else. In 1929 the dictatorship was instituted partly to deal with this state of affairs. Many of the politicians, at least from the old Habsburg empire, were not in reality averse to the new conditions. It allowed them to sink back into the good old ways of opposition with no necessity or even hope of having some day to be responsible for their actions. Thus, they opposed the government's internal and external policies and called the dictator all sorts of names either from inside or outside the country with absolute abandon.

The Serbians were in as bad a state. They had been particularly corrupt and so had been excluded as well as the Croats. Thet took the attitude that the king had destroyed democracy and so they must oppose him root and branch. Nothing he did could be right. So, they too came to hold on to opposition just for its own sake. They could make no compromises with the king unless he gave in entirely to their demands. Thus, many were offered places in the government as time went on but would have nothing to do with it. The trouble was that they did not use their opposition to work out a coherent policy of their own that might be used practically some day. They merely opposed.[485]

The tendency of the regency went against them also. The Prince insisted on viewing himself as a Yugoslav rather than as a Serb. Finally came the Sporazum in 1939. It may have had the effect of decreasing the alienation of the Croats but it increased that of the Serbs. The Croats and Slovenes especially increased their influence in the government and, with it, the number of jobs they held. This decreased the number of those held by Serbs. Their onetime dominance appeared over and so they became more and more frustrated and hostile to the regime. They began to criticize the Prince's personal life and then his relationship to young King Peter and Queen Marie.[486]

All these factors aided in the fall of the regency. The old precedent of military intervention in national affairs; the downgrading by the regency of many old Serbian officers; the regency's refusal to bring back on their own terms the precoup politicians; the regency's agreement with Croats highly offended the Serbs; the regency's insistence on being Yugoslav rather than merely Serbian; the regency's neutral rather than openly pro-allied stand.[487]

The man who first favored a violent solution was General Bora Mirković, assistant to General Simović who was head of the Yugoslav airforce. He was very much in the tradition of Colonel Apis and the regicides of 1903. Like them, he thought the new coup would be strictly a military operation carried out for the public good. ''Deeply imbued with the spirit of Serb nationalism, more shrewd than intelligent, discontented, temperamental, unknown except to a few, he took pride in the military heritage of his family and country ... Like Apis he was energetic and secretive, and would speak his mind only to those he considered trustworthy ... His political ideas, like those of many Serbs of his generation, were fuzzy and romantic, colored by the heroic Serbian past. Like Apis he had many fixed ideas and refused to compromise on those he considered matters of principle.''[488]

From his own testimony, he began to formulate plans for the coup at the time of the signing of the Italo-Yugoslav Pact of 1937. With his great sense of local patriotism, he came to the conclusion that the army must intervene. The officers must resume their historic role and end the drift to disaster. Once more the army must become a force to be reckoned with and must act for the national welfare.

After investigation, he came to the conclusion that no one supported the government's policy. It became a matter of personal honor and duty that something had to be done and that quickly.

At first he tried to turn to the minister of war, General Milan Nedić. He had once seemed personally friendly. Mirković had no success with him. Nedić would only say that no matter what was done all was lost.

Mirković then approached General Stanković, commander of the royal guards, and General Bogoljub Ilić, who was to become minister of war later on. Both expressed themselves as interested. Neither would commit himself. Both said they were incapable of arousing popular enthusiasm and unworthy of a post of such moral responsibility.

Only after four years of searching did he find someone. This was the commander of the airforce, General Dušan Simović. In 1937 he had believed that an honorable solution could be found without the necessity of resorting to force. By 1941 he had come over to the view that force might be necessary but only as a last resort. When Mirković presented his ideas to him he expressed himself as willing to take the lead.[489]

Simović had had a rather checkered career. He was noted for his ambition and his ability to play army politics. These had once caused him to be transferred from the airforce to an army corps in Bosnia. This would be equivalent today to being taken from the Strategic Air Command to commanding a school for cooks in Montana. By 1939 he had risen to be chief of the general staff and desired above all to be minister of war. Instead, he was appointed head of the airforce.[490]

Simović and Mirković together decided the coup would take place when Cvetković returned from Vienna. It has been stated by some of his followers who were closest to him at the time that he had not the slightest idea that the Germans might retaliate if his coup succeeded. Goering was a brother airman whose autographed picture occupied the place of honor in his home. Simović was sure he would understand. Furthermore, they thought the whole thing was secret. Heeren, however, informed Berlin of its likelihood on the 26th.[491] It would appear from what has been published so far about the coup that very few people were actual plotters. There would appear to have been two or three plotters who had felt out support and knew it would be available at a moment's notice. One reason for waiting until the return of the government from signing the treaty was to assure the buildup of popular support. General Simović has stated flatly in his unpublished memoirs that there was no conspiratorial organization. Only in the terminal phase of the plot was a small group of officers informed. Nevertheless, there appear to have been three levels on which the coup was organized. At the top was Mirković who alone knew when things would happen and who would take part. Since part of the armed forces had already been alerted for possible trouble with Germany or Italy and issued live ammunition, it was relatively easy to move them to where they were needed. This was, of course, particularly the case with the airforce. Virtually none of Mirković's lieutenants were in on the plot.[492]

The second level was in the Reserve Officers' Club in Belgrade. The majority of members at this time were airforce officers. Here the British had made considerable inroads in promoting their idea of revolution.[493]

The third level was made up of several parts. One was composed of career officers mainly belonging to the general staff school centering around Major Zivan Knezević, then a commander of a Guards infantry battalion.[494]

Another part of this groups was the liaison between the general staff and the political opposition. One of these was Professor Radoje Knezević, brother of Major Knezević. He had been King Peter's tutor in French and secretary of the Democratic Party's executive committee. Through the Serbian Cultural Club he maintained contact with the intellectual elite of the University of Belgrade clustering around the historian, Slobodan Jovanović.[495]

The Serbian Cultural Club was composed of many of the upper-middle class professionals and intellectuals. A great many of the professors at the University of Belgrade as well as some diplomats were in it. On the edge was Ivo Andrić, Yugoslav minister in Berlin. A few years ago he was the winner of the Nobel Prize for his novels and stories. The older members had lived through the Balkan Wars and World War I and knew first hand the tremendous sacrifices the country had made in order to grow and were deeply committed to the Yugoslav idea. Others wanted to establish the cultural primacy of Serbia and, perhaps establish a new nationalist party.[496]

Professor Knezević was particularly prominant in this. The Stojadinović government had found his ideas too radical. It was believed that he was interlarding his theories into his French lessons to the king. Therefore, they dismissed him. Hurt by this and already a convinced opponent of the status quo, he cast his lot with the opposition. Through his brother, he took it upon himself to bring together the dissidents of the Serbian Cultural Club and the airforce.[497] Thus, the coup represented the coalescing of a number of elements. Mirković had not expected this, visualizing the coup as a strictly military affair, but he was willing to get help from any source. Generally these were Serbs, and some Croats and Slovenes, who believed the Pact betrayed old alliances and doomed Yugoslavia to dishonor once the inevitable allied victory occurred. In addition, they were convinced it would encourage Croat separatism and the claims of Italy thus destroying the Yugoslav state.[498]

On March 26 at 10:00 A.M. Cvetković and Cincar-Marković returned to Belgrade. Maček, acting head of government in their absence, met them at the railroad station. He told them all was calm. He said that as soon as the terms of the treaty were read to the crowds, especially the part about no military help to the Axis, they calmed down and dispersed peacefully.[499]

At 5:00 P.M. that evening, General Simović returned to airforce headquarters and called for Mirković. It was agreed the coup would take place that evening. At 7:00 came news that General Simović was to be placed on the retired list. It was agreed the coup would take place at 2:15 A.M. The General then went home to prevent suspicions by unusual actions. General Mirković remained at headquarters getting forces together for the coup. By the time it was to occur the following forces had been brought together.[500]

Zemun. This was airforce headquarters. Because of that, it was completely motorized and had the central airforce radio for communications with the whole country. The third battalion of the Second Infantry Regiment was here as well and was in the plot.

Belgrade. a) Two battalions of the Royal Guard Infantry Regiment were to surround the royal palace. b) One other battalion of the Guards was to seize the prime minister's office and its neighboring ministries. c) They were to be assisted by a tank battalion. d) A second tank battalion would hold the road to Banjica. e) An artillery battalion was to close the roads to the south. f) In addition, there was to be an anti-aircraft battalion and an anti-aircraft searchlight battalion making up a reserve. All airforce units all over the country were alerted to procede to the capital in case of trouble. The head of the Serbian veterans organization also was in it and was at headquarters ready to bring his men out if necessary. These other units were merely auxiliaries to the airforce. This was the one trusted group.[501]

The coup went off so well that by morning it was essentially over. The only difficulty was over Prince Paul. In the middle of the planning that evening it was learned that the Prince was leaving Belgrade. His destination was unknown. It was speculated that if he headed north he would be over the Hungarian frontier by 2:15 when the coup was supposed to take place. Here he might apply for Axis help in putting down the coup. No one knew what to do about this. A call or any action would warn the forces opposed to the coup that it was about to take place. They could not call Simović since it was known that his phone was tapped, nor could they go to his house since it was watched constantly by the secret police. An attempt was made to stop the train through an anonymous phone call reporting a bomb on the train. It delayed it only forty-five minutes. After this the whole coup threatened to break down in total confusion. The younger officers insisted it be carried out on time, though. Finally, an officer was sent to inquire about the train's route. He learned from the transport department of the general staff that it was due to arrive in Brdo, Slovenia in the morning. This would place it near Zagreb at the time of the coup, well within the country. No danger had to be feared after all.[502]

When everything was over and all military units had reported success, Mirković called Simović by sending a messenger. He was to come and have the government turned over. The coup, then, was entirely successful in Belgrade. Only one person was killed when a gendarme was shot as he reached for his rifle as the shortwave station at Mkis was seized.[503]

Maček, leader of the Croats and vice premier in the old government, had returned to Zagreb the evening of March 26th. There he was informed by a fellow Croat, Finance Minister Sutej, that the coup had taken place. He said that he and the other three Croats in the old government had been arrested and ordered to join the new government. He said they had refused to do so unless Maček gave his approval. Maček told them to do nothing until he could consult with some of his aides. At this point the chief of police of Zagreb came to him and informed him of the Regent's presence in Zagreb and that the Prince wanted to see him at once. After Maček went to the train, they all went to the palace of the Ban of Croatia for a conference at the insistence of Maček.[504]

At the palace Maček said they should not regard the coup as an accomplished fact. He pointed out that at the most the insurgents held only Belgrade and perhaps Serbia. They did not control Croatia. He should immediately see to the loyalty of the Fourth Army, which was made up almost entirely of Croats. With that he would be in a position to negotiate with the rebels. Further, many officers and men in Belgrade itself were not on the side of the rebels and were looking for a place to rally to.[505]

Prince Paul did not welcome these suggestions at all. He pointed out that the king was still in Belgrade. Action by the Prince might endanger the king's life. Furthermore, the Prince's family was still in Belgrade and they might get hurt. He finished by saying that he was tired of the whole thing anyway and welcomed the chance to resign. He would be happy to do so and go to Greece with his whole family. Maček would not act alone and so all chances of a counter coup were gone with the refusal of the Prince to act.[506]

The only other major problem for the coup itself was to gain possession of the king and bring him over to their side. In his memoirs King Peter disclaims all knowledge of the coup before it took place and that he was as surprised as everyone else.[507] This seems surprising when it is considered that the whole plan of the coup could only succeed if the king consented to take control and legitimize the new government. If he did not, Simović would simply be a general who had seized power and could only rule by force. The idea in the first place had been to get rid of the regency and put in the legitimate government of he king. He would then do right and follow a policy good for the country. Thus, they had to get control of him and convince him they were right. From the beginning they called themselves the royal government. When Simović took over, for instance, the cry was "long live the king." For these reasons, some writers seem to assume that the king was in on the plot from the beginning. From the latest material this does not seem to be true. The plotters would appear, as in so much else, to have assumed without question, that he would support them.[508]

There were a number of difficulties in the way. In 1930 King Alexander had moved into a new palace at Dedinje. Most of the royal guard were, of course, moved there as well. One battalion was left at the old palace. This group took part in the coup, taking the office at the prime minister, the ministry of war and general staff headquarters without resistance. There were some serious oversights in going on to take the royal palace. No plans had been made to capture a number of key figures who were to cause trouble: regents Stanković and Perović, Court Minister Antić, the king's aide, General Pavle Barjaktarević, and chief of staff Kosić.[509]

As it turned out, these were all at the royal palace. From there, they tried to hold off the coup. General Barjaktarević deployed the one battalion of the royal guard along the palace wall while the rebel units were spread around the palace outside. The two remaining regents appointed General Kosić as commander of the Belgrade garrison as well as retaining his former position of chief of staff. Shortly after 4:00 A.M. he drove to the headquarters of the Danube Division at Banjica on the outskirts of Belgrade. The officers were mostly loyal to Prince Paul. No one was there, though. He put the unit on alert but did not stay. If he had, and then moved the unit against those besieging the royal palace, he undoubtedly could have broken them and things would have taken a very different turn. He did not,

however, and by the time the troops were ordered to move the officers
knew something was up and refused to move.[510]
At 6:00 A.M. Kosić had the king awakened. Soon after General
Kosić was captured. Then the remainder of the royal guard went over
to the rebels. The remaining resistance soon disappeared, especially
when the king refused to order any action against the rebels.[511]
By now the revolt was a full fledged popular affair. Ambassador
Lane of the United States reported home that Belgrade was full of
wildly enthusiastic crowds including two which demonstrated at the
American Legation.[512] Nevertheless, those around the king who hoped
to stop the coup were still optimistic. When they heard of the capture
of Kosić, they tried to get the king to order the Danube Division to
go against the rebels. He refused to do so.[513] It appeared the only
hope left was to get to the regent before he returned to Belgrade and
persuade him not to resign.

After the talk with Maček and the Ban of Croatia, Ivan Subasić,
the regent and the governor left Zagreb about noon returning to Zemun
that evening. General Simović and a group of officers met his train
there to take the Prince to the ministry of war.[514]

On the way the two men talked. Prince Paul said that he should
have listened to the general reminding him of the earlier talk in which
Simović told him of a plot. He said he was willing to resign and do
anything else that would relieve the internal situation. He was also
willing to help the government from abroad, perhaps from England.
As they came into the center of town, he said he would like to go
immediately to Greece where he had relatives. Simović said the
government would have no objections to that. Asked when he would
like to go, the Prince answered tonight. The general then said he could
leave at midnight. This was the way it happened.[515]

Despite the revolutionaries' supposed conviction that the king would
go along with them, there were problems about establishing their
legitimacy. Under the constitution of 1931 this could only be done
by obtaining the king's written approval.[516] They, of course, could
not get to the king right away while it was imperative to get his
approval immediately. To get to him would have meant fighting which
might endanger his life. Therefore, when this became plain, the officer
charged with getting confirmation gave up and returned to the ministry
of war. They then decided to act as though he had given his approval.
At 9:00 P.M. the king heard a broadcast proclaiming that he had taken
all power into his own hands, that the regents had resigned, and that
he had charged General Simović with forming a new government.
He was amazed to hear how much the voice resembled his own.[517]

There was also some argument about what sort of government the
new one should be. A meeting took place at the ministry of war to
decide this while the revolution was still going on. Despite his earlier
talk about establishing democracy again, Mirković now came out with

a different plan. This was for a government on the lines of that set up by his friend General Antonescu in Rumania. This would be a cabinet of generals headed by a general. Presumably, this would be himself. Radoje Knezević was very much against this plan. He said that the main reason for the coup had been supposedly that all governments since 1929 had not represented the nation. Therefore, the new one should get its roots directly from them. The imposition of the dictatorship, he said, had broken the 1921 consitution and so no government since then had been legitimate. These had been entirely controlled by the royal court and so were oppressive. Thus, all the coup has done has been to destroy the dictatorship and tyrranous government that had oppressed the country. The time had come to get back to a legitimate government. This could only be done by going to the people.[518]

There were certain difficulties here. Presumably, when he talked about the people and the nation he meant the Serbian people and nation. He appears to have been inclined to include Croats and Slovenes in the new government from the old Cvetković government because he apparently thought of them as true representatives of their people. Apparently he never considered what might happen if they were not included.[519]

Another difficulty was his apparently unthinking rejection of the 1931 costitution, again in regard to the nationalities. They had come to accept the 1931 costitution as something they could work with even if they did not like the sort of government it set up. The 1921 constitution, on the other hand, had always been totally unacceptable to them so that they had always totally refused to work within it. After much argument, the Knezević ideas were accepted by all, including the supporters of Mirković.[520]

Finally, after Prince Paul had gone to Greece the rebels could get their government legalized by the king. At about 9:30 P.M. Simovic finally met the king. The proclamation made that morning using an imitation of the king's voice, and the decree for the formation of the new government was signed. The king is reported to have whispered to an aide that Simović did not seem as bad as he thought he would be. It had been rumored earlier in the day that Simović had planned to do away with the monarchy.[521]

According to the constitution, the king could not ascend the throne until his 18th birthday. This would not be until September 6, 1941. On March 28 he was sworn in, however, by the patriarch. With this, the new government, with the young king still only 17, was fully in power.[522] Its final hold on power occurred when Maček agreed to retain his old post of vice-premier. This was on April 3. He had been insisting that adherence to the Tripartite Pact must be kept in order to avert war with Germany. Also, he wanted to make sure that Croats and Slovenes would have a place in the government and the autonomy gained in the Sporazum would be kept up.[523]

The only really important point, of course, was what would
Germany do now? Already on March 27th at 2:30 P.M. Directive 25
was issued to the German armed forces ordering them to prepare for
war with Yugoslavia. In this Hitler stated at the beginning that attempts
could be expected from Yugoslavia to explain this all away but they
would be useless. His decision for war was not reversible. Also, he
decided to make this a national war as well. The Croats were to be
weaned away from any loyalty to the government and constituted as
a fifth column controlled from Germany.[524]

In the meantime, Heeren attempted to get in touch with the new
government and they set out to reassure Germany on their intentions.
Heeren came to the ministry of war on the morning of March 27.
He was able to see the new foreign minister, Momcilo Ninčić, that
morning although he was told that the prime minister was unable to
see him. Heeren was assured that the coup was caused by the lack
of public support for the government of Prince Paul. Ninčić said that
the choice of himself as the new foreign minister would assure continued cooperation with the Axis Powers, particularly with Germany.
He assured him that he would see that all obligations which the
government had assumed would be scrupulously observed. However, he could not state specifically the new government's attitude
to the Tripartite Pact.[525] Heeren had already sent off a telegram to
Berlin at 11:55 A.M. merely informing them that the coup had taken
place, that it had been to place the king on the throne, that it was
highly popular although carried out entirely by the armed forces
and that it appeared to be primarily directed against the Tripartite
Pact.[526]

General Simović talked to him, also, at 9:00 P.M. He tried to
reassure him that there would be no changes. He stressed that the
revolution had been caused by internal politics. He said that the Prince
had not surrounded himself with people respected by the country.
Simović said that he himself had always been a friend of Germany.
He said he was proud of his friendship with Reichsmarschall Goering
and Field Marshall Milch, and he requested that his regards be for-
warded to them.[527]

The next day Simović had a talk with Lane, the American ambassador. Simović told Lane that he wanted to avoid any talk about the
Tripartite Pact since it had not yet been ratified. Yugoslavia was not,
therefore, bound by its terms. He said they did not want to offend
Germany and so would neither ratify nor denounce the Pact. It would
simply be allowed to die a natural death from inaction, as far as
Yugoslavia was concerned. Yugoslavia would, however, resist any
move by force against Salonica.[528] Ninčić, the new foreign minister,
had already had a slightly different conversation with Lane on the
29th. Here he said Yugoslavia could not repudiate the Pact since it
became effective on signing. The question was how it could be applied.

The present government, he said, would not allow the same thing to happen to Yugoslavia as happened to Rumania and Bulgaria.[529]

On the 30th Ninčić called Heeren in and made a formal statement to him as follows:

> The present Royal Yugoslav Government remains true to the principle of respect for international treaties which have been concluded, among which the Protocol signed on the 25th of this month at Vienna belongs. It will insist in the most determined fashion on not being drawn into the present conflict. Its chief attention will be devoted to the maintenance of good and friendly relations with its neighbors the German Reich and the Kingdom of Italy.
>
> The Royal Government is particularly interested in the manner of applying the Protocol mentioned; in connection with this it is mindful of safeguarding all the essential interests of the Yugoslav State and people.[530]

Also, a few days after the formation of the new government Simović summoned the two principle ethnic-German leaders. He explained to them that Yugoslavia wanted only friendly relations with the Reich. He asked them to assure Heeren of this and that the German minority was not being persecuted in any way.[531]

Meanwhile, Italy was also brought into the matter. Mussolini was extremely worried by the turn events had taken. This was shared to some extent in Germany. Ribbentrop was convinced the whole thing was Italy's fault. There never would have been this trouble but for the Italian fiasco in Greece.[532] It certainly seemed to Mussolini that he might be attacked in Albania at any time by a combined Greek-Yugoslav offensive. If he had been so easily defeated by the Greeks alone, what would happen when they were helped by Yugoslavia?[533]

His fear was not lessened by the first communications he had from Germany. On March 28th Hitler warned him of the difficulties. He told him that Yugoslavia had been the prime difficulty in Germany's desire to aid Italy in Greece. Her forces could be a real danger on the flank or rear of any German force moving on Greece through Bulgaria or Salonica. Therefore, he had waited on any move to help Italy until this danger was ended by Yugoslav adherence to the Tripartite Pact. Now the question had been settled by the coup. He went on to say:

> I now urgently request you, Duce, not to carry any further operations in Albania for the next few days. I consider it necessary that you undertake with all available forces to cover and protect the most important passes from Yugoslavia to Albania. It is not a question of measures which need

to remain in effect for a long time, but of emergency measures meant to prevent the development of a crisis in the next 2 to 3 weeks.[534]

The next day, March 29th, Simović had a talk with the Italian Minister to Belgrade, Giorgio Mameli. This did even more to disquiet Mussolini. Simović warned Mameli that if German troops entered Salonica and cut Yugoslavia off from access to the Aegean, Yugoslavia would have to occupy Albania in order to secure an exit through the Adriatic.[535] These two things coming together seem to have convinced Mussolini that all efforts must be made to placate Yugoslavia, at least for the moment.

Stakić, who had been an agent of earlier meetings with Ciano and Mussolini, informed Simović on April 1 that Mameli wished to see him. Later that day they met. The substance of what he had to say was that Mussolini would attempt to mediate the affair with Hitler. He, also, extended an invitation for Simović to come to Rome. The Yugoslav cabinet studied this proposal that same evening. It was agreed it would be too dangerous for Simović to accept such an invitation but that Ninčić and Vice-Prime Minister Jovanović should go instead. The Italians kept trying to get a clarification from Yugoslavia on what would happen if Germany acted in Greece. This they would not give. Finally on April 3 Italy said they would not allow the visitors to come until this was clarified. There the matter rested.[536]

In the meantime connections with Germany had been somewhat broken. On March 29th Berlin ordered Heeren not to attend any official functions in Belgrade. He could give illness as an excuse. He was not to go to the Yugoslav foreign office to receive official communications but was to send an official representative.[537] In Berlin Weiszacker ordered officials of the foreign office to feign absence if the Yugoslav minister or his staff asked for appointments.[538] On April 2nd Ribbentrop told Heeren to reduce the size of the legation staff to four or five persons within 24 hours. When they received from Berlin the code words "Tripartite Pact" they were to destroy all secret materials and codes and to bury the wireless equipment. After that, what was left of the staff was to leave the city for a suitable refuge in the country. In addition, all consulates except that in Zagreb were to close down on April 3. After April 4 Germany would halt all Yugoslav shipping on the Danube found within the German-Hungarian frontier.[539] Also, on March 30th Heeren was ordered home by Ribbentrop for "consultations."[540]

Lane of the United States tried during these days to get a clarification of the Yugoslav attitude to the Tripartite Pact. What he was able to learn was not particularly reassuring. It seemed he had been quite naive, as had Britain, in believing that the Tripartite Pact was the very basis of the coup. From what he could learn, there seemed no idea of repudiating it. Thus, all U.S. and British efforts against it, on Britain's part to the point of fomenting revolution, had been useless. Nincic told him the pact could not be repudiated since it was ratified on being signed. Furthermore, he must consider what might happen to the country. Not only might there be trouble with Germany but it might mean the dissolution of the country. Thus, the vital question now was how the pact was to be applied. This was still in doubt as Lane was convinced he was not yet fully aware of all the secret commitments entered into by the Cvetkovic government in regard to the Pact.

Nincic also expressed unhappiness with all the street demonstrations in favor of the Allies and against the Axis. He said it had embarrassed the government with the Germans. He, also, expressed displeasure at the broadcast by Churchill in which he said that Yugoslavia had now found her soul and that the coup was a blow to the Axis. He said that these were not only embarrassing but unwise. He asked Lane's government to bear this in mind.

Lane was also embarrassed by some of the popular reaction. He had once reported that Yugoslav public opinion supported the coup in its oposition to signing the Pact. Now he had to report that the Croats, Slovenes and Moslems had called on the new government to adhere to the agreement. He tried to maintain, however, that the new government would not give into all demands, as Bulgaria and Rumania had.[541] He would, perhaps, have felt worse if he could have known that earlier the council of ministers had agreed not to decree general mobilization but to continue calling up the men class by class.[542]

Macek was also bothered by these developments. Subasic returned to Zagreb on March 29th. He told Macek that the new government intended to honor all the international commitments of the old government, including the Tripartite Pact. Despite all the demostrations and slogans they would not break the ties to the Axis or go to war for Britain.[542]

Macek was dissatisfied with the report, particularly its conclusion where Subasic predicted there would be no war with the Axis. He became so dissatisfied that he sent his deputy, August Kosutic, to Belgrade to make a new evaluation.[544]

Kosutic returned almost immediately on March 31st with a much less optimistic report than that of Subasic. He reported that it was true that the government was doing everything it could to prevent war. Vice-Premier Jovanovic was going to Berlin and Nincic was going to Rome in attempts to end the growing tension between Yugoslavia and the Axis. He believed, though, that little could come out of these meetings. There had been too many incidents of an unpleasant nature involving the Germans. Heeren had been able to use as one excuse for his departure to Berlin that a mob had spat on him as he returned to his home after attending a Te Deum sung for King Peter.[545]

Maček was furious over all this wondering what it did to the future of Croatia and the way it put in jeopardy the future of all Yugoslavs.[546] In addition, a great many men had started to call on him claiming to be plenipotentiaries, or the agents of men claiming to be plenipotentiaries, of the Germans with all sorts of offers. These he claimed were couched in the vaguest terms. He blamed the revolutionaries for opening him to this sort of thing.[547]

One of these was a man named Derffler. On March 28th he called on Maček. He urged Maček to go to Berlin immediately to find out what they thought there of the Croatian independence movement. He pointed out that their attitude would have a great deal to do with whether or not he entered the Simović government.[548] On March 30th, Berlin instructed Derffler to tell Maček that he had no information yet but to leave the impression that he would have definite news a little later. According to Derffler, Maček completely broke down when he read this because he assumed this would mean he would get no aid.[549]

However, the same message from Ribbentrop to the consul in Zagreb conveying this message gives a different impression to that previously cited, which was Maček's version. In an appendix marked "for your information," it is stated that a Viennese engineer named Derffler had been contacted by Maček on March 28th. Ribbentrop gives the impression here that neither he nor anyone else in the foreign ministry knew anything about him. It was decided, however, to make use of him. It says Derffler should be back in Zagreb from his trip to Berlin and should be used to convey the message given before.

In the main body of the telegram a different story is also told. It starts off by mentioning that inquiries have been received from Maček through various channels. A footnote informs us that one of these was a message from the Foreign Intelligence Department of the OKW of March 27th. It was the transmission of an inquiry from Maček through Abwehr channels on Germany's attitude to the Yugoslav government.[550] Thus, it would appear that Maček initiated the contacts with the Germans and these were not as unwelcome as he would lead us to believe.

The telegram goes on to warn him and the other Croatian leaders against cooperating with the new regime. It goes on to urge the utmost secrecy about these contacts. If he wants to maintain them, he must assure absolute secrecy.[551]

On April 1st, a man named Melletke, with credentials from the German foreign office, informed him that the official policy of Germany now called for an independent Croatia. By now, this complicated Maček's situation and made his decision more difficult. He said that, despite this, he would have to go to Belgrade and take part in the government. Serbian troops were already moving into Croatia. The Croatian militia would be unable to stop them and so it would be impossible for him to form an independent Croatia. Furthermore, he reminded Melletke that he asked Germany for arms for his militia and they had not supplied them. He disclosed that the Yugoslav government had made him an offer too. Belgrade had promised him that the king and two other people not named would form an authoritarian government with the king as a figurehead. Melletke tried to get him to change his mind, showing how impressed he was by this revelation.

Maček replied that he had to join the Simović government whether he wanted to or not in order to prevent a civil war. He was convinced that he could gradually secure autonomy for Croatia and be able to restore orderly relations with Italy and Germany. He was certain, he said, that he could push the government into declaring itself in favor of the Tripartite Pact and into offering a reparation plan that would satisfy the Germans.

Seeing that Maček could not be deterred from joining the government, Melletke asked him to promise that he would not take any new steps until he had consulted Berlin. This he promised to do.[552] On the evening of April 3 he left for Belgrade.

The offer supposedly sent to Maček by the royal government was transmitted to Berlin by the consul in Zagreb on April 1st. It appears here again that instead of being an offer to Maček from Belgrade, it was instead the demands Belgrade must satisfy if Maček were to enter the government. It would appear that Maček had tried to impress the German envoy in order to get more out of him.

> Recognition of the Tripartite Pact and implementation in the spirit of the Treaty; the appointment of two co-regents for the king, one of whom is to be a Croat; the resignation of the Minister of War, and the withdrawal of the military from politics. Maček considers the resignation of the Croatian ministers as tactically inexpedient. He would refrain in principle, in the present situation, from entering the government. He would do this only if war could thereby be averted.[553]

A great deal of information was by now reaching the Yugoslav government that a German attack was more and more likely. The most reliable came from Colonel Vauhnik, Yugoslav military attache in Berlin. His sources brought him many bits of information that could only point to war. A journalist in the Deutsche Allgemeine Zeitung informed him on March 29 that Hitler had told a meeting the night before that Yugoslavia would be destroyed as a military power if she did not decide instantly and unequivocally, to stand with Germany. The same afternoon he was told by his old friend, Dr. Sigismund Bernstorff, the same story except that he said his source was a

SS group leader in the headquarters of the Gestapo. On April 1 he received several messages that trouble could be expected in a week to ten days. That evening a phone call told him the attack would be in the early hours of Sunday, April 6, and would take the form of heavy air raids that would turn Belgrade into a heap of rubble. Vauhnik already had intimations that April 6 was important. There had been news that Germany would launch an attack on Greece through Bulgaria on that date. He now came to the conclusion that both attacks would be coordinated to form parts of one plan. Accordingly he sent a telegram to the general staff in Belgrade that they could expect a German attack on April 6th. This news was sent on April 2 by three different routes to make sure it would reach Belgrade.

After this the information poured in. He came to the conclusion that most Germans must side with Yugoslavia so much information was coming in. From the Gestapo's main office he learned that a large number of case workers were being dispatched to the Yugoslav frontier. From a source in Hamburg he learned that an SS division was being sent to the Rumanina-Yugoslav frontier. Another was going through Hungary.

Again he sent telegrams to Belgrade. Still he received no word from there that his warnings had been received. He tried to phone the general staff but without success. Finally on April 3 he sent his aide. Later he learned that all his messages had been received. This happened only because the German orders to stop all his messages had been lost in red tape for several days. It did not matter anyway since the Yugoslav general staff was convinced he had been taken in and were sure there would be no attack. The last telegram he sent conveyed the information that Germany would attack with 32 divisions. After the affair was all over Hitler disclosed in a speech that 31 divisions and 2 brigades had been readied for the attack.

It would appear that Vauhnik's source was in the very highest German levels. He has disclosed since the war that he received the information from Admiral Canaris, head of the German high command's foreign and counter-intelligence office. It was passed on to Vauhnik through Major-General Hans Oster, chief assistant to Canaris. Although many Yugoslav officers admitted they saw Vauhnik's telegrams, General Ilić, minister of war, has implied that he did not.[554]

Maček arrived in Belgrade on April 4th. His first impression was of a growing fear of war with Germany among the members of the government. Belgrade, Zagreb and Ljubljana had just been declared open cities in case of war. The only one still outwardly expressing the conviction that there would be no war was General Simović. He had staked all on this gamble and he could not very well back down now. If he had the only real excuse for the coup would be gone. Simović assured Maček that the German army would break under

Yugoslav resistance. He appeared convinced that the panzers could not operate in the mountains of the Balkans, especially with the lack of roads to navigate the mountains. He seems to have thought that, if war came, it must necessarily be fought on the same terms as World War I. That could mean that stalemate would result as it had before. The character of the Yugoslav army fighting on home ground with their old tactics was well known. At any rate, he said, he was doing all he could to prevent war. Maček asked him how long it would take the Germans to organize an attack. Simović thought 14 days if they wanted to be sure of success. He said nothing about the warnings of Colonel Vauhnik about the air attacks on Belgrade scheduled for April 6th. He went on to say that Foreign Minister Ninčić would report the next day to the cabinet on his negotiations with Italian Minister, Mamelli. It is to be remembered that Italy had offered to mediate the quarrel.

As far as Ninčić was concerned, the situation with Germany had gone much further than he had expected. As we have seen, he believed that the Tripartite Pact was in force. He told Ambassador Lane that the Pact became law on its signing and that he did not intend to repudiate it. He did not foresee any insurmountable difficulties with Germany.[555] On the morning of April 1st he and Simović had an appointment to see Heeren in order to assure him of that fact. Heeren had it cancelled before it could take place on the grounds that the whole matter was now in the hands of Berlin exclusively. On April 3rd Ninčić notified all Yugoslav missions abroad that he had

informed the German and Italian ministers here that the Royal Government remained faithful to the principle of existing international treaties and, therefore, to the agreement of Vienna of March 25th of this year; that its chief concern was to maintain the policy of good and friendly relations with Germany and Italy; and that it will take most determined steps not to be drawn into the present conflict.[556]

The Yugoslav minister in Berlin was also instructed to see officials of the German foreign office and ''to offer all concessions compatible with national honor.''[557] For five days, including an attempt on the 5th, Andrić tried to see anyone at all in the foreign office. No one would see him. He even tried to see the Italian ambassador to get him to pass his messages along. The Italian ambassador expressed his regret at the whole situation and fervently assured Andrić his government wanted to arrive at a solution.[558]

Meanwhile, the feelers had been revived Italy had put out to mediate the situation when they feared an attack by Yugoslavia on themselves. Ninčić had put out approaches to get them to do so, and would report to the cabinet on their progress.[559]

Late in the afternoon of April 5th the cabinet met. Ninčić reported that Italy was willing to intercede on Yugoslavia's behalf on the condition that Yugoslav troops immediately occupy the Greek-Yugoslav frontier to prevent the entrance into Yugoslavia of British or Greek troops. Ninčić advised that the offer be accepted. Simović agreed but with the proviso that Yugoslavia occupy Salonica. Ninčić was very angry over this, saying that Simović was talking nonsense. He said that this was the only way by which German troops could enter Greece without violating Yugoslav territory. In addition, Salonica was not Yugoslav territory and she would be violating her doctrine of neutrality if she took it.

As the meeting went on, it became obvious that most of the members favored Ninčić's proposals and would vote for them. At this point Simović made a violent speech for war in which he glorified Serbia's military past. At the end Maček said that if Simović kept that sort of thing up he would resign from the cabinet.

In the end Ninčić had to ask the Italians to extend the deadline for the answer from 7:00 P.M. Saturday to noon Sunday. They agreed to do so.[560]

One other last minute attempt was made to convince the Germans that the new government would stick with the treaty. The afternoon of the 5th, the foreign minister's brother went to the German legation twice. He told them that the entire cabinet had agreed that Ninčić should go to Berlin. He asserted that, with the turmoil because of the coup and his own recent operation, he had been unable to really take control of affairs. He assured the Germans, however, that this would now be changed. He said that the foreign minister had a large majority of the cabinet behind him so that it would accept anything he proposed. He assured them that he was a complete and whole hearted adherent of the Pact. It was true, he said, that the country had received proposals for different action from abroad but he assured them that Yugoslavia would only listen to those which came from Berlin. This appears to have been the last contact of Yugoslavia and Berlin. The proposal, of course, was ignored by Berlin.[561]

As has been stated, It would appear that Hitler gave no consideration at all to the sincerity of Yugoslavia's statements that she would continue to adhere to the Pact and that the change of government would not effect her relations with Germany. On being told the news Hitler screamed that this had destroyed his favorite project, the grand coalition against England.[562] Ribbentrop, on April 5th, complained that Germany had done everything possible in the way of concessions. Now the Yugoslavs had turned against Germany without the slightest provocation. This slap in the face had occurred when Hitler was making every effort to persuade the Japanese to attack the British at Singapore.[563] On March 27 Hitler had called a full conference in which he stated that all chance to trust the Yugoslavs was gone. There was no need to wait for declarations of loyalty. They should not be answered if they came. Immediate preparations should begin for war. No ultimatums or declarations of war would be given. The moment the forces were ready to attack Yugoslavia, they should go.[564]

Later that day he called in the Hungarian and Bulgarian ministers to tell them of the situation. He said that those who had engineered the coup had entirely misjudged the military situation and had gone mad. This offered Hungary, as he told the Hungarian ambassador, the golden opportunity to revise her borders as she had wanted to do for so long. Aside from the parts of Styria and Carinthia ceded to Yugoslavia after World War I, Germany wanted no territory. She had no territorial ambitions in the area, he told the ambassadors. Croatia would be independent and there must never again be a Yugoslavia. He went on to tell the Bulgarian ambassador "that this had settled the Macedonian question."[565]

On April 3rd Hitler approved the date of April 6th for the attack.[566] At 4:00 A.M. that morning Ribbentrop radioed the legation in Belgrade the message, "Tripartite Pact. Acknowledge receipt." This was the signal that the attack would begin.[567]

Only two hours later the attack began with an air raid on Belgrade. This continued on a massive scale for several hours. There were virtually no anti-aircraft guns and the Yugoslav air force was smothered by the vast number of German planes. It has been estimated that at least 2000 planes were used by the Germans against Yugoslavia while that country had only 284 old planes that were no match for the Germans. Destruction of these was so great the first day that the Germans gave up bombing raids on air fields after the first day and concentrated on aiding the troops.[568]

To everyone's surprise the war was soon over. The armistice was signed on April 17th to go into effect the next day.[569] It has been said that the advance of the German panzers was so rapid and the whole thing was over so soon that the greater part of the Yugoslav reserves called up and units sent to the frontiers never had a chance to even begin fighting or fire a shot. The bulk were caught on their way to the frontiers. As a result, most of them simply melted off into the mountains, often as complete units under their officers. The German advance was so rapid that the tanks left all these soldiers behind or bypassed them completely. By the time the German infantry could come up on foot, these troops had taken cover in the mountains.[570]

This campaign should have shown the Germans some lessons about the use of armor in such a country as Yugoslavia. Of course, they had not expected such success for armor in those mountains. Such tactics had worked well on the plains of Poland and France where the disorganized troops could be rounded up at leisure.[571] In this case, the tanks easily broke through the poorly equipped Yugoslav army on the frontier and kept going against practically no opposition since the Yugoslav plan was to stop the Germans at the frontier. Then there were so few roads usable by tanks that vast stretches of country were untouched for weeks. This left the largest part of the Yugoslav army absolutely untouched. Most was later rounded up and virtually all Croat units immediately gave up without firing a shot. In a number of cases more untoward incidents occurred. There was active treason from some Croat officers. The most famous is of an air force officer who flew to Graz, Austria a few days before the attack began. There he turned over to the Germans a list of all airports used by the Yugoslav air force. Many Croat units mutinied, threw away their weapons and went home. There were incidents of fighting between Croat and Serb units rather than against the Germans. An entire brigade with its officers surrendered to a German bicycle company. Finally, Belgrade itself fell to a lieutenant and a single SS infantry platoon.[572] Many units were still complete and thousands of individuals simply were untouched and wandered off into the mountains where they began to organize themselves in their traditional military role.

The way in which the army simply disintegrated can be seen from a few statistics. In the twelve days of fighting over 200,000 Yugoslav troops were captured.[573] No one appears to know how many were killed or wounded. For the Germans, the total casualty list for the campaign was 558. Of these 151 were killed, 392 wounded and 15 missing in action.[574] The only heavy resistance came from Serbian and Slovenian soldiers fighting on their own soil and defending their homes against a traditional enemy. Their resistance was so fierce that the German advance was stopped in many areas.[575]

The last question that need concern us in this affair was the fate of the government. The king fled the country to Greece on April 14th. Most of the government had either preceded him or soon followed. The only one who remained in the country was Maček. He had resigned, however, in order to try to save Croatia out of the wreckage.[576] No one was left of the government to surrender to the Germans. Then someone remembered Cincar-Marković and thought he should do it since he had been acceptable to the Germans before. He might be able to save something from the wreckage. He was finally found but indignantly refused to do so. He pointed out that he had managed to preserve peace for the country while the coup had directly repudiated his work and so caused the trouble the country was now in. The irony of the situation was certainly obvious. He finally was persuaded to act, however, and on April 17th he signed the armstice in Belgrade.[577]

CHAPTER 6
CONCLUSIONS

When Yugoslavia was formed after World War I she found herself in a very insecure position. She had only been able to achieve nationhood because of the destruction of the Habsburg Empire, and could only maintain her independence as long as no new state appeared to fill the void. Into the interwar period there were three possible contenders for the place left by the Habsburgs. They were Germany, Italy and Soviet Russia. In most of the period all were too weak to seriously consider a policy of expansion. Not only did it appear that France would undoubtedly act to stop them but each would oppose the others because of jealousy. It was only after 1933 with the rise of Hitler that it seemed likely the vacuum in Central Europe would be filled. This brought forth the predictable responses.

By the time Hitler came to power his dreams for Germany had coalesced along two lines. One was to completely do away with the provisions of the Versailles Treaty. The other was to expand Germany so that she could fill her "rightful" place in the power structure of Europe and the world. His dream seems to have been to create out of eastern Europe a new rural Germany that would create living space for Germans. This meant the conquest of East Europe and the Russian Ukraine.

These plans would in both respects involve Germany in a new war with France. Hitler expected, however, that this time England could be kept out of the hostilities or even, perhaps, be brought over to Germany's side. This would be done by exploiting the differences between France and England and their growing hostility over certain problems. Also, he would guarantee England's empire and even allow her to absorb new territories from France's empire. Thus, England's traditional intervention to prevent hegemony by one power over Europe could be prevented and she could be steered to look where Hitler thought her real interests lay, in her colonial empire. It was very unlikely that France would join with Russia this time considering

French feelings over the soviet system. Thus, Germany could view the likelihood of war calmly since war with France alone or with her eastern allies would not expose Germany to great risks. It would be a short and relatively easy war.

From the beginning he thought of Italy as his major partner in such a war. He felt this would be a natural partnership because all three (Germany, England and Italy) would have interests in areas so far apart that they could not come into conflict. Germany would be interested in East Europe and Italy in the Mediterranean. I will not comment on the inherent over simplicity of these schemes except to say that, of course, his ideas did not take into consideration a number of points about England's attitude to all these questions.

Another point of crucial interest for our story is Italy's dreams of expansion. Besides non-European areas, Mussolini also coveted the Balkans and the Danube section as areas of historic interest for Italy. He looked back at the long interest of Venice and Genoa in the Balkans during the Middle Ages and Renaissance, for instance, and claimed that a new Italian empire must include those same territories. Also, he never forgot that the Roman Empire had once controlled the area. Ultimately, he always dreamed of reviving the Roman Empire. As I show in the body of the paper, Hitler was very concerned in his plans for war that Germany not suffer again as she had in World War I from lack of food and raw materials caused by the British sea blockade. The cutoff in imports was crucial, particularly in their effect on civilian morale. The Danube basin and the Balkans played an important role in his plans to insure an adequate supply of food and raw materials. I went into some detail regarding his efforts to integrate Yugoslavia into an economic system designed to do this. In addition, Hungary and Rumania were very important suppliers of food while Rumania was Germany's sole European supplier of oil. To have Italy endanger these sources of supply could not be allowed.

Thus, Italy and Germany were actually rivals over the Danube Basin and the Balkans. Hitler should certainly have known that after the way Mussolini interfered in his attempted takeover of Austria. It was equally unrealistic not to know that Italy would only be a drain on Germany in the event of a war. She had nothing like the industrial base needed for a modern war. Hitler was well acquainted with the problems of German industry in World War I. He should have known that Germany would still have a big problem in a new war and that the problems would only be worse if they were saddled with supplying Italy also. One of the most interesting aspects of this question is the relations of Hitler and Mussolini. It is known that Hitler's feelings about Mussolini were ambivalent, to say the least. He always respected him as the first fascist leader to become ruler of a state. In all his actions he showed how much he thought of him in that regard. The problem was that he felt contempt for him as a politician. One of the few actually documented times when Hitler got into a real demonic rage was over Mussolini's invasion of Greece. He let all around him know that he thought Mussolini a fool and that he had made a bad mistake. As far as Hitler was concerned, the real evil of the situation was that he then had to get Mussolini out of his self created mess.

Mussolini certainly had bad feelings for Hitler. Before he decided to join Hitler he had regarded him as a bad figure in european affairs. He had sided with the other powers to keep him under control. As mentioned above, the biggest block to Hitler's absorption of Austria for some time was Mussolini. At the time of the assassination of Chancellor Dollfuss, when Hitler had expected to occupy Austria, Mussolini had threatened to meet him with the Italian army. This forced Hitler to stop.

The later shift was because of the Ethiopian Problem when Mussolini was opposed by England and France. In his anger, he went over to support of Hitler. He appears to have expected to be able to dominate Hitler since he saw himself as the more intelligent man and the more experienced politician. It worked out the other way. After Greece Mussolini found himself utterly dependent on Hitler. His status of total subordination to and dependence on Hitler was not permanent. Thus, Germany and Italy were at odds over the area. Mussolini was constantly afraid that Hitler would take it before he could stake his own claim. Yugoslavia attempted to use the situation to keep her independence as long as she could. The situation might have gone on except for Mussolini's jealousy at Hitler's fabulous success. Mussolini decided to act to achieve some gains before Hitler had taken everything. The result was the Greek fiasco. Hitler had to come to rescue him. There no longer was any possibility of Yugoslavia evading the issue. It was a matter of war or joining the Axis. She joined.

It is at this point that the nationality problem rises to its worst height. As I show, Yugoslavia was a federation formed from a number of somewhat related groups. All but the Serbs had hoped for a loose federation that would leave them pretty free to manage their own affairs. The Serbs looked on the new state as their empire. Since they had the monopoly of force, this was the way it turned out. The Vidovdan Constitution, which gave form to the new state, recognized this status of a united state under the control of Serbia. Out of this had risen the divisions that made up the basis of the national question.

The new state seemed, however, to be slowly getting over its birth pains when the leader of the principle opposition party was assassinated. From then on the divisions became rigid. The one event that made the problem almost incurable was the setting up of a dictatorship by the king. With its martial law, police rule and the end of democratic forms, it seemed to many among the minorities as a return to the worst of Serbian rule. Nonetheless, the dictatorship did go far toward ending the corruption and self serving politics which had caused the assassination of Radić. Most people were only too happy to see honest government under an energetic king who was trying his best to cure the difficulties under which the country labored. Possibly, if the king had not been assassinated by the most alienated group of all, the nationality problem might have been well on its way to being cured.

Under the succeeding government of the Regent, Prince Paul, (ruling until young King Peter would reach his majority) the dictatorship was maintained. The Prince was a rather cold man with little real knowledge of the country so that the dictatorship was maintained when it had long outlived its usefulness. The result was a new, greater outburst of the nationality question. It came more and more to international notice also because of its involvement in the death of the king and its continued use by Mussolini to undermine the country.

Those who engineered the coup in 1941 against Prince Paul and the Axis Pact were mainly Serbian officers who felt that the politicians were corrupt and dishonest and that they and the Prince had allowed the minorities too many rights. Their hope was to produce a return to the good old Serbian peasant and military virtues which, in their view, had made Serbia. Therefore, their coup was bound to again alienate the minorities who resumed their fears of Serbian domination.

When it was over the question was what had they really accomplished. They found that, despite all their talk, they had to honor the Axis Pact. It was all the country could do in the circumstances. Probably if the regency had published the whole story the coup would never have happened. Secrecy used in a misguided way and from ignorance about the real mood of the country seems to have been a major ingredient in the situation.

In the meantime, England had intervened in the situation by coming to the aid of Greece with troops. They were also encouraging the Yugoslavs to resist with force. This was bound to provoke Hitler to action. Despite his anger at what he regarded as a deliberate insult, he might have calmed down. The intervention of England was bound to make any solution but war impossible. By this time, Hitler regarded England as his real enemy so that any English presence was enough to set him off. The tragedy of the whole situation was that England made cynical use of these countries. It would appear that Churchill and his advisors well realized that Hitler would intervene and that they would be defeated. The idea was that this would be a process of bleeding that would weaken Germany. Also it would spread his power too thinly so that England could hope that eventually she could take Hitler on a more equal basis. The destruction of Yugoslavia was then inevitable once England had intervened in Greece. The only way for the Germans to get there was through Yugoslavia.

When fighting developed the depth of the nationality problem became clear. The armed forces fell to pieces. Almost the whole navy joined the enemy. It was traditionally a Croat force. The air force was in large part, also, Croat. In some cases Croat and Serb units fought each other rather than the Germans. Because of the rapidity of the conquest, (a mere 12 days) many Serbian units were not captured. They melted off into the mountains before German infantry could come up and take their surrender. In the mountains they became the nucleus of the Chetnik and Partisan guerrillas.

The downfall of Yugoslavia in 1941, thus, takes on a kind of inevitability. The nationality problem does not seem as crucial, as many of those who took part in the affairs of those days have claimed. To them there was a sellout by power hungry men who would do anything to retain their positions or gain even more power. I have shown that no one party or nationality ended with very clean hands. Almost everyone was playing his own little game and attempting to maintain relations with everyone else in order not to lose if plans went wrong. But, I think I have shown that none of the principal players was deliberately playing a game of treason for his own benefit. They all seem to have done what they did from the mistaken notion that they were helping whatever national group they came from.

The position of some Yugoslavs is ambiguous, to say the least of it. Both leaders of the Croatian Peasant Party (Radić and Maček) certainly played politics with wild abandon. Maček had very close relations with the Germans and Italians in 1940 and 1941. He does not seem ready to explain them and now that he is dead there seems little chance of ever finding an explanation. But, all that does not seem to have really effected events. The explanation has to be found in the relations of the governments involved.

The real tragedy in the whole situation is the fate of King Alexander and his son King Peter II. Alexander probably was the only figure in a position of influence who might have saved the situation. His death was the real factor that made the denouement inevitable. I feel that if he had survived the nationality problem could have remained under control and might gradually have withered away under his perhaps stern but even handed government. His death has been called the first shot of World War II. Again war was to come on the world from the tangled problems of the Balkans.

In foreign affairs he seemed astute too. He understood how to keep Mussolini reasonable and had built a good relationship with Hitler. He might have kept things under control there, also. At any rate, Prince Paul did not have the king's ability or authority and so both situations got out of hand. Young King Peter simply never had the chance to show what he could do.

With Alexander's undoubted ability to keep all the factions from blowing the country up he might have been able to keep Yugoslavia neutral as things got worse in the area. If Yugoslavia had been united under such an able king Mussolini might never have dared to act in Greece. A possibly hostile Yugoslavia behind him would have been far too much of a threat. Then the pressure to join the Axis Pact would probably not have come. Without the actions of Italy, Hitler would have been glad to maintain his economic control and would not have needed invasion.

Yet, one has to wonder how things would have turned out. The lack of any real popular desire to have King Peter return after the war shows that the public does not seem to have remembered the royal government with any fondness. The ease with which Tito prevented that is quite unlike other countries where the Communists had a much harder time. Despite Alexander's undoubted popularity, was there really any grassroots love of the monarchy? That is a question still to be answered.

Notes

Preface

1. Hoptner, J. B., *Yugoslavia in Crisis, 1934-41* (New York, 1962); Maček, Vladko, *In the Struggle for Freedom* (University Park, Pa., 1957); Ristić, Dragiša, *Yugoslavia's Revolution of 1941* University Park, Pa., 1966).
2. Čulinović, Ferdo, *Slom Stare Jugoslavije* (Zagreb, 1958)
3. Biber, Dušan, *Nacizem in Nemci v Jugoslaviji, 1933-1941* (Ljubljana, 1966)
4. Wuescht, Johann, *Jugoslawien und das Dritte Reich: Eine dokumentierte Geschichte der deutsch-jugoslawischen Beziehungen von 1933 bis 1945* (Stuttgart, 1969)
5. Roberts, Allen, *The Turning Point: The Assassination of Louis Barthou and King Alexander I of Yugoslavia* (New York, 1970)
6. Pribičević, Svetozar, *Diktatura Kralja Aleksandra* (Belgrade, 1953)
7. Adamić, Louis, *My Native Land* (New York, 1943)
8. Graham, Stephen, *Alexander of Yugoslavia* (London, 1938)
9. Armstrong, Hamilton Fish, *Peace and Counter Peace: Memoirs of H. F. Armstrong* (New York, 1971)

Chapters 1-6

1. The early history of the area may be found in L. S. Stavrianos, *The Balkans since 1453* (N. Y., 1958), R. Ristelhuber, *Histoire des Peuples balkaniques* (Paris, 1950), Arthur J. May, *The Habsburg Monarchy, 1867-1914* (Cambridge, Ma., 1951), C. A. Macartney, *Hungary, A Short History* (Chicago, 1962). For Serbia see particularly the works of Slobadan Jovanović.
2. Stavrianos, *op. cit.*, p. 621.
3. Dimko Tomasić, "Croatia in European Politics," *Journal of Central European Affairs*, II, pp. 64-86.
4. *Ibid.*, p. 117
5. *Ibid.*, p. 119
6. Count Carlo Sforza, *Fifty Years of War and Diplomacy in the Balkans* (N. Y., 1940). Essentially a biography of Pasić. Ivo J. Lederer, *Yugoslavia at the Paris Peace Conference* (New Haven, 1963), pp. 4, 5. Charles Jelavich, "Nikola Pasić: Greater Serbia or Jugoslavia?" *Journal of Central European Affairs*, II (1951), pp. 133-152.

7. Hans Kohn, *Panslavism, Its History and Ideology,* 2nd ed, revised, (N. Y., 1960) p. 253. Ferdinand Sisić, *Jugoslovenska Misao* (Belgrade, 1937). Herman Wendel, *Der Kampf der Südslawen um Freiheit und Einheit* (Frankfurt am Main, 1925). These last two titles are among the best on the subject.

8. May, op. cit., pp. 72-80. J. B. Hoptner, *Yugoslavia in Crisis* (N. Y., 1962), pp. 2-3, Francis Dvornik, *The Slavs: Their early History and Civilization* (Boston, 1956) p. 278 for treaty of 1102 with Hungary.

9. Lederer, *op. cit.,* pp. 24-26; M. Paulova, *Jugoslovenski Odbor* (Zagreb, 1925); Hoptner, *op. cit.,* p. 3; Stephen Graham, *Alexander of Yugoslavia* (London, 1938), pp. 283-284.

10. Sforza, *op. cit.,* p. 185

11. Svetozar Pribičević, *Diktatura Kralja Aleksandra* (Belgrade, 1953)

12. Ferdo Čulinović, *Slom Stare Jugoslavije* (Zagreb, 1958) p. 54. Vladko Maček, *In the Struggle for Freedom* (College Park, Pa., 1957), pp. 41, 42.

13. George G. Jackson, Jr., *Comintern and Peasant in East Europe, 1919-1930* (N. Y., 1966), pp. 40-46. Dimko Tomasić, "The Struggle for Power in Jugoslavia," *Journal of Central European Affairs,* I (July, 1941), p. 150.

14. Graham, *op. cit.,* pp. 127-128. Maček, *op. cit.,* pp. 28, 35, 37. This party wanted to solve the Croatian Problem by a trialistic solution of the Habsburg state. Croatia would become the ruler of a south slavic bloc equal to Austria and Hungary. Tomasić, The Struggle, *op. cit.,* pp. 156-157.

15. Graham, *op. cit.,* pp. 127-128. Leigh White, *The Long Balkan Night* (New York, 1944), p. 179. Tomasić, Croatia, *op. cit.,* p. 81.

16. See Sforza, *op. cit.* for Pasić and the Radical Party.

17. Paul Shoup, *Communism and the Yugoslav National Question* (New York, 1968) pp. 19-21, note p. 51. R. V. Burks, *The Dynamics of Communism in Eastern Europe* (Princeton, 1961), pp. 107-108. Ustavortvorne Skupstine, *statisticki pogled izbora narodnik poslanika* (Belgrade, 1921).

18. Stavrianos, *op. cit.,* p. 628.

19. Maček, *op. cit.,* pp. 109-118.

20. *Ibid.,* pp. 121-125.

21. Malbone Graham, "Constitutional Development, 1914-1942" in *Yugoslavia,* ed. Robert J. Kerner (Berkeley and Los Angeles, 1949), pp. 125-129. For maps showing all the internal changes from 1921 through 1941 see ed. Werner Markert, *Ost-europa Handbuch: Jugoslavia* (Koln, Graz, 1954), pp. 86-88.

22. Earl Mittleman, *The Nationality Problem in Yugoslavia; A Survey of Developments, 1921-1953* (New York, Unpublished Ph.D. dissertation done at N. Y. U., 1954), pp. 69-71. Maček, *op. cit.,* pp. 124-126.

23. Ed. Charles and Barbara Jelavich, *The Balkans in transition* (Berkeley and Los Angeles, 1963), pp. 331-333.

24. Dimko Tomasić, "The Struggle for power in Yugoslavia," *Journal of Central European Affairs,* I, p. 153.

25. Macartney and Palmer, *op. cit.,* pp. 225-226; Malbone Graham, *op. cit.,* p. 126.

26. King Peter II, *A King's Heritage* (London, Cassell and Co., 1955), p. 39.

27. Hamilton Fish Armstrong, "After the Assassination of King Alexander," *Foreign Affairs,* XIII, pp. 206-210.

28. Mittleman, *op. cit.*, p. 84.

29. Tomasić, Struggle, *op. cit.*, p. 158.

30. Elizabeth Wiskemann, "Yugoslavia and the Anschluss," *The Contemporary Review*, vol. 148, pp. 47-51.

31. Lederer, *op. cit.*, pp. 5-11.

32. Sir Ivone Kirkpatrick, *Mussolini, A Study in Power* (New York, Hawthorn Books, 1964) pp. 78-80, 170; Macartney and Palmer, *op. cit.*, pp. 258-271.

33. S. Graham, *op. cit.*, p. 128.

34. Ernst Nolte, *Three Faces of Fascism* (New York, Holt, Rinehart and Winston, 1966) pp. 12-14.

35. King Peter II, *op. cit.*, pp. 40-44

36. Graham, Alexander, *op. cit.*, p. 127.

37. Macartney, *October 15th: A History of Modern Hungary, 1929-1945* (Edinburgh, Edinburgh University Press, 1956), pp. 85-86. Macartney, *Hungary and Her Successors* (London, Oxford University Press, Royal Institute of International Affairs, 1937), pp. 373-375. Graham, Alexander, *op. cit.*, p. 127.

38. Macartney, "October 15th," *op. cit.*, p. 86.

39. S. Graham, *op. cit.*, p. 41.

40. King Peter II, *op, cit.*, p. 41.

41. Tomasić, The Struggle, *op. cit.*, p. 157.

42. S. Graham, *op. cit.*, pp. 127-128; Wiskemann, *op. cit.*, pp. 46, 47, 48, 50.

43. Constantin Fotitch, *The War We Lost* (New York, The Viking Press, 1948), pp. 7-8.

44. John Crane, *The Little Entente* (New York, The Macmillan Co., 1931), pp. VII, 9. Hoptner, *op. cit.*, p. 10.

45. Crane, *op. cit.*, pp. 22-25. Alan Cassels, *Mussolini's Early Diplomacy* (Princeton, 1970), pp. 344-348. The classic account of the Balkan Entente is in *"The Balkan Conferences and the Balkan Entente, 1930-35"* by Robert J. Kerner and Harry Howard (Berkeley, U. of California Press, 1936). It is, however, nothing but a summary of the public record. It says nothing about the Greater Yugoslavia problem.

46. Crane, *op. cit.*, pp. 39-41.

47. Wiskemann, *op. cit.*, p. 47.

48. Pierre Renouvin, *World War II and Its Origins* (New York, 1969), pp. 64-65. A. J. P. Taylor, *The Origins of the Second World War* (New York, 1962), p. 88.

49. The story of this taken essentially from Macartney and Palmer, *op. cit.*, pp. 317-320.

50. *Ibid.*, p. 317.

51. *Ibid.*, pp. 317-318.

52. *Ibid.*, p. 318

53. *Ibid.*, pp. 19-20, 174-175; Hoptner, *op. cit.*, pp. 14-15; Stavrianos, *op. cit.*, pp. 519-523, 648-649.

54. Hoptner, *op. cit.*, p. 14; Markert, *op. cit.*, p. 92.

55. *Ibid.* Kerner and Howard, op. cit., pp. 13-18.

56. *Ibid.*, pp. 14-15; Kerner and Howard, *op. cit.*, This paragraph summarizes most of their work.

57. *Ibid.*, p. 15; Kirkpatrick, *op. cit.*, pp. 286-288; Kerner and Howard, *op. cit.*, pp. 115, 116.
58. *Ibid.*
59. *Ibid.*, p. 16; Markert, *op. cit.*, p. 92.
60. Macartney and Palmer, *op. cit.*, pp. 318-319.
61. Hoptner, *op. cit.*, pp. 16-17; Johann Wuescht, *Jugoslawien und das Dritte Reich: eine dokumentierte Geschichte der deutsch-jugoslawischen Beziehungen* (Stuttgart, 1969), p. 11.
62. For example, Ferdo Čulinović, *Slom Stare Jugoslavije* (Zagreb, 1958). This is the most objective history of the interwar period put out in Yugoslavia after World War II.
63. Nolte, *op. cit.*, p. 14.
64. S. Graham, *op. cit.*, pp. 127-131; Tomasić, Croatia, *op. cit.*, p. 81.
65. S. Graham, *op. cit.*, pp. 127-128.
66. *Ibid.*, p. 129; Cassels, *op. cit.*, pp. 344-348.
67. Graham, *op. cit.*, pp. 127-129; King Peter II, *op. cit.*, pp. 39-43.
68. *Documents of German Foreign Policy,* Dept. of State. (Hereinafter referred to as D. G. F. P.) Series C, II, (Washington, Govt. Printing Office), p. 498; Hoptner, *op. cit.*, p. 24; Graham, *op. cit.*, pp. 283, 237.
69. Andre François-Poncet, *The Fateful Years,* (New York, 1948), pp. 159-161; S. Graham, *op. cit.*, p. 215.
70. François-Poncet, *op. cit.*, pp. 158-161.
71. Taylor, *op. cit.*, p. 69; H. R. Trevor-Roper, ed., *Blitzkrieg to Defeat* (New York, 1964), pp. XIII-XVIII.
72. Alexander Dallin, *German Rule in Russia,* (London, 1957), pp. 20-21.
73. Hoptner, *op. cit.*, p. 24; Wiskemann, *op. cit.*, p. 47.
74. Nolte, *op. cit.*, p. 461; S. Harrison Thomson, *Czechoslovakia in European History,* (London, 1965), pp. 378-379, 403.
75. Macartney, *op. cit.*, p. 136-154.
76. *Ibid.*
77. *Ibid.*, pp. 138-139.
78. Hoptner, *op. cit.*, p. 24
79. S. Graham, *op. cit.*, pp. 127-129
80. *Ibid.*, p. 130.
81. *Ibid.*, pp. 130-168.
82. Pierre Renouvin, *War and Aftermath, 1914-1929,* (New York, 1968), pp. 222-223.
83. Renouvin, Origins, *op. cit.*, pp. 26-28.
84. *Ibid.*, p. 64; Hoptner, *op. cit.*, pp. 22-25
85. Hoptner, *op. cit.*, pp. 22-25.
86. *Ibid.*; Macartney and Palmer, *op. cit.*, pp. 326-327
87. Kirkpatrick, *op. cit.*, p. 298.; Hamilton F. Armstrong, *Peace and Counter Peace,* (New York, 1971), p. 294.
88. Macartney and Palmer, *op. cit.*, p. 276.
89. *Ibid.*
90. Fotitch, *op. cit.*, p. 8.
91. *Ibid.*
92. Kirkpatrick, *op. cit.*, p. 298.

93. Culinović, *op. cit.*, p. 23; *Definitivni regultati popisa stannvistva 31-31-B1 g. Bd. IV* (Sarajevo, 1940), p. VII, Tab. I, II.

94. Jozo Tomasevich, *Peasants, Politics and Economic Change in Yugoslavia* (Stanford, 1955), p. 318.

95. *Ibid.*, p. 309.

96. Culinović, *op. cit.*, p. 23.

97. D. Beatrice McGown, "Agriculture," in *Yugoslavia*, ed. by Robert Kerner, *op. cit.*, p. 161; Tomasevich, *op. cit.*, pp. 160, 171, 172, 211-212, 321-324, 381-382; *Statisticki godisnjak, 1936*, pp. 88, 89.

98. Josef Matl, "Der Gesellschaftliche und Mewtalle Strukturwandel bei den Südslawen im 19 und 20 Jahrhundert," *Südostforschungen XII* (Munich, 1951), p. 111; Vladimar Rozenberg, Jovan Kosić, *Ko finansira jugoslovensku privredu?* (Belgrade, 1940), p. 90.

99. Jackson, *op. cit.*, p. 217; Maček, *op. cit.*, pp. 80-81; Robert Livingston, *Stepan Radić and the Croatian Peasant Party, 1904-1929* (Cambridge, Mass., Unpublished Ph.D. dissertation at Harvard University, 1959), p. 559.

100. Jozo Tomasevich, "Foreign Economic Relations, 1918-1941" in *Yugoslavia* ed. R. Kerner, *op. cit.*, pp. 200-201.

101. Stavrianos, *op. cit.*, pp. 632-633; Seton-Watson, *op. cit.*, pp. 229-230; Tomasevich, *Foreign, op. cit.*, p. 185.

102. Tomasevich, foreign, *op. cit.*, p. 182.

103. *Ibid.*, pp. 182-183.

104. *Ibid.*, p. 170-174

105. *Ibid.*, p. 171; Hoptner, *op. cit.*, p. 95-96.

106. Tomasevich, *op. cit.*, p. 173; Hoptner, *op. cit.*, pp. 95-96; Wilhelm Treue, "Das Dritte Reich und die Westmachte auf dem Balkan," *Vierteljahrhefte fur Zeitgeschichte*, January 1953, pp. 45-64.

107. Wuescht, *op. cit.*, pp. 98-100.

108. Hoptner, *op. cit.*, pp. 105-107.

109. Tomasevich, *op. cit.*, p. 209; *Statisticki godisnjak, 1936*, pp. 242, 243; 1940, pp. 234, 235.

110. *Statisticki godisnjak, 1931, 1936, 1938-1939*.

111. Tomasevich, foreign, *op. cit.*, p. 180.

112. *Ibid.*, p. 206; Wuescht, *op. cit.*, pp. 100-108.

113. *Ibid.*, pp. 96-97; Hoptner, *op. cit.*, pp. 107-108.

114. Hoptner, *op. cit.*, pp. 100-108; Milan Stojadinovic, *Ni Rat ni Pakt* (Buenos Aires, 1963), pp. 544ff.

115. Tomasevich, foreign, *op. cit.*, p. 208; Hoptner, *op. cit.*, p. 201; Paul Einzig, *Bloodless Invasion: German Economic Invasion of the Danubian States and the Balkans* (London, 2nd ed., 1939), p. 18.

116. Einzig, *op. cit.*, p. 18.

117. Tomasević, foreign, *op. cit.*, pp. 205-206-207; M. W. Fodor, *South of Hitler* (Boston, 1939), pp. 261, 263.

118. Franz Neumann, *Behemoth: The Structure and Practice of National Socialism, 1933-1944* (New York, 1966), pp. 328-329, 334-336.

119. Tomasevich, *Peasants, op. cit.*, p. 175; Wuescht, *op. cit.*, p. 99.

120. Hoptner, *op. cit.*, pp. 102-103.

121. Fodor, *op. cit.*, p. 262, See Footnote 117. Stojadinović says 20% above the world price.

122. Hoptner, *op. cit.*, p. 103.
123. Einzig, *op. cit.*, p. 47.
124. Einzig, *op. cit.*, p. 77.
125. Tomasevich, foreign, *op. cit.*, p. 210.
126. Einzig, *op. cit.*, pp. 22-23.
127. *Ibid.*, pp. 31-33.
128. Tomasevich, foreign, *op. cit.*, p. 179; Seton-Watson, *op. cit.*, p. 383.
129. Einzig, *op. cit.*, p. 37.
130. Tomasevich, foreign, *op. cit.*, pp. 208-210.
131. *Ibid.*, p. 210.
132. *Ibid.*
133. Hoptner, *op. cit.*, pp. 104-106.
134. *Ibid.*, pp. 107-108.
135. Tomasevich, foreign, *op. cit.*, p. 213.
136. *Ibid.*, p. 213.
137. *Ibid.*, p. 213.
138. Armstrong, *op. cit.*, pp. 342-343.
139. *Loc. cit.;* Hoptner, *op. cit.*, p. 26.
140. Dragiša N. Ristić, *Yugoslavia's Revolution of 1941* (University Park, Pa., 1966), p. 24; Hoptner, *op. cit.*, pp. 32-33.
141. Hoptner, *op. cit.*, pp. 33-34.
142. Nolte, *op. cit.*, pp. 12-14.
143. Hoptner, *op. cit.*, pp. 121-122; *DGFP.* D, IV, No. 434; Ciano's Diary, 1939-1943, *op. cit.*, p. 13; *Ciano's Diplomatic Papers*, Ed. by Malcolm Muggeridge, Trans, by Stuart Hood (London, Odhams, 1948), p. 104.
144. D. Mitrany, *Marx Against the Peasant: A Study in Social Dogmatism* (Chapel Hill, 1951), p. 122; Nolte, *op. cit.*, pp. 14-15.
145. Dimko Tomasić, "The Struggle for Power in Jugoslavia," *Journal of Central European Affairs,* I (April, 1941), pp. 157-158; Leigh White, *The Long Balkan Night* (New York, 1944), p. 179; Nolte, *op. cit.*, p. 14.
146. Kerner, *op. cit.*, p. 134.
147. Hoptner, *op. cit.*, pp. 46, 47; Fotitch, *op. cit.*, p. 14.
148. Hoptner, *op. cit.*, pp. 59-60; Fotitch *op. cit.*, p. 14.
149. Macartney, *op. cit.*, p. 337; Fotitch, *op. cit.*, pp. 13, 14.
150. Renouvin, World War II, *op. cit.*, p. 27; Hoptner, *op. cit.*, p. 22.
151. *DGFP*, C, II, Nos., 316, 318; III, Nos., 263, 264; Hoptner, *op. cit.*, p. 24.
152. Claude Eylan, *La Vie et la Mort D'Alexandre Ire* (Paris, 1935), p. 183.
153. Anthony Eden, *Facing the Dictators* (Boston, 1962), p. 121.
154. Eden, *Loc. cit.;* M. W. Fodor, *op. cit.*, p. 53; Allen Roberts, *The Turning Point: The Assassination of Louis Barthou and King Alexander of Yugoslavia* (New York, 1970), pp. 135, 141.
155. Eden, *op. cit.*, pp. 120-133; Roberts, *op. cit.*, pp. 36, 66, 92, 128, 135, 166, 171-174; Graham, *op. cit.*, pp. 128, 129; Andre François-Poncet, *The Fateful Years*, trans. by Jacques Le Clercq (New York, 1949), pp. 159-161.
156. Eden, *op. cit.*, pp. 120-133; Roberts, *op. cit.*, pp. 148-158.
157. Eden, *op. cit.*, p. 132.
158. A. J. P. Taylor, *op. cit.*, pp. 84, 85.

159. A. J. Barker, *The Civilizing Mission: A History of the Italo-Ethiopian War* (New York, 1968), pp. 76-80.

160. Eden, *op. cit.*, pp. 139-144.

161. *DGFP*, C, III, Nos. 517, 519; Gerhard Meinck, *Hitler und die deutsche Aufrüstung, 1933-1937* (Wiesbaden, 1959), pp. 92-96.

162. A. J. P. Taylor, *op. cit.*, p. 85.

163. Barker, *op. cit.*, pp. 64-68; Taylor, *op. cit.*, pp. 87-88; Kirkpatrick, *op. cit.*, pp. 319-321.

164. Hoptner, *op. cit.*, p. 28; Graham, *op. cit.*, p. 237; Roberts, *op. cit.*, p. 158.

165. Hoptner, *op. cit.*, pp. 28-30.

166. Graham, *op. cit.*, pp. 237-262.

167. Gerald Weinberg, *The Foreign Policy of Hitler's Germany, 1933-1936* (Chicago, 1970), pp. 228, 229; Hoptner, *op. cit.*, pp. 98-102.

168. Weinberg, *op. cit.*, pp. 216, 217; Barker, *op. cit.*, pp. 78-79.

169. Hoptner, *op. cit.*, pp. 32, 33.

170. *Ibid.*, p. 33

171. *Loc. cit.*

172. *Ibid.*, pp. 33, 34.

173. *Ibid.*, p. 34.

174. *Ibid.*, p. 35.

175. *Ibid.*, p. 36; Weinberg, *op. cit.*, pp. 228, 229.

176. Hoptner, *op. cit.*, p. 36.

177. *Ibid.*, pp. 36, 37.

178. *Ibid.*, p. 37; Eden, *op. cit.*, pp. 309-318.

179. Eden, *op. cit.*, p. 359; Barker, *op. cit.*, p. 321; Arnold Toynbee, ed. *Documents on International Affairs* (London, II, 1935), pp. 487-489. Cited hereafter as DIA.

180. Eden, *op. cit.*, pp. 346, 356.

181. Hoptner, *op. cit.*, p. 39.

182. *DIA*, II (1935), pp. 304-309.

183. Hoptner, *op. cit.*, pp. 39, 40.

184. *Ibid.*, pp. 41, 42.

185. *Ibid.*, p. 43.

186. Mario Cervi, *The Hollow Legions: Mussolini's Blunder in Greece, 1940-41* (New York, 1971) p. 56; Hoptner, *op. cit.*, p. 160.

187. Cervi, *op. cit.*, pp. 271-271; Hoptner, *op. cit.*, pp. 160, 161.

188. Ristić, *op. cit.*, pp. 125, 126; Hoptner, *op. cit.*, p. 43.

189. Macartney, Ind., *op. cit.*, p. 303.

190. Taylor, *op. cit.*, pp. 95, 96.

191. *Ibid.*, p. 97; Weinberg, *op. cit.*, pp. 239-254.

192. Weinberg, *op. cit.*, p. 239; Erich Eyck, *A History of the Weimar Republic, vol. I* (Cambridge, Ma., 1962), pp. 85, 86; Eden, *op. cit.*, p. 370.

193. Eden, *op. cit.*, p. 379.

194. Eden, *op. cit.*, p. 370.

195. *Ibid.*, pp. 108, 109; Weinberg, *op. cit.*, pp. 74, 184.

196. Eden, *op. cit.*, pp. 378-382.

197. Weinberg, *op. cit.*, pp. 251, 252.

144 NOTES

198. This became pretty general in the 1930's. Everyone was so hypnotized with the horror of air war and supposed German efficiency that, if anything, German propaganda claims were universally believed to be too low. Thus, efforts to catch up with or challenge Germany were given up before they could begin. Charles Lindbergh, *The Wartime Journals of C. Lindbergh* (New York, 1970), pp. 26, 35-36, 70, 73, 82-83. Compare with Alastair Horne, *To Lose a Battle: France 1940* (Boston, 1969), pp. 81, 185.
199. Renouvin, *op. cit.*, pp. 78-85; Eden, *op. cit.*, p. 393.
200. Hoptner, *op. cit.*, p. 44.
201. *Ibid.*, p. 44.
202. Weinberg, *op. cit.*, p. 252; Donald C. Watt, "German Plans for the Reoccupation of the Rhineland: A Note." *Journal of Contemporary History*, vol, I, 4, p. 193.
203. Weinberg, *op. cit.*, p. 252; Watt, *op. cit.*, p. 199.
204. Hoptner, *op. cit.*, pp. 44-45.
205. *Ibid.*, p. 45.
206. *DGFP*, C, IV, Nos. 91, 93, 198, 261.
207. Hoptner, *op. cit.*, pp. 44-47; U. S. State Dept., *Foreign Relations of the United States* (Washington, D. C., Government Printing Office, vol. I (1936), p. 289. Hereafter cited as FRUS; *DGFP*, C, V, Nos. 48, 56, 202, 216; IV, Nos. 191, 434, 446, 447.
208. Hoptner, *op. cit.*, p. 47; Weinberg, *op. cit.*, pp. 226-228; *DGFP*, C, IV, Nos. 444, 533, 550, 576.
209. Hoptner, *op. cit.*, pp. 54-55; Weinberg, *op. cit.*, pp. 230, 231; *DGFP*, C, II, Nos. 322, 387,; IV, Nos. 64, 110, 153, 160, 175, 339, 353, 362, 385, 393, 401, 405, 427, 431, 478, 516, 535, 561, 572, 581.
210. Hoptner, *op. cit.*, p. 55.
211. *Ibid.*, pp. 55-56.
212. *Ibid.*, pp. 55-60.
213. *Ibid.*, pp. 294, 110, 62; *DGFP*, C, V, Nos, 374, 540.
214. Hoptner, *op. cit.*, p. 83.
215. *Ibid.*, p. 62.
216. *Ibid.*, pp. 62-81.
217. *Ibid.*, pp. 65-67, 71, 74.
218. *Ibid.*, pp. 76-81.
219. *Ibid.*, pp. 81-82. Full text of the treaty in *Ibid.*, pp. 301-303.
220. *FRUS*, I (1937), p. 71.
221. Ciano's Diary 1937-38, *op. cit.*, p. 41.
222. Hoptner, *op. cit.*, pp. 82, 89; Ciano's Diary 1937-38, *op. cit.*, pp. 41-42.
223. Quoted in Hoptner from Galeazzo Ciano, *L'Europa Verso la Catastrofe* (Verona, 1948), pp. 151-162.
224. *Ibid.*, p. 82.
225. Ferdo Culinović, *Slom Stare Jugoslavije* (Zagreb, 1958), pp. 89-91; Hoptner, *op. cit.*, pp. 87, 121-122; Ciano's Diary 1937-38, *op. cit.*, pp. 41-42; *DGFP*, D, V, No. 163.
226. Vladko Maček, *In the Struggle for Freedom* (University Park, Pa., 1957), pp. 202, 203; Hoptner, *op. cit.*, p. 127.
227. *DGFP*, D, V, No. 163.
228. *FRUS*, I, (1937), 208; *DGFP*, C, I, No. 279.

229. *Statisticki godisnjak,* 1930, 1936, 1940.
230. *Loc. cit.*
231. Hoptner, *op. cit.,* pp. 105-106; Tomasevich, *op. cit.,* pp. 207-209.
232. *Ibid.,* pp. 104-105.
233. *DGFP,* D, V, No. 159.
234. Hoptner, *op. cit.,* pp. 105-106.
235. *Ibid.,* p. 107.
236. *Ibid.,* p. 105; Kerner, *op. cit.,* pp. 208-212.
237. Hoptner, *op. cit.,* p. 106; Toynbee, Survey, *op. cit.,* 1938. p. 62.
238. Hoptner, *op. cit.,* pp. 106-107.
239. *Ibid.,* pp. 107-108.
240. *DGFP,* D, IX, No. 442.
241. Hoptner, *op. cit.,* p. 121.
242. *Ibid.,* pp. 129-130.
243. Maček, *op. cit.,* pp. 154-155.
244. *Ibid.,* p. 164; Hoptner, *op. cit.,* p. 130.
245. Hoptner, *op. cit.,* pp. 130-131.
246. *Ibid.,* p. 131; Maček, *op. cit.,* pp. 181-182.
247. Maček, *op. cit.,* pp. 183-185; Hoptner, *op. cit.,* pp. 131-133.
248. *DGFP,* D, V, No. 291.
249. *DGFP,* D, V, Nos. 291, 310, 311, 385.
250. Ciano's Diary, 1939-43, *op. cit.,* pp. 23-24; Hoptner, *op. cit.,* p. 133.
251. Hoptner, *op. cit.,* pp. 134-135.
252. *Ibid.,* p. 136; Wuescht, *op. cit.,* pp. 183-184.
253. Hoptner, *op. cit.,* p. 136; Wuescht, *op. cit.,* p. 183 quotes the Zagreb Resolution.
254. *DGFP,* D, V, Nos. 300, 310, 205.
255. Ciano's Diary, 1939-43, *op. cit.,* pp. 48-49.
256. Hoptner, *op. cit.,* p. 137; Ciano's Diary, 1939-43, *op. cit.,* p. 49; *DGFP,* D, VI, No. 15.
257. *DGFP,* D, IV, No. 37.
258. Hoptner, *op. cit.,* p. 138.
259. Ciano's Diary, 1939-43, *op. cit.,* pp. 41-42.
260. Ciano's Diary, 1939-43, *op. cit.,* pp. 247-248; Walter Hagen, *Die Geheime Front* (Linz and Vienna, 1950), pp. 209-210.
261. Maček, *op. cit.,* pp. 186-187.
262. Ciano's Diary, 1939-43, *op. cit.,* p. 51.
263. Maček, *op. cit.,* pp. 187-189.
264. Ciano's Diary, 1939-43, *op. cit.,* p. 89.
265. *Ibid.,* p. 93. Agreement given in full in Wuescht, *op. cit.,* p. 288. However, the date is given as April 26, 1939. This seems an error since Ciano gives May 26 as the date of this agreement. The negotiations for it apparently only began in May as well. Since this is a translation into German, it is probably a translation error.
266. Maček, *op. cit.,* pp. 189-190; Ciano, *op. cit.,* pp. 96-97.
267. *DGFP,* III, 4, No. 378.
268. *Ibid.,* No. 379.
269. Ciano's Diary, 1939-43, *op. cit.,* pp. 54, 58.
270. *Ibid.,* pp. 61-63.
271. *Ibid.,* p. 64.

272. *DGFP*, D, VI, No. 192.
273. *Ibid.*, No. 256; Ciano, *op. cit.*, pp. 75-76; *DGFP*, III, 5, No. 544.
274. Hoptner, *op. cit.*, p. 144 in footnote 25.
275. *DGFP*, III, 4, Nos. 426, 511, 542.
276. Hoptner, *op. cit.*, p. 147; Ristić, *op. cit.*, pp. 30-31.
277. *DGFP*, D, VI, Nos. 262, 474; Hoptner, *op. cit.*, p. 148.
278. Hoptner, *op. cit.*, p. 148.
279. *DGFP*, III, 6, pp. 11-12, 438-39; Dragiša Cvetković, *Dokumenty o Jugoslaviji* (Paris, 1939), vol. 9, No. 1034; *FRUS*, I (1939), pp. 198-200, 287-288.
280. Cvetković, *op. cit.*, No. 7, pp. 8-12; Hoptner, *op. cit.*, p. 149; Ristić, *op. cit.*, p. 32.
281. Hoptner, *op. cit.*, p. 149.
282. Cvetković, *op. cit.*, *"Srpsko-Hrvatski Sporazum, 1939"* (1952), pp. 18-26.
283. Maček, *op. cit.*, pp. 186, 187-188; Hoptner, *op. cit.*, p. 150.
284. Maček, *op. cit.*, pp. 187-188; Hoptner, *op. cit.*, p. 150.
285. Maček, *op. cit.*, p. 188; Hoptner, *op. cit.*, pp. 150-151.
286. Maček, *op. cit.*, p. 189; Hoptner, *op. cit.*, p. 151.
287. Maček, *op. cit.*, p. 189.
288. *DGFP*, D, VI, No. 295.
289. Maček, *op. cit.*, pp. 190-191; Hoptner, *op. cit.*, pp. 151-152.
290. Hoptner, *op. cit.*, p. 152.
291. *New York Times*, August 2, 1939, pp. 10, 18.
292. Maček, *op. cit.*, p. 191; Hoptner, *op. cit.*, p. 153.
293. Maček, *op. cit.*, pp. 192-195; Hoptner, *op. cit.*, pp. 153-155.
294. Hoptner, *op. cit.*, pp. 154-155.
295. *Loc. cit.*
296. *Ibid.*, pp. 155-156.
297. *Loc, cit.*
298. *DGFP*, D, VI, No. 680.
299. *Ibid.*, No. 691.
300. Hoptner, *op. cit.*, pp. 156-157.
301. *Ibid.*, p. 158.
302. *DGFP*, D, V, Nos. 288, 300, 307, 409, 683.
303. *Ibid.*, VI, Nos. 573, 615, 620, 686, 210, 279, 687, 703, 758.
304. *Ibid.*, VIII, Nos. 53, 117; VII, No. 532.
305. Fotitch, *op. cit.*, pp. 22-24.
306. *FRUS*, II (1939), pp. 888-890.
307. Tomasevich, *op. cit.*, p. 242.
308. Branko Lazić, *Tito et la Revolution, 1937-1956* (Paris, 1957), p. 53.
309. Hoptner, *op. cit.*, p. 161.
310. *DGFP*, D, V, No. 304.
311. Macartney, *op. cit.*, p. 145.
312. *DIA*, I (1938), pp. 287-288.
313. *DGFP*, D, VI, No. 67.
314. *Ibid.*, No. 884.
315. Cvetković, *op. cit.*, No. 8.
316. *DGFP*, D, VI, No. 689.
317. *DGFP*, III, 6, Nos. 393, 534.

318. Grigoire Gafencu, *Prelude to the Russian Campaign* (London, 1945), pp. 124, 260.

319. *DGFP*, D, IX, No. 198.

320. Hoptner, *op. cit.*, pp. 165-166; Ciano's Diary, *op. cit.*, pp. 124, 125; Ciano's Diplomatic Papers, *op. cit.*, pp. 297-304.

321. Ciano's Diary, *op. cit.*, p. 125.

322. Hoptner, *op. cit.*, pp. 166-167.

323. Ciano's Diary, *op. cit.*, p. 131.

324. Ciano's Diary, *op. cit.*, pp. 143, 183.

325. Ciano's Diary, *op. cit.*, p. 183; Pietro Badoglio, *Italy in the Second World War* (London, 1948), pp. 6, 8; Kirkpatrick, *op. cit.*, pp. 424-427.

326. Kirkpatrick, *op. cit.*, pp. 431-432; Ciano's Diary, *op. cit.*, p. 142.

327. *DGFP*, III, 6, No. 393; 7, Nos. 554-556.

328. *DGFP*, D, VII, No. 112.

329. *FRUS*, I (1939), pp. 420-421.

330. Raymond Brugère, *Veni, Vidi, Vichy* (Paris, 1944), pp. 165-166.

331. *FRUS*, I (1939), p. 238.

332. Brugère, *op. cit.*, p. 4.

333. Maxime Weygand, *Memoires: Rappele au Service* (Paris, 1950), vol. III, p. 41.

334. Sir LLewellyn Woodward, *British Foreign Policy in the Second World War* (London, 1970), vol. I, p. 23; J. R. M. Butler, *Grand Strategy* (London, 1957), vol. II, p. 70.

335. Woodward, *op. cit.*, vol. I, pp. 28-29.

336. Butler, *op. cit.*, p. 299.

337. Germany, Auswartiges Amt, *Dokumente zum Konflikt mit Jugoslawien und Greichenland* (Berlin, 1941), Nos. 51, 58-60; Weygand, *op. cit.*, p. 64.

338. *DGFP*, D, IX, Nos. 100, 191.

339. Ciano's Diary, *op. cit.*, p. 234.

340. Churchill, *Their Finest Hour: Vol. II, The History of the Second World War* (Boston, 1948), pp. 128-129.

341. *DGFP*, D, VIII, No. 669.

342. Hoptner, *op. cit.*, p. 172; F. W. Deakin, *The Brutal Friendship* (New York, 1962), pp. 7, 8, 12; Cervi, *op. cit.*, pp. XI, XVIII.

343. *Ibid.*, p. 173; Deakin, *op. cit.*, p. 13.

344. Ciano's Diary, *op. cit.*, pp. 243-244, 246-249.

345. Hoptner, *op. cit.*, pp. 173-174.

346. *Ibid.*, p. 174.

347. *Ibid.*, pp. 174-175; *DGFP*, D, VIII, No. 155.

348. Hoptner, *op. cit.*, p. 175.

349. *Ibid.*, p. 176.

350. Brugère, *op. cit.*, pp. 167-168.

351. Hoptner, *op. cit.*, p. 177.

352. *Loc. cit.*

353. *Ibid.*, pp. 177-178.

354. Raymond Sontag, *Nazi-Soviet Relations, 1939-41* (Washington, D. C., Dept. of State, Government Printing Office, 1948) pp. 166-168.

355. Hoptner, *op. cit.*, pp. 178-179.

356. Sontag, *op. cit.*, pp. 178-181, 190-194.

357. Sontag, *op. cit.*, pp. 226-254.

358. Adam B. Ulam, *Expansion and Coexistence: The History of Soviet Foreign Policy, 1917-1967* (New York, 1969), pp. 302-303.
359. Hoptner, *op. cit.*, p. 180.
360. *DGFP*, D, IX, Nos, 341; Ciano's Diary, *op. cit.*, pp. 256-257.
361. *DGFP*, D, IX, Nos., 356, 360, 373.
362. Ciano's Diary, *op. cit.*, pp. 263-264; Kirkpatrick, *op. cit.*, p. 264; Hoptner, *op. cit.*, p. 180.
363. Hoptner, *op. cit.*, see footnote p. 181; For documents see Auswartiges Amt, Dokumente zum Konflikt, *op. cit.*
364. Ciano's Diary, *op. cit.*, p. 275; *DGFP*, D, X, No. 129.
365. *DGFP*, D, X, Nos. 343, 353.
366. Ciano's Diary, *op. cit.*, p. 284.
367. Hoptner, *op. cit.*, p. 182.
368. Ciano's Diary, *op. cit.*, pp. 297, 299, 300; *DGFP*, D, X, Nos. 357, 388; XI, Nos. 12, 123, 136, 277, 324-325; Cervi, *op. cit.*, pp. 59-61.
369. Deakin, *op. cit.*, p. 12; Ciano's Diary, *op. cit.*, p. 298.
370. Hoptner, *op. cit.*, pp. 183-187; *DGFP*, D, XI, pp. 110, 231, 320, 334, 418.
371. Hoptner, *op. cit.*, pp. 186-187.
372. Quoted in Ristić, *op. cit.*, p. 44.
373. Hoptner, *op. cit.*, pp. 187-188; Ciano's Diary, *op. cit.*, pp. 304-305; Velimir Terzić, *Jugoslavija u Aprilskom Ratu, 1941* (Titograd, 1963), pp. 96-97.
374. Hoptner, *op. cit.*, p. 188; Terzić, *op. cit.*, pp. 96-97.
375. Ristić, *op. cit.*, pp. 46-47; Martin van Creveld, "25 October 1940: A Historical Puzzle," *Journal of Contemporary History*, London, vol. 6, No. 3, pp. 87-88.
376. Sontag, *op. cit.*, pp. 207-213.
277. *Ibid.*, p. 216.
378. *Ibid.*, pp. 217-254.
379. Ciano's Diary, *op. cit.*, pp. 307-308.
380. Sontag, *op. cit.*, pp. 258-259.
381. Ristić, *op. cit.*, pp. 47-48.
382. *Ibid.*, p. 48.
383. Ciano's Diary, *op. cit.*, pp. 307-308; Danilo Gregorić, *So Endete Jugoslawien* (Leipzig, 1943), pp. 95-98; *DGFP*, D, XI, pp. 532-533, 608.
384. Hoptner, *op. cit.*, pp. 188-189.
385. *Ibid.*, p. 189.
386. Ciano's Diary. *op. cit.*, p. 308.
387. Gregorić, *op. cit.*, pp. 108-116; Terzić *op. cit.*, pp. 92, 93.
388. *DGFP*, D, XI, p. 637.
389. Ristić, *op. cit.*, p. 49.
390. *DGFP*, D, XI, No. 692.
391. *Ibid.*, pp. 728-735; Terzić, *op. cit.*, pp. 93, 94.
392. *Ibid.*, p. 672.
393. *Ibid.*, p. 735.
394. *Ibid.*, p. 820.
395. *Ibid.*, p. 927.
396. *Ibid.*, p. 930.
397. *Ibid.*, p. 641.

398. *Ibid.*, pp. 803-804.
399. *Ibid.*, p. 993.
400. Hoptner, *op. cit.*, p. 190.
401. *Ibid.*, pp. 190-191.
402. *Ibid.*, p. 191.
403. *Ibid.*, pp. 191-192.
404. *DGFP*, D, XI, p. 641.
405. Hoptner, *op. cit.*, p. 198.
406. *Ibid.*, pp. 198-199.
407. *Ibid.*, p. 199.
408. *Ibid.*, p. 200.
409. *Loc. cit.*
410. *Loc. cit.*
411. *Ibid.*, p. 201.
412. Ciano's Diary, *op. cit.*, pp. 329-330; *FRUS*, II (1941), p. 937; *DGFP*, D, XI, pp. 1018, 1114, 1127.
413. Hoptner, *op. cit.*, p. 202.
414. *Ibid.*, pp. 202-203.
415. *Ibid.*, p. 203.
416. *DGFP*, D, XI, No. 708.
417. *Ibid.*, D, XI, No. 20.
418. *Loc. cit.;* Gregorić, *op. cit.*, pp. 119-122.
419. *DGFP*, D, XII, No. 10; Gregorić *op. cit.*, pp. 119-122.
420. *DGFP*, D, XII, No. 10; Gregorić, *op. cit.*, pp. 119-122.
421. *DGFP*, D, XII, No. 15; Ristić, *op. cit.*, p. 54.
422. Hoptner, *op. cit.*, pp. 208-209.
423. *DGFP*, D, XII, No. 45.
424. *Ibid.*, Nos. 47, 48; Cvetković, *op. cit.*, "Razgovori u Berchtesgadenu" (July, 1956), No. 8, pp. 7-17.
425. Hoptner, *op. cit.*, pp. 204-205.
426. *Ibid.*, p. 205; Terzi, *op. cit.*, pp. 105, 106.
427. *Ibid.*, pp. 210-211; Terzić, *op. cit.*, pp. 102-104.
428. *Ibid.*, pp. 211-212; *DGFP*, D, XII, No. 85.
429. *DGFP*, D, XII, No. 97.
430. Leonardo Simoni, *Berlin, Ambassade D'Italie* (Paris, 1947), p. 249.
431. Woodward, *op. cit.*, pp. 525-536; Hoptner, *op. cit.*, pp. 212-213; Churchill, *op. cit.*, pp. 10 and 95.
432. *FRUS*, II (1941), pp. 943-948, 957.
433. Hoptner, *op. cit.*, p. 216.
434. *Ibid.*, pp. 216-218.
435. *DGFP*, D, XII, No. 84.
436. *Ibid.*, No. 130.
437. *Ibid.*, No. 131; Hoptner, *op. cit.*, pp. 218-221.
438. *DGFP*, D, XII, No. 131.
439. *Ibid.*, No. 138.
440. Referred to in footnote 3, page 257, *DGFP*, D, XII.
441. *Ibid.*, No. 144.
442. *Ibid.*, No. 145.
443. *Ibid.*, No. 149.
444. *Ibid.*, No. 151.

445. *Ibid.*, No. 156.
446. *Ibid.*, no. 165.
447. *Ibid.*, No. 178 refers to this agreement by Mussolini.
448. *Ibid.*, footnote 2 to above document; Ristić, *op. cit.*, pp. 62-63.
449. Hoptner, *op. cit.*, pp. 231-233.
450. *FRUS*, II (1941), pp. 954, 957.
451. Ristić, *op. cit.*, p. 63.
452. *DGFP*, D, XII, No. 173.
453. There is confusion on the date of this meeting. Fotić, in his memoirs, (*op. cit.*, p. 64) and Maček (*op. cit.*, p. 209) say there was a secret meeting with Hitler by Prince Paul on March 18. Hoptner could find no evidence of this meeting and so puts the Crown Council meeting on March 6 (*op. cit.*, p. 219). This makes it conform with the meeting with Hitler about which he knew. The German documents are no help. The last document known about calls for a last meeting whose only purpose, according to the document, is to sign the treaty. Thus, a further meeting of the two seems pointless. Ristić, *op. cit.*, pp. 64-65; Hoptner, *op. cit.*, pp. 219-221.
454. *DGFP*, D, XII, No. 187.
455. Hoptner *op. cit.*, p. 239.
456. *DGFP*, D, XII, Nos. 192, 194.
457. Hoptner, *op. cit.*, pp. 239-240; Ristić, *op. cit.*, pp. 74-78; This account is from a manuscript account by General Simović in Hoptner's possession. Maček, *op. cit.*, pp. 214-215.
458. Ristić, *op. cit.*, pp. 66-67.; Woodward, *op. cit.*, pp. 517-521.
459. Ristić, *op. cit.*, p. 67; Woodward, *op. cit.*, pp. 521-522.
460. Woodward, *op. cit.*, p. 530.
461. *Ibid.*, pp. 533-534.
462. *Ibid.*, pp. 535-536.
463. *FRUS*, II (1941), pp. 951-952.
464. *Ibid.*, pp. 955-956, 960, 962-963.
465. *Ibid.*, pp. 959-966.
466. Ristić, *op. cit.*, pp. 71-72. This account is mainly drawn from General Simović's Memoirs.
467. *Ibid.*, p. 72.
468. *DGFP*, D, XII, Nos. 192, 194; Ristić, *op. cit.*, p. 73; Ulrich von Hassell, *Diaries* (Garden City, N. Y., 1947), p. 178.
469. *FRUS*, II (1941), pp. 966-967.
470. Ristić, *op. cit.*, pp. 74-78; *DGFP*, D, XII. In footnote 3 to document 156, telegram 219 of March 13 reports a conversation of Heeren with Cvetković in which the prime minister said that precautions were being taken against a possible uprising.
471. Ristić, *op. cit.*, p. 79.
472. *DGFP*, D, XII, No. 208.
473. Ristić, *op. cit.*, p. 81.
474. *DGFP*, D, XII, No. 178.
475. *Ibid.*, Nos. 205, 206.
476. *FRUS*, II (1941), p. 972; Ristić, *op. cit.*, p. 83.
477. *FRUS*, II, *loc. cit.*
478. *DGFP*, D, XII, No. 259.
479. Hoptner, *op. cit.*, pp. 242-243.

480. *Ibid.*, p. 247.
481. *Ibid.*, pp. 247-248.
482. *Ibid.*, pp. 248-249.
483. *Ibid.*, p. 249.
484. *Ibid.*, pp. 249-250.
485. *Ibid.*, p. 250.
486. *Loc. cit.*
487. *Ibid.*, pp. 250-251.
488. *Ibid.*, pp. 251-253; Ristić *op. cit.*, p. 84. Ristić's account becomes particularly valuable from this point since he took part in the events he describes as aide de camp to General Simović.
489. Hoptner, *op. cit.*, p. 253.
490. Ristić, *op. cit.*, pp. 84-85; Hoptner, *op. cit.*, p. 253.
491. Hoptner, *op. cit.*, p. 254, footnote 6.
492. Hoptner, *op. cit.*, pp. 253-254; Ristić, *op. cit.*, pp. 86-87.
493. Hoptner, *op. cit.*, p. 254; Ristić *op. cit.*, p. 88.
494. Hoptner, *op. cit.*, p. 254; Ristić, *op. cit.*, p. 87.
495. Hoptner, *op. cit.*, pp. 254-255.
496. *Loc. cit.*
497. *Loc. cit.*
498. *Ibid.*, pp. 255-256.
499. Hoptner, *op. cit.*, pp. 245-246; Maček, *op. cit.*, pp. 215-216.
500. Ristić, *op. cit.*, pp. 85-86.
501. *Ibid.*, pp. 87-88.
502. *Ibid.*, pp. 88-89.
503. *Ibid.*, pp. 92-93.
504. Maček, *op. cit.*, pp. 216-217.
505. *Ibid.*, pp. 217-218.
506. *Ibid.*, p. 218.
507. King Peter II, *op. cit.*, p. 62.
508. Hoptner, *op. cit.*, pp. 262-263.
509. Ristić, *op. cit.*, p. 95.
510. *Ibid.*, pp. 95-96.
511. *Ibid.*, pp. 96-100.
512. *FRUS*, II (1941), p. 969.
513. King Peter II, *op. cit.*, p. 78.
514. Ristić, *op. cit.*, p. 102; Maček, *op. cit.*, pp. 218-219.
515. Ristić, *op. cit.*, p. 103.
516. Hoptner, *op. cit.*, p. 262.
517. *Ibid.*, pp. 262-263.
518. *Ibid.*, p. 263.
519. *Ibid.*, pp. 263-264.
520. *Ibid.*, p. 264.
521. Ristić, *op. cit.*, p. 107.
522. King Peter II, *op. cit.*, p. 81.
523. Ristić, *op. cit.*, pp. 111-112; Maček, *op. cit.*, pp. 220-221; *DGFP*, D, XII, Nos. 238, 239, 241, 243, 246, 262.
524. *DGFP*, D, XII, Nos. 217-223.
525. *Ibid.*, No. 219.
526. *Ibid.*, No. 214.

527. *Ibid.*, No. 225.
528. *FRUS*, II (1941), pp. 971-972.
529. *Loc. cit.*
530. *DGFP*, D, XII, No. 235.
531. Dušan Biber, *Nacizm in Nemci v Jugoslaviji, 1933-1941* (Ljubljana, 1966), pp. 262-263; Ristić, *op. cit.*, pp. 114-115. The author states that he was present at this conversation.
532. Hoptner, *op. cit.*, p. 268.
533. Ristić, *op. cit.*, p. 115.
534. *DGFP*, D, XII, No. 224.
535. Hoptner, *op. cit.*, pp. 268-269; Ristić, *op. cit.*, p. 115; *DGFP*, D, XII, No. 235, footnote 2.
536. Ristić *op. cit.*, pp. 115-116; *DGFP*, D, XII, Nos. 252, 253.
537. *DGFP*, D, XII, No. 232.
538. Hoptner, *op. cit.*, p. 267.
539. *DGFP*, D, XII, No. 248.
540. *Ibid.*, No. 236.
541. *FRUS*, II (1941), pp. 969-972.
942. Hoptner, *op. cit.*, p. 271.
543. *Ibid.*, p. 271; Maček, *op. cit.*, pp. 218-219.
544. Maček, *op. cit.*, p. 219; Hoptner, *op. cit.*, p. 271.
545. Maček, *op. cit.*, pp. 219-220; Hoptner, *op. cit.*, pp. 271-272; *DGFP*, D, XII, No. 232, Footnote 1.
546. Maček, *op. cit.*, p. 219; Hoptner, *op. cit.*, p. 272.
547. Hoptner, *op. cit.*, p. 272.
548. *Ibid.*, p. 272; *DGFP*, D, XII, No. 238 and footnote 1.
549. *DGFP*, D, XII, No. 238; Hoptner, *op. cit.*, p. 272.
550. *DGFP*, D, XII, No. 238.
551. *Loc. cit.*
552. Maček, *op. cit.*, pp. 220-221; *DGFP*, D, XII, No. 243, 262.
553. *DGFP*, D, XII, No. 241.
554. Hoptner, *op. cit.*, pp. 281-283.
555. Ristić, *op. cit.*, pp. 118-120; Hoptner, *op. cit.*, p. 283; Maček, *op. cit.*, pp. 221-222.
556. Hoptner, *op. cit.*, pp. 283-284.
557. *Ibid.*, p. 284.
558. *Loc. cit.*
559. *Loc. cit.*; *DGFP*, D, XII, No. 279.
560. *DGFP*, D, XII, No. 253 and footnote 1; Hoptner, *op. cit.*, p. 284.
561. Ristić, *op. cit.*, pp. 118-119; Hoptner, *op. cit.*, pp. 284-285; Maček, *op. cit.*, pp. 222-223.
562. *DGFP*, D, XII, Nos. 271, 272.
563. Ristić, *op. cit.*, p. 121.
564. *DGFP*, D, XII, No. 278.
565. *Ibid.*, No. 217.
566. *Ibid.*, Nos. 215, 216.
567. Hoptner, *op. cit.*, p. 282.
568. *DGFP*, D, XII, No. 283; Ristić, *op. cit.*, p. 124.
569. Ristić, *op. cit.*, pp. 124-126.

570. Hoptner, *op. cit.*, p. 292; Wuescht, *op. cit.*, p. 49. Cites the major provisions of the armistice.
571. Ristić, *op. cit.*, pp. 126-127; Čulinović, *op. cit.*, p. 334; Terzić, *op. cit.*, pp. 287-288; Hoptner, *op. cit.*, pp. 287-288.
572. Hoptner, *op. cit.*, pp. 287-288; Halder, Franz, *Diary,* 6 vols, (Nuremberg, 1946), entries for April 7-11, 1941.
573. Hoptner, *op. cit.*, p. 288.
574. *Ibid.*, p. 286, footnote 62.
575. *Ibid.*, p. 288.
576. *Ibid.*, p. 290.
577. *Ibid.*, pp. 290-292.

BIBLIOGRAPHY

Documents

Germany Auswärtiges Amt; *Documents Relating to the Conflict with Yugoslavia and Greece.* Berlin; Deutscher Verlag, 1941

Gilbert, D.M., *The Nuremberg Diary.* New York; Farrar, Straus and Co., 1947

International Military Tribunal. *Trial of the Major War Criminals before the International Military Tribunal, 1945-1948.* London; His Majesty's Stationery Office, 1947-49, 42 volumes

International Military Tribunal. *Trials of War Criminals.* London; His Majesty's Stationery Office, 1946-1953, 16 volumes

Ministry of Foreign Affairs of the USSR. *Documents and Materials Relating to the Eve of the 2nd World War.* 2 volumes. Moscow, 1948

Ministry of Foreign Affairs of the USSR. *Dokumentry Ministerstva Inostranykh del Germanii.* 3 volumes. Moscow, 1946

Muggeridge, Malcolm, ed.; Hood, Stuart, trans. *Ciano's Diplomatic Papers.* London; Odhams, 1948

Toynbee, Arnold J. *Survey of International Affairs.* London; Oxford U. Press for the Royal Institute of International Affairs, 1933-1942

Trevor-Roper, H. R. ed. *Blitzkrieg to Defeat.* New York; Holt, Rinehart and Winston, 1964

U. S. Dept. of State. *Documents on German Foreign Policy, 1918-1945, Series C and D* Washington, D. C.; Government Printing Office

U.S. Dept. of State. *Foreign Relations of the United States.* Washington, D. C.; Government Printing Office, 1861

U. S. Dept. of State. *Nazi-Soviet Relations, 1939-41.* Edited by Raymond J. Sontag and James S. Biddie. Washington, D. C.; Government Printing Office, 1948

Primary Sources
Diaries and Personal Accounts

Adamić, Louis. *My Native Land.* New York, Harper and Brothers, 1943

Beard, Charles A. and Radin, George. *The Balkan Pivot.* New York; the Macmillan Co., 1929

Ciano, Count Galeazzo. *Ciano's Diary,* edited by Malcolm Muggeridge. London; Heinemann Ltd., 1947

Ciano, Count Galeazzo. *Ciano's Hidden Diary, 1937-38,* trans. and notes by Andreas Mayor, introduction by Malcolm Muggeridge. New York; E. P. Dutton and Co., 1953

Fodor, M. W. *South of Hitler.* Boston; Houghton, Mifflin Co., 1939

Fotitch, Constantin. *The War We Lost.* New York, The Viking Press, 1948

François-Poncet, Andre. *The Fateful Years.* trans. by Jacques Le Clercq. New York; Harcourt, Brace and World. 1949

Glosarić, Mirko. *Borba Hrvata.* Zagreb; Antun Vilzik, 1940

Goebbels, Joseph, ed. and trans. by Louis P Lockner. *The Goebbels Diaries, 1942-43.* Garden City, Doubleday and Co., Inc., 1948

Lindbergh, Charles. *The Wartime Journals of C. Lindbergh.* New York, Harcourt, Brace, Jovanovich, Inc., 1970

Roucek, Joseph S. The Politics of the Balkans. New York; McGraw Hill, 1939

von Hassell, Ulrich. *Diaries.* Garden City, Doubleday, 1947

West, Rebecca. *Black Lamb and Grey Falcon.* New York, The Viking Press, 1940

White, Leigh. *The Long Balkan Night.* New York, Charles Scribner's Sons, 1944

Wiskemann, Elizabeth. *Prologue to War.* London; Oxford U. Press, 1940

Memoirs

Badoglio, Pietro. *Italy in the Second World War.* London; Oxford U. Press, 1948

Churchill, Winston. *Their Finest Hour: Volume I of the History of the Second World War.* Boston; Houghton, Mifflin Co., 1948

Eden, Anthony. *Facing the Dictators: The Memoirs of Anthony Eden, 1923-1938.* Boston; Houghton, Mifflin Co.

Gafencu, Grigoire. *Prelude to the Russian Campaign.* London; Muller, 1945

Maček, Vladko. *In the Struggle for Freedom: the Memoirs of.* University Park, Pa.: the U. of Pennsylvania Press, 1957

Pavelić, Dr Ante Smith. *Dr Ante Trumbić, Problemi Hrvatsko-Srpskih Odnosa.* Munich, Knjižnica Hrvatske Rivije, 1959

King Peter II. *A. King's Heritage.* London; Cassell and Co., Ltd., 1955

Ristić, Dragiša N. *Yugoslavia's Revolution of 1941.* University Park, Pa.: The Pennsylvania State U. Press, 1966

Rosenberg, Alfred, ed. by Sergi Lang and Ernst von Schenck, trans. by Eric Posselt. *The Memoirs of A. Rosenberg.* Chicago and New York: Ziff-Davis Publishing Co., 1949.

Schmidt, Dr Paul, *Hitler's Interpreter,* ed. by R. H. C. Steed, London: Heinemann, 1951.

Sforza, Count Carlo. *Fifty Years of War and Diplomacy in the Balkans.* New York: Columbia U. Press, 1940.

Stojadinović, Milan. *Ni Rat Ni Pakt.* Rijeka, Otokar Kersovani, 1970.

Cvetković, Dragiša. *Dokumenty o Jugoslaviji,* 10 vols., Paris: 1951-57.

Lord Vansittart. *The Mist Procession.* London: Hutchinson, 1958.

von Papen, Franz, trans. by Brian Connell. *Memoirs.* London: Andre Deutsch, 1952.

Weygand, Maxime. *Rappele au Service,* 3 vols. Paris: Flammarion, 1950.

Secondary Sources

Barber, A. J. *The Civilizing Mission: A History of the Italo-Ethiopian War.* New York: The Dial Press, 1968

Bauer, Helmut. *Ein Vielvolkerstaat Zerbricht: Werden und Vergehen Jugoslawiens.* Leipzig: Luhe, 1941

Beloff, Max. *The Foreign Policy of Soviet Russia,* 2 vols. London: Oxford U. Press, 1947

Biber, Dušan, *Nacizem in Nemci v Jugoslaviji, 1933-1941.* Ljubljana, Cankarjeva Zolažba v Ljubljani, 1966

Bonifačić, Antun and Mihanovich, Clement, eds., *The Croatian Nation in Its Struggle for Freedom and Independence.* Chicago: "Croatia" Cultural Publishing Center, 1955

Brisson, Charles. *Alexandre de Yougoslavia.* Paris: Elbeuf, 1934

Burks, R. V. *The Dynamics of Communism in Eastern Europe.* Princeton: Princeton U. Press, 1961

Butler, J. R. M. *Grand Strategy.* London: His Majesty's Stationery Office, 1957

Cassels, Alan. *Mussolini's Early Diplomacy.* Princeton: Princeton U. Press, 1970

Cervi, Mario. *The Hollow Legions: Mussolini's Blunder in Greece, 1940-41.* New York: Doubleday, 1971

Colton, Joel. *Leon Blum, Humanist in Politics.* New York: Alfred A. Knopf, 1966

Crane, John. *The Little Entente.* New York: The Macmillan Co. 1931

Čubrilović, Vaso. *Politika Proslost Hrvata.* Belgrade: Politika A. D., 1939

Čulinović, Ferdo. *Drzavnopravna Historija Jugoslovenshikh Zimalja XIX i XX Vijeka.* Zagreb: Skolska Knjiga, 1953-1954

Čulinović, F. *27 Mart.* Zagreb: Historijski Institut Jugoslovenske Akademije u Zagrebu, 1965

Čulinović, F. *Slom Stare Jugoslaviji.* Zagreb: Skolska Knjiga, 1958

Dallin, Alexander, *German Rule in Russia.* London: Macmillan and Co., 1957

Deakin, F. W. *The Brutal Friendship: Mussolini, Hitler and the Fall of Italian Fascism.* New York: Harper and Row, 1962

Dorpalen, Andreas, *The World of General Haushofer: Geopolitics in Action.* New York: Farrar and Rinehart, Inc., 1942

Dresler, Adolf. *Kroatien.* Essen: Essener Verlagsanstalt, 1944

Dvornik, Francis. *The Slavs: Their Early History and Civilization.* Boston, 1956

Einzig. Paul. *Bloodless Invasion: German Economic Penetration into the Danubian States and the Balkans.* London: Duckworth, 1939, 2nd edition.

Eyck, Erich. *A History of the Weimar Republic,* 2 vols. Cambridge, Mass.: Harvard U. Press, 1962

Gartner, Emil. *Kroatien in Sudslaven.* Berlin: Junker und Dunnhaupt, 1944

Gisevius, Hans., trans. by Richard and Clara Winston. *To the Bitter End.* Boston: Houghton, Mifflin Co., 1947

Glojnarić, Mirko. *Borba Hrvata.* Zagreb: Antun Vilzik, 1940

Graham, Stephen. *Alexander of Jugoslavia.* London: Cassell and Co., 1938

Hagen, Walter. *Die Geheime Front.* Linz and Vienna: Nibelungen, 1950

Hamblock, Ernest. *Germany Rampant: A Study in Economic Militarism.* New York: Carrick and Evans, Inc., 1939

Hamilton, F. E. Ian. *Yugoslavia: Patterns of Economic Activity.* New York: Frederick A. Praeger, 1968

Hauptmann, Ludmil. *Die Kroaten im Wandel der Jahrhundert.* Berlin: Wiking Verlag, 1943

Hoptner, J. B. *Yugoslavia in Crisis, 1934-1941.* New York: Columbia U. Press, 1962

Horne, Alaistair. *To Lose A Battle: France 1940.* Boston: Little, Brown and Co., 1969

In der Maur, Gilbert. *Die Jugoslawien einst und jetzt,* 3 vols. Berlin: 1936-1938

Jackson, George D., Jr. *Comintern and Peasant in East Europe, 1919-1930.* New York: Columbia U. Press, 1966

Jelavich, Charles and Barbara. *The Balkans in Transition.* Berkeley: U. Of California Press, 1963

Katić, Dr Lovre. *Pregled Povijesti Hrvata.* Zagreb: Redovno Izdanje Matice Hrvatske, 1938

Kerner, Robert J. and Howard, Harry. *The Balkan Conferences and the Balkan Entente, 1930-1935.* Berkeley: U. Of California Press, 1936

Kerner, Robert J., editor. *Yugoslavia.* Berkeley: U. Of California Press, 1949

Kirkpatrick, Sir Ivone. *Mussolini: A Study in Power.* New York: Hawthorn Books, Inc., 1964

Kiszling, Rudolf. *Die Kroaten: Der Schicksalsweg innes Südslawenvolkes.* Verlag Hermann Bohlans Nachf., 1956

Lazitch, Branko. *Tito et la Revolution Yougoslave.* Paris: Fasquelle Editeurs, 1957

Lederer, Ivo J. *Yugoslavia at the Paris Peace Conference.* New Haven: Yale U. Press, 1963

Livingstone, Robert. *Stjepan Radić and the Croatian Peasant Party, 1904-1929.* (Unpublished PhD dissertation). Cambridge, Mass., Harvard University.

Macartney, C. A. *A History of Hungary, 1929-1945.* New York: Frederick A. Praeger, Inc., 1956

Macartney, C. A. *Hungary: A Short History.* Chicago: Aldine and Co., 1962

Macartney, C. A. *Hungary and Her Successors.* London: Oxford U. Press, for the Royal Institute of International Affairs, 1937

Macartney, C. A. *October 15th: A History of Modern Hungary, 1929-1945.* Edinburgh: Edinburgh U. Press, 1956

Macartney, C. A. and Palmer, A. W. *Independent Eastern Europe.* New York: Macmillan and Co., 1962

Shoup, Paul, *Communism and the Yugoslav National Question.* New York: Columbia U. Press, 1968

Sington, Derek and Weidenfeld, Arthur. *The Goebbels Experiment: A Study of the Nazi Propaganda Machine.* New Haven: Yale U. Press, 1943

Stavrianos, L. S. *The Balkans since 1453.* New York: Holt, Rinehart and Winston, 1958

Taylor, A. J. P. *The Origins of the Second World War.* New York: Athenaeum, 1962

Terzić, Velimir *Jugoslavija u Aprilskom Ratu.* Titograd: Graficki Zavod, 1963

Thomson, S. Harrison. *Czechoslovakia in European History.* London: Frank Cass and Co., Ltd., 1965

Tomasević, Jozo. *Peasants, Politics and Economic Change in Yugoslavia.* Stanford: Stanford U. Press, 1955

Čekić, Milutin. *Jugoslawien am Scheidewege das Serbo-Kroatische Problem und Jugoslawiens Aussenpolitik.* Leipzig: F. Meiner, 1939

Ulam, Adam B. *Expansion and Coexistence: The History of Soviet Foreign Policy, 1917-1967.* New York: Frederick A. Praeger, 1969

von Südland, L. (von Pilar, Ivo). *Die Südslawische Frage und der Weltkrieg.* Zagreb: 1944

Weber, Eugen. *The Varieties of Fascism.* Princeton: D. van Nostrand Co., Anvil Books. 1964

Weinberg, Gerald. *The Foreign Policy of Hitler's Germany: The Diplomatic Revolution in Europe, 1933-1936.* Chicago: U. of Chicago Press, 1970

Wiskemann, Elizabeth. *The Rome-Berlin Axis.* London: Oxford U. Press, 1949

Wolfe, Henry C. *The German Octopus.* Garden City, New York: Doubleday, Doran and Co., 1938

Woodward, Sir Llwellyn. *British Foreign Policy in the Second World War.* London: Her Majesty's Stationery Office, 1970

Yarochevitch, Milorad. *La Yougoslavie dans les Balkans.* Paris: Les Editions Internationals, 1935

Zivančević, Mihailo M. *Jugoslavija i Federacija.* Belgrade: Stamparja Privredni Pregled. 1938

Journals

Armstrong, Hamilton Fish. After the Assassination of King Alexander. *Foreign Affairs,* vol. 13, no. 2

Armstrong, H. F. Jugoslavia in Transition, *Foreign Affairs,* vol. 14, no. 1, October, 1935

Armstrong, H. F. The New Kingdom of Yugoslavia, *Foreign Affairs,* vol. 8, 1930

Biber, Dušan. Ustaše i Treci Reich, *Jugoslovenski Istoriski Časopis,* 1964, vol. 2

Graham, M. W. The Dictatorship in Yugoslavia, *American Political Science Review,* vol. 23, 1929

Jelavich, Charles. Nikola Pasić: Greater Serbia or Jugoslavia? *Journal of Central European Affairs,* vol. II, 1951

Pribičević, Stojan. The Nazi Drive to the East. New York: *Foreign Policy Association, Inc.,* 1938 *Foreign Policy Reports,* Vol. XIV, no. 15, October 15, 1938

Raditsa, Bogdan. Yugoslav Nationalism Revisited: History and Dogma, *Journal of Central European Affairs,* vol 21, no. 4, January 1962

Roucek, Joseph S. The Social Character of Yugoslav Politics, *Social Sciences,* vol. 9, 1934

Schacker, Gerhard. The Little Entente Between the two Fascisms, *The Contemporary Review,* vol. 150, August 1936

Sweet, Paul. Recent German Literature on Mitteleuropa, *Journal of Central European Affairs,* vol. 3, April 1943

Tomasić, Dimko. Croatia in European Politics, *The Journal of Central European Affairs,* vol. 2, April 1942, January 1943 von Creveld, Martin. 25 October 1940: A Historical Puzzle, *The Journal of Contemporary History,* vol. 6, no. 3

Watt, Donald C. German Plans for the Reoccupation of the Rhineland: A Note., *Journal of Contemporary History,* vol. I, no. 4

Wiskemann, Elizabeth. Yugoslavia and the Anschluss, *The Contemporary Review,* vol. 148, July 1935

Newspapers

Le Temps, Paris
New York Times, New York
Politika, Belgrade and Zagreb
Völkischer Beobachter, Berlin and Munich